THEY LOC
A Comparative Analysis of the Ideal of Community
in the Thought of Howard Thurman and Martin Luther King, Jr.

Walter E. Fluker

UNIVERSITY
PRESS OF
AMERICA

Lanham • New York • London

Library of Congress Cataloging-in-Publication Data

Fluker, Walter E., 1951-
They looked for a city: a comparative analysis of the ideal of
community in the thought of Howard Thurman and
Martin Luther King, Jr. / Walter E. Fluker.
p. cm.
Bibliography: p.
1. Sociology, Christian (Baptist)—History of doctrines—20th
century. 2. Afro-American Baptists—Doctrines—History—20th
century. 3. Thurman, Howard, 1900-1981—Views on community.
4. King, Martin Luther, Jr., 1929-1968—Views on community.
I. Title
BX6447.F57   1988
307'.092'2—dc19   88-31335 CIP

ISBN 0-8191-7262-6 (alk. paper)
ISBN 0-8191-7263-4 (pbk.:alk. paper)

All University Press of America books are produced on acid-free paper.
The paper used in this publication meets the minimum requirements of American
National Standard for Information Sciences—Permanence of Paper for Printed Library
Materials, ANSI Z39.48–1984.   ∞

But as it is, they desire a better country, that is a heavenly one. Therefore God is not ashamed to be called their God, for the Lord has prepared for them a city.

Hebrews 11:16

DEDICATION

This book is dedicated to my parents, Clinton and Zettie Fluker, from whom I first learned the meaning of "community." Especially to my father, who passed away during the early stages of my writing, this book is a pledge and token of the vows between us.

ACKNOWLEDGEMENTS

The love and labors of many special people have been a part of this study. The project began as my Ph.D. dissertation, "A Comparative Analysis of the Ideal of Community in the Thought of Howard Thurman and Martin Luther King, Jr." (Boston University, 1988). Although there have been revisions in the format, language and additional work on historical details, the substance of the book is essentially the same. Therefore, my gratitude is expressed to my major professor and first reader of the dissertation, John H. Cartwright, for his supervision of the study; and to Professor Harold H. Oliver, the second reader, for his valuable assistance and suggestions along the way. I owe a great debt to Dean Emeritus Walter G. Muelder for his early encouragement and resourcefulness in the conceptualization of the dissertation and his willingness throughout the work to offer critical commentary on methodological problems and content.

For the publication of the book in its present form, I am especially indebted to Dean H. Jackson Forstman of the Vanderbilt Divinity School and to the University Research Council of the Vanderbilt University Graduate School for a small grant that enabled me to return to the King and Thurman Papers at the Mugar Memorial Library of Boston University during the Fall of 1987. My colleagues at Vanderbilt University, Professors Jimmie Lewis Franklin and Lewis V. Baldwin, provided an invaluable service in reading the revised manuscript and making thoughtful corrections.

Among the many people outside the academic environment who contributed in special ways to the completion of this work, I offer special thanks to the St. John's Congregational Church, United Church of Christ, in Springfield, Massachusetts, for their prayers and support. It would have been impossible to write the dissertation without the early sabbatical they granted during the summer of 1985. Also, the Hampden Association of the Massachusetts Conference, United Church of Christ, awarded a scholarship from the Harold and Mary Johnson Memorial Trust to assist in costs incurred during my leave from pastoral duties. I deeply appreciate the support of the Howard Thurman Educational Trust Fund, and in particular Sue Bailey Thurman, for making available the Thurman materials and for providing the quiet space and opportunity to begin my research during August of 1982. I also wish to thank Mrs. Thurman for permission to quote from "Freedom Under God," Second Century Convocation, Washington University, February, 1955. My beloved in-laws, Dr. and Mrs. Melvin H. Watson, served as pivotal sources and benefactors throughout my research and writing.

Mrs. Elyse Downs, my landlady and mother-in-residence, provided a home away from home during my early years in Boston, and she continues to serve as a strong pillar for my family. My gratitude is also extended to Ms. Judy Matthews-Taylor for the typing and copy-editing of the manuscript. Her devotion to this task is indeed the "stuff" which makes community possible.

Finally, a special thanks to a true "blues brother," Tom Hughes, for the handsome frontispiece.

A wonderful thing happened during the early stages of my writing. Our son, Clinton Rahman, was born. Many a night, he provided the stimulus and the love to complete the work, for which I am indeed grateful. Finally, I am thankful for and to my wife and best friend, Sharon Watson Fluker. Through it all, she was there with words of encouragement, a critical mind, and "a whole lot of love."

CONTENTS

INTRODUCTION

Howard Thurman and Martin Luther King, Jr. were Christian ministers and social prophets who made significant contributions to the religious and social life of America and the world. The search for community was a life-long quest for both men, and the single, underlying thesis of their thoughts and ministries.[1] Although Howard Thurman is the lesser known of the two, his life and ministry have influenced many highly visible individuals (including King) in American society and the larger world community.[2]

Both thinkers were also black Americans whose earliest experiences of community and non-community in the segregated South had a profound impact on their quests and interpretations of human community. These early experiences, and later ones, are given in autobiographical statements throughout their writings, sermons, and speeches. This dimension of their lives and its influence on the development of their understandings of community is a major concern of this work.[3] The fundamental problem addressed here, however, is the ideal of community in Thurman and King. Its significance lies in its examination of their respective approaches to the explication and application of the ideal of community. A central contention in the discussion is that a comparative analysis of the problem in Thurman and King can yield fruitful insight into the conception, character, and actualization of human community.

Before discussing the specific use of *community* in Thurman and King, it should be noted that it is a many *splendored* and *splintered* thing. Like most of our ordinary discourse, its meaning varies with context and usage. Among various settings and situations, there are different dimensions of meaning. Presupposed in such usage, however, is the idea that the word *community* denotes some determinate object, a particular type of social life and experience, e.g., a sense of belonging, a sense of place, a sense of identity, or shared values.[4] Such a common sense view of language, however, fails to address the problem of multi-dimensional levels and varieties of experiences covered in the broad terminology of *community*. In this sense, *community*, like love, covers a multitude of definitional and methodological sins.[5] Because of the highly complex and conflated usage of the term *community*, it is a futile enterprise to talk about it without first recognizing that empirical and evaluative dimensions in the idea are intertwined along with a host of other interrelated problems. Therefore, examining the notion of *community* necessarily involves careful attention to the socio-historical contexts from which the idea arises and how its normative character is understood within that framework. It would be extremely difficult, for instance, to talk intelligently about the notions of community in Plato and Aristotle without some appreciation for the decline of the Athenian city-state. The two philosophers' politico-ethical construals of community are directly related to their respective socio-historical contexts. One of our tasks, therefore, will be to examine the relationship between socio-historical contexts and politico-ethical claims associated with community in Thurman and King and their foundations in the black community in the United States.

In the following discussion, *black community* refers to the definition presented by James E. Blackwell. He defines the *black community* as "a highly diversified, interrelated aggregate of people who unite into relatively cohesive structures in response to white oppression, racism, and patterned repression."[6] He also contends that

> There is no single authentic black experience in America except that which is developed as a consequence of ubiquitous white racism and the prevalent color consciousness. Because of variations in manifestations of racism and color consciousness, multiple black experiences occurred, each one as authentic as the other. The common denominator for all of them, however, is the coalescence of racism and color.[7]

While this working definition will receive elaboration later, it is important to indicate here the *descriptive* function it performs in underscoring the initial problematic which informed these two black American thinkers' *normative* claims for community. Their conceptions of community did not arise from an historical vacuum, rather their understandings of the interrelated structure of human existence and life were born and nurtured in the empirical settings of their families, churches, and larger social contexts where black people had to deal daily with the existential struggles wrought by segregation in the Deep South.

The normative use of *community* in Thurman and King is founded upon philosophical and theological idealism, which maintains that mind and spiritual values are fundamental in the world as a whole.[8] The "idealism" referred to here, however, is deeply entrenched in what Cornel West calls "the prophetic tradition in Afro-America." West argues that

> Black prophetic practices can be generally characterized by three basic features: *a deep-seated moralism, an inescapable opportunism, and an aggressive pessimism*... Afro-American prophetic practices have been and, for the most part, remain ensconced in a moralistic mood: that is, they are grounded in a moralistic conception of the world in which the rightness or wrongness of human actions—be they individually or collectively understood—are measured by ethical ideals or moral standards...[and] black pro-

phetic Americans have tended to assume that such ideals and standards ought to make a difference in regard to how individuals act and operate. In short, black prophetic practices assume that—after the most intense scrutiny—some ultimate sense of a morally grounded sense of justice ought to prevail in personal and social affairs.[9]

Thurman's and King's general metaphysical views are teleological and it is in this context that their definitions of community are best understood. In this discussion, therefore, the term "ideal of community" refers to community in two respects: as the norm for ethical reflection and the goal toward which all of life strives. Thurman's and King's conceptions of community fall appropriately in the mutual/personal model outlined by Frank Kirkpatrick as one of three traditionally held views of community in Western social philosophy and religion. Here community is understood as "a mutuality in which distinct persons find fulfillment in and through living for each other in loving fellowship."[10]

The Approach

Analytic and comparative modes are utilized to interpret each thinker's understanding of community. Basic questions are raised for each which form the analytical construct for the comparison. Since Thurman and King gave autobiographical clues about their personal quests for community, the first question is concerned with the experiential and intellectual sources of the ideal of community in their searches: What were the social and intellectual sources which informed and shaped their understandings of community? The second question is concerned with the nature of community: How is community conceived? What is its character? Third, the question of the actualization of community is raised: What are the barriers to be overcome in the actualization of community? How is community actualized?

The book is divided into three parts. Parts I and II will be devoted to the ideal of community in Howard Thurman and Martin Luther King, Jr., respectively. They will include the experiential and intellectual sources of the ideal of community, the nature of community, and the actualization of community in each thinker. Part III will be devoted to the comparative analysis of the ideal in each clergyman and will present findings and conclusions.

The *experiential and intellectual sources of community* in Thurman and King are examined in Chapters 1 and 4. Biographical profiles, emphasizing significant periods and influences in their quests for community, will be given. Intellectual sources are examined, with special emphasis upon their relationship to the development of the ideal in each thinker. The formative influences of the black community also receive special attention.

Chapters 2 and 5 will treat the *nature of community* in Thurman and King. The task of these chapters is to analyze each thinker's particular conception of community in respect to his definition and treatment of the normative and empirical dimensions of the problem. Also, the character of community is explored in reference to the triadic relationship between God, self and the world.

Chapters 3 and 6 examine each thinker's recommendations for the *actualization of community*. These chapters include an analysis of the barriers to community and the means for overcoming them. The barriers refer to Thurman's and King's interpretations of the personal and social manifestations of evil and sin. This discussion also includes a brief descriptive analysis of their treatments of theodicy. Included under each thinker's recommendation for overcoming the barriers to community is an examination of community as the norm and goal of the moral life, love as the means of actualization, and the nature and role of the church and religion in the actualization of community.

Chapter 7 is the comparative analysis of the ideal of community in the subjects of our study. The comparison will identify continuities and discontinuities in Thurman and King in respect to the sources, nature and actualization of community. Chapter 8 is the final chapter on findings and conclusions.

The author is acutely aware of the use of sexist language by Thurman and King. Needless to say, both were products of their times and culture. Given their committments to the communitarian ideal, it is my firm conviction that if they were alive today, they would be advocates of inclusive language in respect to gender as they were with race and class.

Finally, our claims in this endeavor are modest. The problem of community does not receive a definitive answer from Thurman and King. Their recommendations for the actualization of community will be found severely lacking by some readers. This should not come as a surprise to anyone who has an appreciation of the profundity of the problem. In fact, as they did not solve it in their lifetimes, neither will we in this generation—yet *community* remains the fundamental problem of human existence. Therefore, we dare to *look for the city* through the eyes of these two black American thinkers, who, as fellow pilgrims, remind us that we have no other choice—because, like it or not, we are caught in the web of the spider. To ignore the problem is suicide—to attempt to understand it and to make some contribution to its solution and realization is to choose to live humanely and authentically in the world.

Part I

The Search for Common Ground:
The Ideal Of Community
In Howard Thurman

For he looked for a city which has foundations, whose builder and maker is God.
— Hebrews 11:10

1

Chapter 1

Beggar at the Gate

The years, the months, the days, and the hours have flown by my open window. Here and there an incident, a towering moment, a naked memory, an etched countenance, a whisper in the dark, a golden glow—these and much, much more are the woven fabric of time I have lived. What I have written is but a fleeting imitation of the outside of what one man sees and may tell about the path he walks. No one shares the secret of life; no one enters into the heart of the mystery. There are telltale signs that mark the passing of one's appointed days. Always we are on the outside of the story, always we are the beggars who seek entrance to the kingdom of our dwelling place. When we are admitted, the price exacted us is the sealing of our lips. And this is the strangest of all the paradoxes of the human adventure: we live <u>inside</u> all experience, but we are permitted to bear witness only to the <u>outside</u>. Such is the riddle of life and the story of the passing of our days.

—Howard Thurman

Deep river, my home is over Jordan,
Deep river, Lord; I want to cross over into campground.
O children, O, don't you want to go to the gospel feast,
That promised land, that land, where all is peace?
Deep river, my home is over Jordan,
Deep river, Lord; I want to cross over into campground.

—Negro Spiritual

Teacher, mystic, writer, visionary — Howard Thurman was a man who influenced countless individuals, and whose quiet and powerful idiom still rings in the hearts of prophets of social justice like Jesse Jackson who says, "[W]e knew it was a blessing to give this prophet a glass of water or to touch the hem of his garment."[1] Benjamin Mays, the stalwart and scholarly president of Morehouse College and once Thurman's student advisor, remarked, "[H]e generated in the minds of young Negroes the idea of freedom. When they saw Howard Thurman, most of them, for the first time, saw a free man. When they heard or read Howard Thurman, for the first time they experienced a free man and this freedom was conta-

3

gious."[2] Perhaps this is why Martin Luther King, Jr. is reported to have carried a copy of Thurman's *Jesus and the Disinherited* in his briefcase.[3]

Thurman's presence penetrated the core of those whom he met and with whom he shared. The testimonies are endless. Once in an interview with a founding member of the Fellowship Church in San Francisco which he pastored from 1944- 1953, I asked, "What was the impact of Howard Thurman on your life?" Tears welled up in her eyes and with the deepest expression of sincerity, she softly uttered, "He made me feel that I had worth." I had to shut off the recorder because she could not speak for some time afterwards.[4]

He was a person who loved children. Samuel DuBois Cook, President of Dillard University, reports that Thurman was often the guest preacher at his school's baccalaureate service. On one occasion, President Cook invited prestigious persons from the community to dine with Thurman and his wife. He said he will never forget how the Thurmans quietly excused themselves "from the company of the `high and mighty'" for nearly two hours to visit with his children. Cook says, "The experience disclosed something profound and supremely beautiful about Howard Thurman. It was symbolic of his love of children, his love of life, the magic of his power, and his sense of continuity, the flow, the drama, and `aliveness' of life."[5]

He was a man whose hearty laughter filled the air with gusto that remained long after he had departed. Vincent Harding, the great historian of the black struggle, remembers his laughter. "Sometimes," writes Harding, "his stocky frame would shake with laughter. This was an earthly mystic, filled with pranks and jokes, ever ready to laugh at himself, at life, and at anything else close at hand." His love was as free as his laughter. Harding continues, "I remember our silences. They were filled with his wisdom and compassion. Indeed, it may be that he was the wisest and most compassionate man I have ever known."[6]

Perhaps his wife, Sue Bailey Thurman, states it best when she says, "He leads people home."

Thurman's quest for community was the central defining category of his life and thought. In his "search for common ground" it can be seen how the development of his thinking emerged from the particularity of the black experience of community to a more universal understanding of the interrelatedness of all of life. His earliest experiences with nature, his family, the black church and community of Daytona, Florida, and his education in black schools form the background for his later intellectual pursuits at Rochester Theological Seminary and Haverford College. The influences during this latter period of Thurman's intellectual development confirmed for him the profound truth that he had already discovered in his early years in the black community: that all life is interrelated, it is *one thing*.

4

A key theme in Thurman's development is his intensely personal understanding of community. In Thurman's search for common ground, he sees himself as both subject and object in a parabolic journey towards community.[7] His teaching and ministerial positions as pastor and chaplain, and later his work with the Howard Thurman Educational Trust Fund, served as spiritual and intellectual laboratories in which his vision of community could be tested and revised.

While it is difficult to separate the experiential dimension of his development from his intellectual formation, for the purposes of analysis, this chapter is divided into two sections. First, there is a biographical profile, which emphasizes significant periods and influences in his personal development. This section will follow the basic outline: 1) early years; 2) education; 3) early ministry and teaching; 4) a greater vision; and 5) the wider ministry. The following section will examine the major intellectual sources which contributed to the formal character and expression of his thought: 1) Morehouse College; 2) George Cross; 3) Olive Schreiner; and 4) Rufus M. Jones.

The Experiential Sources
of Community

The Early Years

Affinity With Nature

Howard Thurman was born at the turn of the century on November 18, 1900 in Daytona Beach, Florida. The second child and only son, born to Saul Solomon and Alice Ambrose Thurman, young Howard was an unusual child whose closest companions were found in the world of nature.[8] The deep, dark woods, the lonely solitude of the Florida nights, the rhythmic movement of the Halifax River, the pounding surf and majestic stillness of the Atlantic Ocean, the terrible mystery and fascination of tropical storms, and the resiliency and strength of the old oak tree in his backyard—all these early childhood experiences with nature provided Thurman with clues to the inner unity of all living things that would constitute the central concern of his life. [9]

The Family

Thurman's early affinity with nature can be explained, in part, by the extreme hardships of his family environment and his inner need for security and affirmation.[10] His early years were beset by a number of adversities and tragedies which left their scars on his tender spirit. The experience which left its profoundest mark was the funeral service of his father.[11] At the funeral, a local evangelist, Reverend Sam Cromarte, seized the opportunity as an occasion to illustrate the fate of those who died "outside of Christ." Thurman says, "I listened with wonderment, then anger, and finally mounting rage as Sam Cromarte preached my father into hell."[12] In his need to find a sense of meaning and immunity against the onslaught of this devastating event, he turned to the huge oak tree in his backyard. Many years later, he was to describe it as his "windbreak against existence." As the tree was able to withstand the raging storms, he sought a similar strength.[13]

While the circumstances associated with his father's death cut deeply into the developing personality of Thurman, his mother's constant struggle to provide for her family after her husband's death had a significant impact upon the sensitive young boy. Alice Thurman was a quiet, devoutly Christian woman, who, after her husband's death, went to work as a domestic for a white family in downtown Daytona.[14] Her responsibilities to her employer took away much of the valuable time which Howard and his two sisters needed, and which she wanted so badly to share with them, but could not.[15]

The sudden death of Thurman's father, followed closely by the death of his stepfather, and the terrible burden of his mother's work situation which separated her from her children, contributed greatly to his close identification with nature and his need to develop his inner world. These circumstances were compounded by his own self-perception and the absence of close childhood acquaintances. In an unpublished manuscript, Thurman shares the loneliness and sense of rejection:

> I seemed to be passed over unnoticed, my company was not welcomed by girls nor by the boys in choosing sides for games. Among my peers I seemed to be an 'extra,' but never quite so.... I was ever haunted by a feeling of awkwardness in all my relationships, I felt clumsy. As I walked, it was as if my feet felt fearful of being together. I've told how under stress, the toe of my right foot would rub against my left heel, and that I was fat... I had no older brother or father to defend me, only Momma, Grandma, and my sisters. Yet somehow I did not feel I was a failure just because I did not 'belong' with boys and girls my age. The humiliations of my youth threatened me, but did not undermine my self-worth.[16]

If there was one dominant force, outside of Thurman's companionship with nature, which was responsible for his sense of self-worth in the face of overwhelming difficulties, it was his maternal grandmother, Nancy Ambrose. She "was the first to teach Thurman that spirituality sustains one in the midst of life's many predicaments."[17]

"Grandma Nancy" came to live with her daughter and children after the death of Saul Thurman and was actually the person who reared Howard and his sisters. He refers to her as "the anchor person in our family" who "brooded over our lives."[18] It was his grandmother who helped to instill in him a sense of self-worth in spite of the indignities he suffered from his peers and his painful encounters with the crushing reality of segregation in the Deep South.[19] She was able to inspire in her grandson a belief that life mattered. Thurman writes that whenever his grandmother would sense that he and his sisters were experiencing a loss of personal worth, she would tell them a story of a slave preacher who once or twice a year would visit her plantation. At the close of his delivery, he would pause and tell them: "You are not niggers! You are not slaves! You are God's children!" He says that "When my grandmother got to that part of the story there would be a slight stiffening in her spine and we sucked in our breath. When she finished, our spirits were restored."[20]

Although Nancy Ambrose was illiterate, she had great appreciation for education. She had discovered early that there was something "magic" about learning. When she was a slave, her mistress found her daughter teaching Nancy to read. The little girl was chastised and sent to bed without supper. This experience affected her deeply and convinced her that education was a means of liberation. She assumed responsibility for seeing that Thurman and his sisters excelled in school. Grandma Nancy's concern and diligence in monitoring Howard's educational progress reaped high benefits. He was the first black student in Daytona to take and pass the eighth grade examination which qualified him for high school.[21]

The Black Church

These formative influences from the world of nature and his family environment, especially from his grandmother, did much to kindle a growing sense of personal worth and mission in young Thurman. The chief experiential source, however, in his early search for "common ground" was the black church. Both his mother and grandmother were faithful church members, and it was through their examples and tutelage that Thurman found a context through which he could pursue and actualize what he would later call "the hunger of the heart."[22] Although at his father's funeral he had sworn out of confusion and anger that he would never have anything to do with the church, at twelve years old he joined Mount Bethel Baptist Church. The attendant ceremonies and rites of passage were, and still are, integral parts of the black church tradition and did much to give him a strong sense of "somebodiness." Thurman's experience of baptism and later of discipline by a "sponsor" in the church had an inestimable impact upon his sense of self. The significance of living in a community which genuinely supported his personal worth against the

7

ravages of a larger and hostile society was important to his developing personality. He explains the meaning of these early church experiences:

> In the fellowship of the church, particularly in the experience of worship, there was a feeling of sharing in primary community. Not only did church membership seem to bear heavily upon one's ultimate destiny beyond death and the grave; more than all the communal ties, it also undergirded one's sense of personal identity. It was summed up in the familiar phrase, 'If God is for you, who can prevail against you?'[23]

The Black Community of Daytona

Finally, there was the black community of Daytona, Florida. The Thurmans lived in a section called Waycross, one of the three population pockets for Negroes in those days.[24] Thurman described his neighborhood as an "extended family."[25] According to him, all children in Waycross were under the general supervision of the adults:

> Any child belonged to the whole immediate community, so that if an adult saw me and wanted me to do an errand, I did not have to go home and ask my mother's permission. I would simply do it because Mrs. Thomas told me and that was all that was necessary.[26]

Despite the extreme hardships endured by the people of Waycross because of segregation, they were enabled to transcend their situation through caring and sharing in community. Thurman highlights the community's response to his father's death as one example of this genuine sense of community in which the black people of Waycross lived and worked.

> My father's death was only one of many experiences I recall that bore the aura of the caring of all, the sharing of all, during times of illness or suffering. The sick were cared for at home for no hospitals were open to us (black people) other than the "pesthouse" on the outskirts of town, where smallpox victims were isolated. *In every aspect of the common life, there was a sense of shared responsibility.*[27]

There were three individuals in the black community of Daytona, outside the family context, who served as outstanding models for Thurman during his early years.[28] They were Thornton Smith, a Dr. Stockings, and Mary McLeod Bethune. Thurman refers to Smith and Stockings as his

8

"masculine idols in these early years." Mary McLeod Bethune, one of the outstanding personages of the twentieth century and the founder of Bethune Cookman College in Daytona, was another important model of excellence and community for Thurman. He was aware of her struggles in starting the school and knew of her unrelenting faith which enabled her to realize the vision of creating a center of quality education for young Negro women in the South. He and his family knew Mrs. Bethune personally and often attended commencement exercises of the school. He would hear her speak of her trials and victories at his church on fifth Sunday nights, which were undoubtedly Missionary nights. He speaks of the significance of the school for local youth even though many young women in Daytona could not afford to attend. "The very presence of the school, and the inner strength and authority of Mrs. Bethune, gave boys like me a view of possibilities to be realized in some distant future."[29]

Experiences of Non-Community

These experiences of primary community in the contexts of the family, church and the black community of Waycross were at least equalled by the overwhelming experiences of non-community wrought by segregation in these early years of Thurman's development. The psychological toll of these experiences, according to Thurman, could have been devastating, but he chose early to treat white people indifferently and to cast them outside of the scope of "the magnetic field of his morality."

> To all white persons, the category of exception applied. I did not regard them as involved in my religious reference. They were read out of the human race—they simply did not belong to it in the first place. Behavior toward them was amoral.[30]

It was not until later years, particularly during his experiences in seminary, that Thurman was able to overcome this moral indifference to white people.[31]

The early experiences with nature, the family environment, the black church, and the black community of Waycross served as the wellsprings for the formative years of Howard Thurman. His experiences of community and non- community in these early years laid the foundation for the vision of community which was the central theme of his life and ministry. The intellectual pursuits which followed find their source in this period of his life and must be understood as emerging from this context.

Education

Early Educational Experiences

Thurman's formal education began in the local Negro school in Daytona which only extended through the seventh grade. After completing his seventh year, his grandmother appealed to the local authorities to allow Howard to take the eighth grade examination. The principal, Professor Howard, taught the promising young student on his own time and the results had revolutionary implications for education among Negroes in Daytona. As mentioned earlier, after Thurman's successful examination, the eighth grade was added to the Negro public school of Daytona.

Thurman attended high school in Jacksonville at the Florida Baptist Academy, one of only three public high schools for Negroes in the entire state. His experience at the Academy was one of the most critical periods of his educational career. The four years at the Academy proved invaluable, not only in respect to his immediate goal of receiving an education, but they also provided precious opportunities for him to develop leadership skills and personal relationships which shaped his career. It was during his junior year at the Academy that Thurman met Dr. Mordecai Johnson, a man who would make a singular impact upon his professional development.[32] He was also valedictorian of his senior class.[33]

Morehouse College

Upon graduation from Florida Baptist Academy, Thurman was awarded a tuition scholarship to Morehouse College in Atlanta, Georgia. The churning intellectual energies which began to emerge at the Academy found greater focus and maturation at Morehouse. Since its humble beginnings during Reconstruction, Morehouse College has been a veritable "candle in the dark" for generations of black men who have sought higher learning and greater visions of service to the black community.[34] Morehouse men learned early a sense of personal worth and their responsibility to those less fortunate in the black community. Thurman says, "We understood that our job was to learn so that we could go back into our communities and teach others."[35]

The two men whom Thurman acknowledged as chiefly responsible for uplifting these values before him and his classmates were President John Hope and Dean Samuel Archer. Dr. John Hope was the fourth president of Morehouse and the first black man to head that institution. His long and distinguished leadership, from 1906-1931, established Morehouse as one of the leading institutions of higher education in the United States.[36] President Hope's scholarly and genteel demeanor won the respect and admiration of young black men like Thurman who saw in him a model

10

of black masculinity in a racist society which devalued their self-worth and mocked their manhood. Thurman says that Hope accomplished this in two outstanding ways. One was that he addressed them as "young gentlemen."

> What this term of respect meant to our faltering egos can only be understood against the backdrop of the South of the 1920s. We were black men in Atlanta during a period when the state of Georgia was infamous for its racial brutality. Lynchings, burnings, unspeakable cruelties were fundamentals of existence for black people. Our physical lives were of little value. Any encounter with a white person was inherently dangerous and frequently fatal. Those of us who managed to remain physically whole found our lives defined in less than human terms.[37]

Hope influenced Morehouse men in another way which instilled self-confidence. Morehouse men were not graduated until they had conceived and memorized an original oration. Students were required to prepare and present an oration before the faculty and student body each year for four years. This early training in oratorical skills helped develop personal character and confidence through disciplined drills and critiques from professors and classmates. These forums gave Thurman some of his earliest opportunities to develop and sharpen his supreme oratorical gifts. He comments:

> Later, during my early postgraduate years, members of the audience would frequently come up to me after one of my talks to say, 'You're one of John Hope's men, aren't you?' The Morehouse training was unmistakable.[38]

Samuel H. Archer was the other figure who made a lasting impression upon Thurman during his Morehouse years. Archer succeeded Hope in the presidency of Morehouse in 1931 and saw the school through the turbulent years of the Depression. Although Archer reluctantly accepted the charge from his friend and colleague, he steered the school through one of the most difficult financial periods of its history.[39] Before assuming the presidency, Archer was Professor of Mathematics and coached the football team. His close identification with the students on both intellectual and personal levels earned him a place of high respect in the hearts of generations of young black men, chief among them being Howard Thurman. Archer was in many ways a father figure for Thurman and other Morehouse men. His wise and compassionate counsel guided Thurman through a period in his personal and intellectual pilgrimage which could have been disastrous.[40]

The Morehouse years reinforced two important lessons which he had learned during his early years in Daytona: a sense of personal worth and a calling to shared responsibility for the black community. Upon graduation from Morehouse in 1923, the school offered him a faculty position in economics, but he declined. He had already decided to attend seminary.[41]

Rochester Theological Seminary

The Morehouse years prepared Thurman well for the intellectual and personal challenges he was to encounter at the Rochester Theological Seminary in Rochester, New York. Thurman had also applied to the Newton Theological Seminary in Massachusetts but his application was declined because he was a Negro.[42] The Rochester Seminary had a more liberal admissions policy which allowed two Negroes to be enrolled in any given year. Also, Thurman knew two other black men who had been graduated from Rochester, Dr. Charles Hubert, who taught religion at Morehouse, and Dr. Mordecai Johnson, whom he had met while a student at Florida Baptist Academy.

In the fall of 1923, Thurman entered Rochester Theological Seminary with feelings of uncertainty and anticipation. He describes the early days there as "the most radical period of adjustment of my life up to that moment."[43] This was his first time living in a totally white environment. Unlike Morehouse, where his professors and fellow students were black men with keen interests in the hopes and aspirations of black people, here he discovered an atmosphere which "contrasted sharply with the more personal and responsive ambience of Morehouse College."[44] At first, Thurman felt some anxiety about his own ability to compete intellectually in this strange, new world, but time proved him well prepared for the academic challenges of Rochester. He was graduated at the head of his class.

The professor who had the most influence upon his personal and intellectual development during this stage was George Cross.[45] Cross taught Thurman during his last year and a half at Rochester (1925-1926). Thurman says that Cross "had a greater influence on my life than any other person who ever lived. Everything about me was alive when I came into his presence."[46] The two met frequently on Saturday mornings for private conferences in which Thurman raised questions which arose from the weekly lectures. Here the young scholar would air his disagreements with Cross, who would listen patiently and then, according to Thurman, proceed to "reduce my arguments to ash."[47]

Toward the end of his last year at Rochester, Thurman met with Cross to share his future plans of marriage and to pastor the Mount Zion Baptist Church in Oberlin, Ohio. He also planned to study with Edward Increase Bosworth and Kemper Fullerton at Oberlin. At this meeting Cross unveiled his own plans for Thurman's future, which later proved a source of encouragement and bewilderment for his brilliant young student. Cross said:

> You are a very sensitive Negro man, and doubtless feel under great obligation to put all the weight of your mind and spirit at the disposal of the struggle of your people for full citizenship. But let me remind you that all social questions are transitory in nature and it would be a terrible waste for you to limit your creative energy to the solution of the race problem, however insistent its nature. Give yourself to the timeless issues of the human spirit. Perhaps I have no right to say this to you because as a white man I can never know what it is to be in your situation.[48]

Thurman says that he "pondered the meaning of his words, and wondered what kind of response I could make to this man who did not know that a man and his black skin must face the `timeless issues of the human spirit' together."[49] Cross told Thurman that he was going to find a teacher abroad for him, but these plans were never realized. Cross died during the spring of 1929 before consummating the arrangements, even though he had found the teacher.

Another major intellectual connection in Thurman's odyssey towards community took place during his seminary tenure. In 1925, at an informal retreat in Pawling, New York, he was introduced to the writings of Olive Schreiner (1855- 1920). A fellow participant, George Collins, read a selection entitled, "The Hunter," from Schreiner's *Dreams*. This was the beginning of a life-long spiritual and intellectual relationship with the South African writer.[50]

Early Ministry and Teaching

Mt. Zion Baptist Church

Thurman was graduated from seminary in June 1926 and married one week later to Kate Kelley of La Grange, Georgia. Shortly after the wedding, he began pastoral duties at the Mt. Zion Baptist Church in Oberlin, Ohio. The brief one and a half years in Oberlin were to be a period of great discovery and sorrow for the young pastor. While at the church, he had his first opportunity to test his religious sensibilities in an institutional setting. He discovered through the experiences of worship and pastoral care an inner unity of fellowship that went beyond the barriers of race, class, and tradition. This was most acutely manifest in his inner life of prayer and meditation.[51] Of particular significance was the response he received from a Chinese gentleman who regularly visited the worship services. His comments were, "When I close my eyes and listen to my spirit I am in a Buddhist temple experiencing the renewing of my own spirit." Thurman remarks: "I knew then what I had only sensed before. The barriers were crumbling. I was breaking new ground. Yet, it would be years before I would understand the nature of the breakthrough."[52]

Rufus M. Jones

These new discoveries of the spirit were offset by the very sad news that his new wife had contracted tuberculosis from her days as a social worker. The doctors recommended that she return South for treatment and convalescence with her family. In the meanwhile, Thurman resigned from the church and went to study with another person who would become another major influence in his spiritual and intellectual pilgrimage towards community. In January 1929, Thurman went to Haverford College to study with the mystic scholar and teacher, Rufus M. Jones.[53] The period at Haverford with Jones came about through a personal request to the professor by Thurman after reading Jones's little book entitled *Finding the Trail of Life*.[54] In that work, Jones recounts his childhood experiences and personal religious quest. Although Thurman had never heard of Jones, the book resonated at such a deep level with the religious experiences of his own childhood that he immediately sought him as a teacher. "When I finished (reading)," he writes, "I knew that if this man were alive, I wanted to study with him."[55]

Morehouse and Spelman Colleges

After his period of study with Jones, Thurman returned to his alma mater, Morehouse College, in the fall of 1929 to teach philosophy and religion. He also taught at Morehouse's sister college, Spelman, and served as religious adviser to the students and faculty. While at Spelman, he began to work on the religious insights of the Negro spirituals, which culminated in the 1947 *Ingersoll Lectures on Immortality*, later published as *Deep River* in 1955.

Morehouse and Spelman, like Mt. Zion Church in Oberlin, provided Thurman with the opportunity to test his religious inclinations and training in a structured environment. In teaching the substance of religion and philosophy courses, Thurman felt his immediate responsibility was to inspire and encourage the student in his/her own personal quest for truth.[56] Of particular interest was the development of self-esteem and confidence in the black students whom he encouraged to use education to enhance the quality of life for their people. It was during this time that he began his popular informal discussions on Saturday nights with young

14

black men who struggled with self-realization in the midst of an intensely bitter and segregated society. He writes:

> Invariably we asked, Why are we in college? What are we trying to find? How can we immunize ourselves against the destructive aspects of the environment? How manage the carking fear of the white man's power and not be defeated by our own rage and hatred?[57]

The last year at Morehouse marked great sorrow for Thurman. His wife, Kate, died of tuberculosis. Her death hurled him into deep depression. Exhausted, emotionally and physically, he managed to teach the second semester, but when June finally came, he took a leave of absence and traveled to Europe. He journeyed to London, Scotland, Geneva, and Paris. He spent the bulk of his time in Scotland where he lived as a paid guest with a family. It was during his sojourn there that he experienced an inner healing that brought his shattered life and dream back into perspective.[58]

Howard University

In June 1932, Thurman married Sue Bailey, the daughter of a Baptist minister and an Arkansas legislator, who added the touch of final healing to his reviving spirit. Their common dreams and aspirations made them a unique combination for the long and productive years which lay ahead. Mrs. Thurman's background in music and the arts, her teaching experience, and skills as a national YWCA secretary blended well with the sensitive, artistic spirit of Thurman. It was this dynamic and creative partnership that went to Howard University in July 1932. At the invitation of his old friend and counselor, Mordecai Johnson, who was now President of Howard University, Thurman assumed duties as a faculty member in the School of Religion and later as chairman of the University Committee on Religious Life. He would, in time, be given the prestigious honor of Dean of Rankin Chapel. Thurman, like many other young black scholars, "was caught up in Mordecai Johnson's vision to create the first real community of black scholars, to build an authentic university in America dedicated primarily to the education of black youth."[59]

During his twelve years at Howard University, 1932-1944, Thurman began to experiment more freely with what he had begun to explore in his earlier ministry. When he first assumed duties as Dean of Rankin Chapel in 1936, he completely redesigned the traditional order of service and included special music, sacred dance, poetry and prose selections, and periods of meditation.

Gradually Sunday morning service at Rankin Chapel became a watering place for a wide range of worshippers, not only from within the university community, but also from the District of Columbia. Despite the fact that the District at that time was as segregated racially as Atlanta or Jackson, the Sunday morning chapel service provided a time and place where race, sex, culture, material belongings, and earlier religious orientation became undifferentiated in the presence of God.[60]

A Greater Vision

India, Burma, and Ceylon

During his early years at Howard University, Thurman had the opportunity to experience a vision of the possibility of human community which would shape the direction of the rest of his life and ministry. In 1935, the national YMCA and YWCA International Committee, acting in behalf of the World Student Christian Federation, invited him to serve as chairman of a delegation of black Americans on a "pilgrimage of friendship" as guests of the Student Christian Movement in India, Burma, and Ceylon. Other members of the delegation were Mrs. Thurman and The Reverend (later Bishop) and Mrs. Edward G. Carroll. This trip was crucial because it provided him with concrete instances in an international setting in which he had to come to terms with his own commitment to the Christian faith in light of the issues of race, culture, and religion. It also gave him an opportunity to experiment further with his developing sense of the power of religious experience to create human community among diverse groups, religions, and cultures.

There were four significant events on this pilgrimage which informed his growing perspective on "common ground." One was centered upon his initial reticence about accepting the invitation to go as a representative of "American Christianity." Thurman was deeply concerned that his acceptance of the invitation would relegate his role to that of an apologist for the segregated practices of the American Christian Church. He reasoned, however, that unless he was personally convinced that the essence of the Christian religion could transcend all national, international, racial, cultural, and religious boundaries that he could not continue as a part of it even in his own country. He resolved to go.[61] Throughout the entire journey, the issue of segregation within the Christian church and its inability to change the color bar was raised in sharp and critical relief by many of the indigenous peoples he met. Thurman was called upon to give his interpretation of the religion of Jesus and its answer to the perennial question of the oppressed: "What does the religion of Jesus say to those

16

whose backs are against the wall, those who are the poor, the disinherited, and the dispossessed?"[62]

Second, Thurman had opportunities to experiment with his developing sense of the "common ground" between different religions.[63] Such an experience occurred while Thurman was at Shantiniketan. He met with the head of the division of Oriental Studies in the university. His meeting with the Hindu professor was "the most primary, naked fusing of total religious experience with another human being of which I have ever been capable." He said that:

> It was as if we had stepped out of social, political frames of reference, and allowed two human spirits to unite on a ground of reality that was unmarked by separateness and differences. This was a watershed experience in my life. We had become a part of each other even as we remained essentially individual. I was able to stand secure in my place and enter into his place without diminishing myself or threatening him.[64]

A third event which contributed to his vision of community was the delegation's meeting with Mahatma Gandhi. Two comments of Gandhi's had lasting significance for Thurman. One was the belief that "the unadulterated message of non-violence could be delivered to men everywhere" through the Afro–American.[65] The other remark was in response to a question by Thurman regarding the greatest obstacle to Christianity in India. Gandhi replied that Christianity as practiced and identified with Western culture and colonialism was the greatest enemy to Jesus Christ in India.[66]

The final event, and the most profound, was the moment of vision that the Thurmans experienced at Khyber Pass. In a flash of transcendence, there was brought into clear perspective the dream of community to which Thurman and his wife would dedicate their lives. He writes:

> Near the end of our journey we spent a day in Khyber Pass on the border of the northwest frontier. It was an experience of vision. We stood looking at a distance into Afghanistan, while to our right, and close at hand, passed a long camel train bringing goods and ideas to the bazaars of North India. Here was the gateway through which Roman and Mogul conquerors had come in other days bringing with them goods, new concepts, and the violence of armed might. All that we had seen and felt in India seemed to be brought miraculously into focus. We saw clearly what we must do somehow when we returned to America. We knew that we must test whether a religious fellowship could be developed in Amer-

ica that was capable of cutting across all racial barriers, with a carry-over into the common life, a fellowship that would alter the behavior patterns of those involved. It became imperative now to find out if experiences of spiritual unity among people could be more compelling than the experiences which divide them.[67]

The Fellowship Church for All Peoples

It was this powerful revelation of the potential of community through religious experience that led Thurman to embark upon the bold adventure of establishing The Church for the Fellowship of All Peoples in 1944. In the fall of 1943, he received a letter from Dr. Alfred G. Fisk, a Presbyterian clergyman and professor of philosophy at San Francisco State College. In the letter, Fisk related the experiences of a small group of people in the San Francisco area who were committed to the idea of creating an interracial church. He requested that Thurman recommend a young Negro man, preferably just out of seminary, to come and serve as co-pastor with him. The individual whom Thurman recommended declined the offer and to the surprise of Fisk, Thurman, who was a tenured professor and Dean of the Chapel at Howard, indicated interest in the part-time position which paid only $200 per month. Thurman noted that "I felt the touch on my shoulder that was one with the creative encounter with the Khyber Pass dream of several years earlier."[68] The idea of an interracial church in America kindled in his mind the possibility that this could be the opportunity toward which his life had been moving.[69]

Thurman served as co-pastor with Fisk until the latter resigned a few years after the church started. Thurman later assumed the title of Minister-In-Residence until his resignation in 1953. At the Fellowship Church, Thurman further developed his inner necessity to demonstrate that the power of religious experience can remove racial, cultural, and religious barriers which impede the actualization of human community.[70]

Marsh Chapel, Boston University

The years at the Fellowship Church (1944-1953) prepared Thurman for what was to be another daring adventure in his search for "common ground." In 1953, at the invitation of President Harold Chase, Thurman resigned as Minister-In-Residence of the Fellowship Church to become the Dean of Marsh Chapel at Boston University. This pioneering move was not without great inner struggle and deliberation, but Thurman marveled at the opportunity to translate the idea of an inclusive fellowship which he had successfully demonstrated in San Francisco to a large university setting where the potential for greater outreach and dissemination was present. He also felt that the move had significant social implications in that he was the first black man ever to hold such a position. Thurman was also appointed Professor of Spiritual Disciplines and Resources at the School of Theology and taught a course in homiletics. He had some ambivalence about his role as a teacher in a structured academic setting because he felt that spirituality was not something that could be taught as an academic discipline, but had to be "caught."[71]

The tenure at Marsh Chapel abounded both with successes and conflict. He continued, in essence, what he had begun at Mt. Zion Baptist Church, Howard University and the Fellowship Church. The worship service at Marsh Chapel was filled with creative and artistic liturgies, special music and dance, and long periods of meditation and silence. Meditation became increasingly important to the worship service at Marsh Chapel.[72] Thurman's popularity as a pulpiteer was recognized in *Life* magazine, and several other journals and magazines carried stories on this unusually gifted preacher.[73] In a short time, his popularity reached far beyond the university setting. Thurman was heard over the university radio station WBUR and became a regular contributor to a local television series entitled "We Believe."[74] The chapel attendance consisted of a diverse grouping of students and faculty from the university and surrounding schools and the greater Boston community. The experience of Marsh Chapel was for Thurman a confirmation of the power of religious experience to overcome religious, cultural, classist, and racial barriers that militate against community. It was also a revelation of the problematic nature of religious freedom within an institutional arrangement. This problem surfaced with the growing vitality of the religious fellowship at Marsh Chapel and the concomitant desire by congregants to organize the chapel program for membership. The university rejected a proposal set forth by an *ad hoc* committee comprised of representatives of the university and community on the grounds that the autonomous nature of such an organization would set a dangerous precedent. The university felt that the chapel as an autonomous institution would in time become unmanageable and undermine the university charter.[75] Thurman saw himself as the greatest stumbling block to the proposed organization. A salutary statement by Walter Meulder, Dean of the School of Theology during Thurman's tenure, is insightful. Referring to Thurman at a retirement celebration in Thurman's honor, he says:

> I may note in passing that it is no secret to historians and sociologists of the church that mystical devotion is a very dangerous phenomenon. Mysticism is generally verging on heresy and the mystic is seldom an organization man. Those who avoid the securities of mediated grace, whether in doctrine or sacrament or institution—and insist on speaking in public—give uneasy hours to the ecclesiastical bureaucrat.[76]

The Wider Ministry

Thurman officially resigned from the deanship of Marsh Chapel in 1965, but before his formal resignation, he took a leave of absence in 1962. For the first two years, he was designated Dean on Leave and the last year he was Minister-at-Large. During the first two years, which he refers to as his "wider ministry," he and his wife took two trips around the world. They traveled to Nigeria where he served as visiting lecturer in philosophy and religion at the University of Ibadan. They also journeyed to Israel, Japan, the Philippines, Egypt, and Hawaii. These trips abroad had a profound effect upon Thurman, particularly the trip to Africa.[77] In captivating prose, he described the awe-inspiring experience of his first view of the West Coast of Africa:

> From my cabin window I look out on the full moon and the ghosts of my forefathers rise and fall with the undulating waves. Across these same waters, how many years ago they came. What were the inchoate mutterings locked tight within the circle of their hearts? In the deep, heavy darkness of the foul- smelling hole of the ship, where they could not see the sky nor hear the night noises nor feel the warm compassion of the tribe, they held their breath against the agony.
>
> How does the human spirit accommodate itself to desolation? How did they? What tools of the spirit were in their hands with which to cut a path through the wilderness of their despair? If only death of the body could come to deliver the soul from dying.... If death had come, being ushered into life by a terrible paroxysm of pain, all the assurance of the Way of the Tribe would have carried the spirit home on the wings of precious ceremony and holy ritual. But this! Nothing anywhere in all the myths, in all the stories, in all the ancient memory of the race, had given hint of this tortuous convulsion. There were no gods to hear, no magic spell of witch doctor to summon, even one's companion in chains muttered his quivering misery in a tongue unknown and a sound unfamiliar.
>
> O my fathers, what was it like to be stripped of all supports of life save the beating of the heart and the ebb and flow of fetid air in the lungs? In a strange moment when you suddenly caught your breath, did some intimation from the future give to your spirit a wink of promise? In the darkness, did you hear the silent feet of your children beating a melody of freedom to words which you would never know, in a land in which your bones would be warmed again in the depths of the cold earth in which you would sleep, unrealized and alone? [78]

Thurman's latter years were devoted to the ministry of the Howard Thurman Educational Trust, which he founded in 1965. The Trust is a charitable and eleemosynary foundation that provides a channel for the enlistment of funds for those who share the dream of community. It disburses funds in a carefully planned program of support for religious, charitable, scientific, literary, and educational causes. The Trust, located in San Francisco, houses Thurman's private library and over 800 tapes of meditations, sermons, addresses, lectures, and discussions which represent over forty years of his spiritual pilgrimage toward community. Through the auspices of the Trust, Howard Thurman Listening Rooms have been located throughout the United States and in seventeen countries. Boston University's Special Collections Division in the Mugar Memorial Library houses the original Thurman papers, tapes, and other printed materials.

The establishment of the Trust marked Thurman's last formal endeavor in creating a place where his dream of community could be realized. After a long illness, he died at his home in San Francisco where the Trust is located, during the early morning hours of April 10, 1981. His vision of a "friendly world underneath friendly skies"[79] continues in his rich legacy of the written and oral word. His own words describe best the depth and significance of his life and ministry:

> My testimony is that life is against all dualism. Life is One. Therefore, a way of life that is worth living must be a way worthy of life itself. Nothing less than that can abide. Always, against all that fragments and shatters and against all things that separate and divide within and without, life labors to meld together into a single harmony...in all these things there is a secret door which leads into the central place, where the Creator of life and the God of the human heart are one and the same. I take my stand for the future and for generations who follow over the bridges we already have crossed. It is here that the meaning of the hunger of the heart is unified. The Head and the Heart at last inseparable; they are lost in wonder in the One.[80]

The Intellectual Sources of Community

Morehouse College

Thurman's student years at Morehouse College, from 1919 to 1923, were perhaps the most crucial period of his intellectual development. Although he credits George Cross as the most influential intellectual source in his life, his four years at Morehouse College represent his introduction into a new world of ideas which would whet his intellectual appetite and encourage him to pursue higher learning beyond the limited expectations imposed by the greater society. The rich fraternal atmosphere and the stimulating intellectual climate of Morehouse College found a willing and enthusiastic participant in the searching spirit of the young student. Thurman was a member of the student YMCA, the Debating Society, and the editor of the first senior yearbook in the history of the school. It is Thurman's claim that he and his classmate, Jim Nabrit, read every book in the small but respectable college library.[81]

The Morehouse faculty set high levels of expectation for their students, both academically and spiritually. Thurman was privileged to study with some of the most distinguished black scholars of his day. Among these was the noted sociologist, E. Franklin Frazier, from whom Thurman took a course in Social Origins.[82] Another noted educator whose influence and friendship were to continue throughout Thurman's life was Benjamin Mays. Mays's remarkable career as a teacher, preacher, social activist, and president of Morehouse College touched the lives of many young black leaders, including Martin Luther King, Jr.[83] Mays coached Thurman on the Debating Society and was responsible for kindling his interest in philosophy.[84] Thurman maintained that the absence of formal philosophy courses in the missionary colleges of the South was not an accident, but was systematically designed by the "shapers of our minds" to control the level of consciousness among the black masses.[85] It was, in part, because of Mays's encouragement that Thurman won scholarship monies to study philosophy at Columbia University at the end of his sophomore year. The summer at Columbia was Thurman's first formal introduction to philosophy. He refers to this summer as a very critical period in his intellectual development. In fact, he states that the course at Columbia University in reflective thinking, which was taught by E.A. Burt, was the most significant single course he ever took.[86] Many years later, Thurman credited Mays with the foresight to create the environment whereby young black men could experience themselves as human beings with dignity and worth and their minds as their own.[87] This remarkable friendship between these black intellectual titans lasted nearly 60 years. Beyond their personal appreciation for one another was the common struggle against the demeaning and vicious attacks against their humanity

22

meted out by the racist culture in which they lived. Mays's personal reflection is insightful:

> Howard and I were both determined that lynching, segregation, and degradation would not beat us down. We were not going to believe that we and our people were inferior as the white man intended. We knew by instinct that we were free. We knew that we were created by God and that God, being God, would not and could not create people as slaves.[88]

These men and others, like Professor Gary Moore, who taught sociology, and Professor Lorimer Milton, who guided Thurman through his major in economics, helped to shape the intellectual and spiritual resources that would pilot him in his search for community.[89] He says, "They placed over our heads a crown that for the rest of our lives we would be trying to grow tall enough to wear."[90]

George Cross

Thurman named three professors at Rochester Theological Seminary as influences in his intellectual development. They were Dr. Conrad Moehlman, Professor of the History of Christianity; Dr. Henry Robins, Professor of Religious Education and The History of Philosophy and Religion and Missions; and Dr. George Cross, Professor of Systematic Theology. In this brief discussion, attention will be given only to Professor George Cross, who, according to Thurman, made the most significant contribution to his developing thought.[91]

The dominant concern of Cross's thought was the infinite worth of the individual and her/his relationship to the creation of human community. For Cross, this theme is most definitively demonstrated in the person and work of Jesus Christ.[92] The emphasis is on the unique nature and potential of the individual, i.e., the supremacy of personality that is rooted in its self-consciousness and infinite worth. Cross wrote:

> The whole story of human life becomes the story of the manner in which human creative personality has wrought through the transformation of the race by seeking to impart to every member of it his or her own very selfhood in all its worth.[93]

According to Smith, Cross's thought can be located in evangelical liberalism, which stressed "a personality-centered Christianity, reason and experience, witness to moral and social issues, theological personalism, and an evolutionary revelation of faith."[94] Smith claims that Cross's thought can be viewed in three distinct yet interrelated ways. First, Cross endeavored to define "the essence of the Christian faith," i.e., "the basic, unchanging, unifying truth which characterizes and genuinely manifests the faith."[95] Second, the purpose of this essence is to lead the individual and community toward salvation.[96] Cross believed that the "perfect personality" represented in Jesus Christ is the ideal toward which humanity strives.[97] In the idealization of this perfect personality lies the ground for community. It is the key to the question of the individual's relationship to community:

> By virtue of its estimate of personality the Christian faith is a radically reconstructive force in those relations of man to man we call social. For that very reason it is constitutive of the better community and works toward the permanency of human community life.[98]

Third, Cross maintained that the theological understanding of the essence of Christian faith must be creative and open to truth through rational inquiry and revelation.[99] For him, Christianity is primarily concerned with the inner life, rather than external creeds and dogma. He writes: "For our forms of worship, doctrine, order, and conduct are not truly our religion. They are the outer of which our real religion is the inner."[100] Yet, these externalities have their purpose in "clothing the faith" or providing the faith experience with form and making it possible to be passed on from one generation to the other. Cross identified four historic forms of the Christian faith as the social, liturgical, ecclesiastical, and doctrinal. He interpreted them within the evolutionary model of Protestant liberalism suggested by Smith.[101] He states:

> Creeds are necessary to salvation; but a stereotyped creed? Never. Creeds, moral customs, churches, liturgies, belong together. The same kind of necessity that calls for their creation calls again for their transformation.[102]

A careful reading of Cross's three books suggests that Thurman's early conceptualization of the theological themes that would nurture his understanding of the nature of community could have had their genesis during this fruitful period. These themes are the sacredness of human personality, the primacy of the individual in the creation of community, the dynamic, teleological nature of revelation, the distinction between the "inner" and "outer" dimensions of religious experience, the consciousness of sin, and reconciliation as love.[103]

24

Olive Schreiner

Another important source in the intellectual development of Howard Thurman was Olive Schreiner. Mozella Gordon Mitchell contends that Schreiner influenced Thurman in two vital respects: 1) through her philosophy concerning the universality of truth and the oneness of all life, and 2) through her outstanding literary form and creative expression.[104] Smith argues that although Thurman edited and published Schreiner's writings, they serve more as a creative source of inspiration for him than a seminal intellectual influence. He notes that Schreiner's concern with the unity of all life expresses what Thurman already believed and felt, but did not add any new theological perspective to his thinking. Her influence, according to Smith, belongs in another category, namely, that of providing nourishment to the theme of the unity of all life which was already the heart of Thurman's concern.[105]

While one is inclined to agree with Smith's position in reference to the intellectual influence of Schreiner on Thurman,[106] there seems to be a more profound level of affinity. The fact that Olive Schreiner was a white South African woman who openly and fearlessly denounced racism and sexism had a powerful impact on Thurman. He was not merely drawn to Schreiner by her articulation of the unity of life theme, but also by her identification with the radical moral implications of that theme for the black experience of racism and violence he encountered in his own life situation.[107] A critical question for Thurman in his initial investigation of Schreiner's life and writings was, "How could a white woman born and reared in South Africa think as she thinks and feel about man as she felt?" Thurman never quite resolved this question nor the issue of Schreiner's use of derogatory language to describe black South Africans.[108] Despite these concerns, she served as a fellow traveler and a fount of inspiration for Thurman in his search for "common ground."

There are two significant themes in Schreiner which can also be found in Thurman's thought: the unity of all life and the redemptive role of the solitary individual and his/her responsibility to lay the foundation for the collective destiny of humanity.[109] These two pivotal ideas are also in Cross, but in Schreiner they receive the literary and artistic stroke characteristic of Thurman's own temperament and style.

Rufus M. Jones

Thurman's semester with Jones during the spring of 1929 was his first formal introduction to the study of mysticism. He attended all of Jones's lectures in philosophy and was a special student in a seminar on Meister Eckhart. He was given special reading assignments and met for weekly conferences with Jones. He also had access to Jones's extensive library on mysticism, which was one of the most comprehensive in America.[110] The time he spent with Jones was one of the most important periods of his development. He refers to it as:

> A watershed from which flowed much of the thought and endeavor to which I was to commit the rest of my working life. These months defined my deepest religious urges and framed in meaning much of what I had learned over the years.[111]

While Thurman acknowledges Cross as the most important influence upon him intellectually, it was Jones who provided him with a methodology that did not violate the validity of spirituality and its relationship to social transformation. It should be noted here that Cross's statement that Thurman should devote himself to "the timeless issues of the human spirit" and not waste his energies on the racial problem remained a source of concern for this sensitive young black man. On the one hand, he wanted to honor the counsel of his mentor, but on the other, he felt the keen and urgent need to deal with the reality of being a black man in American society. Jones's most valuable contribution to the development of Thurman's thinking at this critical point of his search for community, therefore, was his demonstration that one could devote oneself to the ultimate concerns of the human spirit without neglecting the pressing moral issues of society. With Jones, Thurman was able to more clearly define the relationship between the inner and outer experiences of religious life. In his opening remarks at the *Rufus Jones Memorial Lectures* in 1961, he shares his indebtedness to his teacher:

> He gave to me the confidence in the insight that the religion of the inner life could deal with the empirical experience of man without retreating from the demands of such experience. To state what I mean categorically, the religion of the inner life at its best is *life affirming* rather than *life denying* and must forever be involved in the Master's instruction, 'Be ye perfect, even as your heavenly father is perfect.'[112]

Smith argues that Jones, like Cross and Robins, can be located within the theological stream of evangelical liberalism, and as Cross and Robins are concerned respectively with the essence of Christian faith and religion, Jones's concern is with the essence of Christian mysticism.[113] The distinctive feature of Jones's mysticism is that it provides the basis for social transformation. Mystical consciousness, for Jones, does not call the believer to spiritual retreat but rather it reveals the Divine will for "a fellowship of mutual caring and serving, and a Divine which dwells in humanity."[114] Jones's mysticism has deep roots in theological personalism. He refers to religious experience as the "conjunct life," which is the divine-human

26

fellowship between persons and a Person. Personality cannot exist without other persons, and a society of finite selves cannot exist without a Consciousness which transcends the entire group of selves.[115]

Jones makes a distinction between two types of mystics which he refers to as "negation mystics" and "affirmation mystics." The negation mystics are those who believe that God cannot be found in finite, transitory experience, but only by a *via negativa*, i.e., by withdrawing from the world of senses and achieving union with God through loss of personality. The fallacy of this position, according to Jones, is that "this mystic is asking for something which could not be known or attained. The Absolute is postulated as precisely the negation of all finiteness [and] turns out to be for us mortals only an absolute zero—a limitless sum-total of negation."[116] The affirmation mystics, on the other hand, do not make the beatific vision the end of life, but rather the beginning. For the affirmation mystic, the Infinite is found in the finite. Jones writes:

> It is the primary fact for him (the affirmative mystic) that he partakes of God, that his personal life has come out of the life of God and that he is never beyond the reach of God who is his source. But his true being is to be wrought out in the world where he can know only finite and imperfect things. His mission on earth is to be a fellow-worker with God—contributing in a normal daily life his human powers to the divine Spirit who works in him and about him, bringing to reality a Kingdom of God.[117]

Jones's rich understanding of the relationship between the inner life and social transformation is a significant element in Thurman's treatment of the committed individual's responsibility to society. As noted, Thurman makes a crucial distinction between the inner and outer modes of existence. Much of his understanding in this respect should be credited to the influence of Rufus M. Jones. James Massey identifies several areas of correspondence between Jones's and Thurman's thought reflected in their doctrines of God and human persons, their reverence for human personality, their suspicion of formal creeds as being usually divisive, their search for ultimates, and their conviction that truth is not defined by contexts of belief.[118]

In summary, this section has been devoted to the experiential and intellectual sources of Thurman's search for common ground. From his early years in the black community of Daytona Beach through his later years with the Howard Thurman Educational Trust, there is a progressive line of development in his quest for community. Specifically, this biographical profile has sought to illustrate a pattern which begins with the particularity of the black American experience of segregation and oppression and emerges into a universal vision which incorporates all humanity. This should not be interpreted as a casual observation, but as a profound insight into the development of the ideal of community in the thinking of Howard Thurman. It should also be noted that from this brief overview of Thurman's quest for community, two significant concerns are present: *the relationship of Christian faith to the color bar*, and *the determination to find a moral and practical method to overcome racism in American society.* These two concerns are critical for a proper interpretation of Thurman's intellectual endeavors.

While the four intellectual sources (Morehouse, Cross, Schreiner, and Jones) represent major influences in his development, Thurman also drew from a wide range of philosophical, theological, and literary insights. The intellectual sources examined above are significant in that they contributed most profoundly to the conception, character, and means of actualization of human community in his thought. These sources will be referred to at appropriate places throughout this examination.

Chapter 2

I Heard of a City

"I have sought," he said, "for long years I have laboured; but I have not found her. I have not rested, I have not repined, and I have not seen her; now my strength is gone. Where I lie down worn out, other men will stand, young and fresh. By the steps that I have cut they will climb; by the stairs that I have built, they will mount. They will never know the name of the man who made them. At the clumsy work they will laugh; when the stones roll they will curse me. But they will mount, and on _my_ work; they will climb, and by _my_ stair! They will find her, and through me! And no man liveth to himself, and no man dieth to himself.

The tears rolled from beneath the shrivelled eyelids. If Truth had appeared above him in the clouds now he would not have seen her, the mist of death was in his eyes.

"My soul hears their glad coming," he said; "and they shall mount! They shall mount!" He raised his shrivelled hand to his eyes.

Then slowly from the sky above, through the still air, came something falling, falling, falling. Softly it fluttered down, and dropped on to the breast of the dying man. He felt it with his hands. It was a feather. He died holding it.

—Olive Schreiner, "The Hunter"

I am a po' pilgrim of sorrow,
I'm in dis world alone,
No hope have I for tomorrow,
But I've started to make heav'n my home.

Sometimes I'm tossed and driven, Lord.
Sometimes I don't know where to roam,
But I heard of a city called heav'n,
And I've started to make heav'n my home.

—Negro Spiritual

Howard Thurman identified his life-long quest for community as "the search for common ground." For him, the ideal of community served both as the goal or _telos_ toward which all life strives and the norm for ethical reflection. In this chapter, the nature of community in the thought of

Thurman is examined in reference to his conception of community and the triadic character of community.

The Conception of Community

For Thurman, community refers to wholeness, integration, and harmony. Fundamental to his conception of community is the teleological nature of life. All life, according to him, is involved in goal-seeking. In each particular manifestation of life, there is the potential for it to realize its proper form, or to come to itself. The actualization of any form of life is synonymous with community. Community as "actualized potential" is true at all levels of life, from tiny cells to human society.[1]

Life serves as a hermeneutical principle in his analysis of the nature of community. He argues that the most obvious characteristic of life, one which is often overlooked, gives the initial clue to the nature of community. This inherent quality is that "life is alive."

> One of the simplest and for me the most profound observations is that life itself is alive. This is a living, pulsing, breathing dimension of experience...this is in essence a dynamic universe and wherever there is life there is some kind of structure and dependability, some inner logic that gives meaning and structure and viability and purpose, not in a metaphysical sense, but purpose in the sense that is expressed when you notice that a house plant finds a way to turn towards the sun without any guidance from you.[2]

Attention to the processes at work in living things all around us reveals that there is hard purposefulness, a determination to live in life itself.[3] This "directiveness"[4] in life that is at work in nature also manifests itself in the personal and social dimensions of human existence. There is a fundamental structure of interrelatedness and interdependability inherent in all living things, including the social arrangements by which human beings relate to one another.

> It is not an overstatement that the purpose of all the arrangements and conventions that make up the formal and informal agreements under which men live in society, is to nourish one another with one another. The safeguards by which individuals or groups of men establish the boundaries of intimate and collective belonging are meant ultimately to guarantee self-nourishment.[5]

The Sources of Community

The sources for Thurman's thinking regarding the nature of community are found in racial memory, living structures, utopias, common consciousness, and identity.[6] He begins his examination of the ideal of community in racial memory by analyzing creation myths. His purpose is to explore what the memory of the human race has to say about the nature of community and its ageless concern for "lost harmony." His central question is, "What is there that seems to be implicit, or inherent in racial memory that is on the side of community?"[7] In attempting to answer that question, Thurman examined the creation myths of the Judeo-Christian tradition and the Hopi Indians. He concluded that a consistent theme in both accounts is "creation with the harmony of innocence; the loss of innocence with the disintegration of harmony."[8] This theme has significant implications for his understanding of innocence and good, and community as an ideal or goal that must be achieved.[9] In each account, the original experience of community by humans is both potential and actualized potential within the framework of innocence. In this state of innocence, the things that work against community are dormant or unactualized, but once they are actualized by the agency of human free will, disharmony results and innocence is lost.[10] The loss of innocence marks the loss of community within persons, in interpersonal relationships, in divine-human relationships, and in nature. He argues that once innocence is lost it can never be restored. After the fall from innocence, the divine-human project of "goodness" or "community" becomes the goal toward which human endeavor must be directed. Unlike innocence, "community" or "goodness" must be achieved through free, responsible actions. Goodness as achieved community is predicated on the radical freedom of the individual to make a conscious, deliberate choice to strive for wholeness, harmony, and integration within the self and in relations with others and the world. This is a key concept in Thurman's anthropology and ethical theory. Innocence is given without knowledge; goodness, however, is achieved through knowledge and responsibility.

When the quality of goodness has been reestablished, a great change has taken place. Eyes are opened, knowledge is defined, and what results is the triumph of the quality of innocence over the quality of discord; a new synthesis is achieved that has in it the element of triumph. That is, a child is innocent, but a man who has learned how to winnow beauty out of ugliness, purity out of stain, tranquility out of tempest, joy out of sorrow, life out of death— only such a man may be said to be good. But he is no longer innocent.[11]

The creation myths demonstrate that this sense of lost harmony is still a part of the collective consciousness of the human race, Thurman contends, and therefore, we can never accept the absence of community as the human destiny.[12]

Second, Thurman examines the nature of community in living structures. He argues that community can be analyzed at two levels of living structures. The first is life in the sense of existence, i.e., in process, in its manifold forms and configurations that manifest themselves in time and space, in an orderly and purposeful universe. Here the concern is with living structures without any particular consciousness as we experience them. There is present at this level a discernible order or pattern that seems to be realizing itself in time. This can be understood without reference to religious characterizations or presuppositions. Order is a given of existence, a part of the facticity of life.[13]

A second dimension of living structures are those entities which exhibit "consciousness."[14] Here Thurman explores the relationship between the biosphere, ecosystems, and organisms in their respective functions and interrelatedness. He stresses that structural dependability, which is characteristic of all life as it strives toward community, can be observed in these conscious living structures as they seek to develop their own unique capabilities.

> The potential in any given expression of life is actualized and becomes involved in this very process in the actualizing of the potential of some other form of life upon which it is dependent. The cycle is endless, and the integration of any form cannot be thought of as independent of a similar process in other forms. Here is structural dependency expressive of an exquisite harmony—the very genius of the concept of community.[15]

Thurman is particularly concerned with the human organism, and seeks to demonstrate its empirical workings of interdependability and interrelatedness with other living phenomena. The human organism reveals an evolutionary process characterized by directiveness and purpose. The emergence of mind in the human organism may be a product of the species' response to the history of the organism itself. The human mind does directly and deliberately what nature has done through ages of trial and error. He suggests that the "mind *as* mind" evolved from the body as part of the unfolding process of potential resident in life and that mind as such is the basis for the evolution of "spirit." The imagination as *mind-evolved spirit* continued the same inherent quest for community which is resident in nature and the body.[16] When an individual consciously seeks community, therefore, s/he will discover that "what he is seeking deliberately is but the logic of meaning that has gone into his creation."[17]

The third source of his reflection on the nature of community is the notion of utopia or "the prophet's dream." He examines the utopias in Isaiah 11:1-9, Plato's *Republic*, The New Jerusalem of *The Apocalypse* (Revelation 21), and Sir Thomas More's *Utopia*. Utopias arise, according to Thurman, out of the individual's experience of disharmony in the present. The utopian dream of harmony and order, therefore, is a projection of the ideal of community which is instinctively a part of the human race.[18] The utopian literary form represents the quality of hope about the human situation and the future. It demonstrates the rational necessity and possibility of a realized future that must be honored as long as the potential for community in the individual, society, or the world has not been actualized. It does not matter, says Thurman, whether the dreamers believe the dream will come to pass in the particular historical context in which they live, but "they dare to say, nevertheless, that it will come to pass, sometime, somewhere."[19]

The fourth source for Thurman's investigation of the nature of community is "common consciousness." The notion of "common consciousness" refers to the affinity between human consciousness and other forms of conscious existence evident in nature. The theme of the kinship of all living things extends even into the realm of communication between animals, plants, and human beings. He reasons that if life is one, then there ought to be a fundamental sense of unity at all levels of existence. Since life in any form cannot be fundamentally alien to life, then more than two forms may share the same moment in time without resistance and without threat.[20] This understanding of "common consciousness" is fundamental to his understanding of love and the role of imagination.[21]

The fifth source is the notion of identity. A sense of self, according to Thurman, is the clue and ground for community with others. Identity is rooted in self-awareness. The self-conscious experience of one's body as a part of nature and being sustained by other forms of life sheds light on the individual's kinship with all living things. An individual's body is also his/her unique, private possession.[22]

The quest for personal identity is also part of the mind's inherent logic, which seeks wholeness and integration. As stated, the mind is part of the evolution of the body.[23] He rejects the notion that the mind appeared by a particular act, decree or fiat. An individual's identity stands in direct relationship to the mind's actualization of its inherent potential. He argues that "in this sense a man's journey into life may be characterized as a quest for community within himself."[24] The dynamic push for order and harmony at the self-conscious level bears striking affinity with what occurs instinctively in subhuman forms of life. The family and society are the communal contexts in which the individual finds his/her identity.[25]

Thurman's understanding of community as "actualized potential" rooted in the dynamic, teleological nature of life has been examined. The triadic character of community is the concern of the second part of this chapter.

The Triadic Character of Community

In Thurman's understanding of the nature of community, there is a triadic relationship between the individual, God, and the world. These three elements are integrally related and form the basic analytical construct for the dynamic character of community. Community is a cooperative project involving all three elements. However, the relationship between the individual and God is primary. Religious experience is *the* fundamental category for all his thinking regarding community. The world, though positive and salient, remains secondary in relation to the centrality of religious experience.[26] His ordering of the respective elements informs this analysis. This discussion will proceed as follows: 1) the individual: the nature of the self, human freedom and responsibility; 2) God: the nature of God, community as the will of God, the immanence of God, and the power of God's love to create the basis for community within the individual and the world; 3) the world: the universe, nature, human society, and the state; and 4) the totality of experience: the nature of religious experience, world-mindedness and disciplines for preparation.

The Individual

The Nature of the Individual

In Thurman's conceptualization of the nature of community, the individual is the point of departure. A persistent note is that the individual must begin with with her/his own "working paper."[27] The development of a sense of self is the basis upon which one comes to understand one's own unique potential and self-worth. Without a sense of self, one drifts aimlessly through life without a true understanding of one's place in existence.[28] A healthy sense of self is garnered out of a dynamic tension between the individual's self-fact and self-image. The person's self-fact is her/his inherent worth as a child of God; it is the central fact that s/he is part of the very movement of life itself.[29] The individual's self-image is formed by relationships with others, and to a large extent, self-image determines one's destiny. However, the individual's case must ultimately rest with her/his self-fact of intrinsic worth. He writes, "The responsibility for living with meaning and dignity can never be taken away from the individual."[30] This is a significant point for his treatment of the individual's

34

response to dehumanizing onslaughts like racism and other forces that work against human potential and community.[31]

The "sense of self" is rooted in the nature of the self. Thurman makes a distinction between the inner and outer dimensions of the self. The individual is both a child of nature and a child of spirit. The outer dimension of the self is part of the external world of nature and human society.[32] The clue to the outer world of relations, however, is found in the inner world of experience. The mind is the place to begin in understanding the inner dimension of the self. For Thurman, the terms "inner life" or "inner awareness" refer to more than the mere formal discursive activity of the mind, but include the entire range of self-awareness of the individual.[33] "Inner life" means:

> The awareness of the individual's responsiveness to realities that are transcendent in character, emanating from a core of Reality which the individual is aware and of which the individual is also aware that he is a part. The inner life, therefore, is activity that takes place within consciousness, but does not originate there and is a part of a Reality central to all life and is at once the ground of all awareness. It is there that man becomes conscious of his meaning and destiny as a child, an offspring of God.[34]

The cultivation of the inner life is the basis for the development of a genuine sense of self and authentic existence in the world. Thurman is acutely aware of the danger of subjectivism and privatization of meaning implied in the emphasis on the development of inner consciousness and tries to guard against this tendency by accentuating the need for external empirical verification of what one experiences in one's inner life. "The real questions at issue here," he contends, "are, how may a man know he is not being deceived? Is there any way by which he may know beyond doubt, and therefore with verification, that what he experiences is authentic and genuine?"[35] Rational coherence between the inner experience of self and the external world is the methodology employed to test for self-deception. He argues that "Whatever seems to deny a fundamental structure of orderliness upon which rationality seems to depend cannot be countenanced."[36]

Human Freedom and Responsibility

Thurman's distinction between the inner and outer modes of self-existence is helpful in understanding his notion of human freedom and responsibility. Human freedom is a key concept in his anthropology and the individual's role in creating community. In defining freedom, he utilizes the inner and outer dimensions of the self to contrast the notions of "liberty" and "freedom." Liberty refers to the external prerogatives, privileges, and grants that a particular social arrangement or context confers upon the individual. "Its locus is outside of the individual and can be given or withheld in accordance to the judgment and the will and behavior of those external to oneself who grant it."[37] Freedom, unlike liberty, is located within the very being of the individual. It is a quality of being and spirit; it is what the individual becomes aware of in the development of a sense of self. Although the external environment may deny the individual's liberty, it cannot deny the fundamental fact of freedom which is the individual's birthright as a child of God. Likewise, the individual cannot deny the fact of his/her freedom. In this sense, like Sartre, Thurman would maintain that one is "condemned to be free."

Thurman utilizes a two-part working definition for freedom. Freedom is first "the will and the ability to act at any moment in time as to influence or determine the future."[38] Implied in this view of freedom is the autonomy of the individual in the midst of social, physical and natural forces. Although the individual's destiny is to a large extent determined by these forces, ultimately he or she cannot be defined by them. The second part of his definition of freedom sheds light on this important point. Freedom is "the sense of options or alternatives."[39] Freedom as a *sense of options* or alternatives is to be differentiated from freedom as an *exercise of options*. There are instances when the exercise of options is impossible, e.g., against natural, impersonal forces. Freedom as a sense of options or alternatives refers to the experience of the inner self located in the will, in the personal place where only the individual as individual can produce effect. He illustrates this view of freedom with a story from childhood in which he cornered a snake and placed his foot on it to hold it still. Even under the weight of his foot he could still feel the small creature resisting by wiggling its tiny body. Thurman says that even though the snake could not escape, it kept alive a sense of option. This sense of option that the individual possesses as a part of his/her being is fundamental to freedom "and wherever this dies, wherever elements in the environment are internalized by people so as to paralyze this sense, then all the lights go out and the soul of the people begins to rot."[40]

Freedom, then is a quality of being; it is part of the "givenness" of the individual. Ultimately, even the individual cannot deny her/his freedom. Thurman believed that freedom understood in this way enables the individual to experience a proper sense of self despite the ravages and insults heaped upon her/him by society and the world.

> 'Freedom under God' means the recognition of the essential dignity of the human spirit; therefore it is inherent in man's experience with life and is a basic ingredient in personality. This is so universal that it is the key to the intrinsic worthfulness which

every man ascribes, at long last, to himself. There is a strange and mighty potency in the elemental knowledge that resides deep in the heart of everyman that freedom under God is his birthright as a child of God.[41]

Freedom also entails responsibility.[42] The individual who is aware of personal freedom is responsible not only for her/his *actions*, but also for her/his *reactions*. The individual is responsible for her/his actions because s/he is free. Therefore, one can never place the blame for what one does on forces outside oneself. Responsibility is a corollary of freedom because when the individual assumes responsibility for her/his actions, s/he confirms the grounds of her/his own self and authenticity. Therefore, one can never unshoulder responsibility for one's actions without forfeiting one's own being.[43] Despite a person's history and the external forces that shape and mold one's fate and story, the individual remains responsible for her/his actions. This emphasis on responsibility has profound implications for the moral imperatives to love and to be sincere ("truth-telling") in *all* encounters and situations. For the oppressed, claiming responsibility for one's own destiny is the initial act of freedom and selfhood. Thurman writes, "If I let anyone take responsibility for my own actions, then I give them power of veto and certification over my life."[44]

The other side of responsibility is the individual's *reaction* to the events of her/his life. There is no escape or rationalization which releases one from the responsibility entailed in free being. At all times, the individual maintains the right of veto and certification over how s/he *responds* to the circumstances of her/his life, even those the individual cannot control.

> I can become a prisoner of events, I can cry aloud at the miscarriage of justice in the universe. I can do a whole range of things, but when I get through all my exhortations, my protestations, my agonizing, I am still left with the tight logic of my personal responsibility to say 'yes' or 'no' to my situation. Yes or no and make it stick. This is the freedom man has. He does not have to say 'yes' even to events he cannot control.[45]

Responsibility exists at both personal and social levels of existence. It is always a shared experience. The prerogative that the individual ascribes to her/himself must be carried over into relations with others. The individual is responsible as a member of the group and/or society in which s/he lives and functions. The privatization of responsibility is a denial of freedom. "Free men must be responsible to themselves and to each other for the personal and collective life which marks their days."[46]

Finally, responsibility is ultimately to God, the ground and guarantor of the individual's freedom. The individual, therefore, is ultimately responsible to God for all her/his *actions* and *reactions*. "God is the Creator of life," says Thurman, "and the ultimate responsibility of life is to God. Man's responsibility to God is personal and solitary, but it is not experienced in isolation or detachment."[47] Society is not exempt from responsibility to God. As societies participate in the dynamics and ends of life, they are also accountable to the God of life. America as a nation is morally responsible for its actions toward its citizens of color and the disinherited.[48]

In summary, the individual is the point of departure for Thurman in his thought regarding the dynamic character of community. His anthropology stresses the centrality of personality and the inherent worth of the individual as a child of God. Developing a sense of self, which is the primary project of the individual, involves maintaining a healthy balance between one's self-fact and self-image. This is rooted in Thurman's distinction between the inner and outer dimensions of the self. The individual is a child of nature and a child of spirit. While the outer world of relations informs the inner life, the latter is the place where the commitment to community is made and the realization of harmony, integration, and wholeness begins. At the core of Thurman's anthropology is his interpretation of human freedom and responsibility. Freedom is part of the "givenness" of being; it is neither conferred upon the individual from authorities or external sources, nor can it be ultimately denied by the individual. It is the individual's birthright as a child of God. Responsibility is entailed in the notion of freedom. The individual is responsible both for her/his actions and reactions. To relinquish responsibility for one's actions or reactions is to forfeit one's being and freedom. Individuals and societies are ultimately accountable to God, who is the Creator of Life.

God

The second principal in the triadic relationship involved in the actualization of community is God.[49] For Thurman, God is the sovereign Lord of human history and the universe. Nothing is outside of the divine context. God's power is absolute, and God's love is omnipresent.[50] God is the Creator and Sustainer of life and existence. God is not merely the Creator of creatures, but is the "Bottomer of existence," i.e., transcendent, all-inclusive, all-comprehending, and universal.[51] God is the Subject of which all living things are predicates. This "subject quality of life," writes Thurman, "seems always to be previous in time to all particular living things or all particular manifestations."[52]

God is related to all existence as Mind in a way similar to the human mind in its relation to time-space existence. The Mind of God seeks to realize Itself in time-space manifestations, therefore existence itself is understood as divine activity. The divine activity is the basis for the rational order which is observable in life.[53] This inherent logic in existence provides the framework for the individual's interpretation of the will of God.[54]

> I am interpreting all manifestations of order or process or plan as an expression of the Will of God coming to Itself in time and space. The order in creation, thought of as a rational principle on the basis of which all man's study of the external world is projected is the will of God in nature and the external world. What is observed as a structure of orderliness or dependability in any and all experiences of life, from the simplest to the most complex, is seen most dramatically in the ability of man to create, plan, to function purposefully, and to implement in time and space what is idea and thought in the mind.[55]

Second, God is also personal and immanent. One of the crucial demands of the religious experience is that the individual is addressed by God at a personal and intimate level. God can never be understood abstractly, but must be experienced as Presence.[56] The Presence of God can be encountered at any level of experience, in the commonplace or through religious discipline and preparation.[57] God is immanent in the world of nature, persons, and things. The divine *imprimatur* is on all of creation. In persons, God is resident within the human mind and spirit. Thurman believed that within the individual there is an "uncreated element" which is the basis for the person's identification with God as a child of God. This "uncreated element" is the seat of intuition[58] and the meeting place between God and the individual. [59]

The life and ministry of Jesus is the great example of the immanence of God operative in the human personality.[60] Jesus, according to Thurman,

> erected a pyramid out of the funded insights of all the prophets, scaled its heights and brought God down out of the clouds, and found him to be an intimate part of the warp and woof of human experience and human struggle.[61]

Third, the love of God is the basis and the assurance of the actualization of community in the individual and society.[62] There is within the individual a basic need to be cared for and understood in a relationship with another at a point that is beyond all good and evil. Much of an individual's time and energy is spent trying to fulfill this need and to guarantee that s/he is not alone. In the religious experience this inner necessity of love is fulfilled by the love of God. In the Presence of God, the person is affirmed and becomes aware of being dealt with totally.

Whether he is a good person or a bad person, he is being dealt with at a point beyond all that is limiting, and all that is creative within him. He is dealt with at the core of his being, and at that core he is touched and released.[63]

Consequently, the individual is enabled to deal honestly and lovingly with her/himself and others. What is experienced in encounter with the love of God becomes the basis for her/his relating to others. "What is disclosed in his religious experience he must define in community."[64] When the individual experiences the love of God, s/he finds the basis and the method for authenticating the vision of community within her/himself and in the world.

In summary, Thurman's vision of reality is theocentric.[65] God is the sovereign Lord of human history and the universe. Nothing is outside the divine context; God's power is absolute, and God's love is omnipresent. God is also the Creator and sustainer of life and existence. The divine activity in life, which is expressed in a rational and intelligible order, discloses the "intent" or the will of God for harmony, wholeness, and integration, in fine, community. The immanence of God is in nature, persons, and things; the divine signature is upon all of life. Within the individual, God exists as the ground of his/her being, the "uncreated element" that transcends time-space manifestations and creaturely concerns. This is the meeting place between the Infinite and the finite, the ground of the religious encounter between God and the individual. It is here that the love of God both enables and requires the individual to seek community within her/himself and in the world.

The World

The third element in the triadic relationship involved in the creation of community is the world. The idea of world, in Thurman, includes the universe, nature, human society, and the state.

The universe is the immensity of life manifesting itself in the totality. Here the creative act of God is understood as the all-pervasive quality of life with an infinite number of configurations and forms. The universe is dynamic and evolving; it expresses itself in creative order as life seeks to come to itself in time and space. In this dimension, there is no origin or end. Such notions are introduced by the human mind in order to give meaning and coherence to the vast totality of life in which it exists.[66]

Second, the notion of world includes nature. Nature is part of the creative activity of God in which life reveals itself in interrelated structures of dependability. Nature is characterized by an impersonal order that operates without consciousness or values.[67] Nature, however, is involved in the movement of life towards community.[68] The human person, as a physical being, is part of nature, and is therefore subject to natural laws.[69] Yet, the individual is capable of self-transcendence and is able to stand over and against nature to manipulate it to her/his own ends. This power over nature has had both positive and negative consequences. Positively, the human race has been able to implement technology that has brought us closer to community; the world is now a veritable neighborhood. But, negatively, modern science has created weapons of destruction that threaten to annihilate human life on the planet. Thurman suggests that the essential problem between human beings and nature is spiritual, and that it is possible for humanity to restore the lost harmony or sense of community with nature. The restored community would include harmonious relationships with animals as well.[70]

This notion of the world also includes human society. He writes, "In human society, the experience of community, or realized potential, is rooted in life itself because the intuitive human urge for community reflects a characteristic of life."[71] Society finds its basis in the individual's need to be cared for and assured that s/he is not isolated from others.[72] All social arrangements by which individuals live are predicated on a common need for "self-nourishment" so that the organism (body, mind, and spirit) can grow and develop. The family is the basic social unit where the process of self-nourishment and acculturation begins;[73] it is a microcosm of the larger society.[74] The family is but part of a larger social unit which insures the sense of belonging and identity for the individual.

The nature and the function of the state in Thurman is remarkably positive. The state is responsible for the affirmation and care of the individual and the creation of a healthy social environment in which the human personality can fulfill its potential. The modern state has tremendous power over the individuals who make up the common life. It manifests this power in three important ways: 1) the state assumes a transcendent role and becomes an object of religious devotion; 2) it gives the individual citizen an integrated basis for her/his behavior so that there is always a normative standard that enables him/her to determine when s/he is out of community; and 3) the notion of the state carries with it the idea of a collective and transcendent destiny, thus reaffirming in crisis experiences the individual's sense of belonging to and participating in something greater than her/himself.[75] The transcendent character of the state and the religious loyalty that it inspires and demands has been a major problem for the American Christian church. The unreconciled conflict between loyalty to God and loyalty to the state is responsible for the American church's silence on issues of racism, segregation, and war. This thesis has serious implications for the American civil religion debate.[76]

41

A critical concern for the state is the presence of minorities who exist as "outsiders" in the midst of "insiders." Minorities are required to honor the same demands of sovereignty, but are denied the basic rewards of that allegiance. This creates two pressing problems for the state: 1) it creates a condition of guilt in the collective consciousness of the society that threatens the vitality of the body politic; and 2) it fosters an environment of power politics between world states which compete for the loyalties of minority groups.[77] The greatest challenge for the state, particularly the United States and the Soviet Union, is to create a social environment in which the individual and minorities have an authentic sense of belonging to the society. Such a climate would be one in which each person has the opportunity to actualize his/her potential, "thereby experiencing community within himself as part and parcel of the experience of community within the State."[78]

In summary, the idea of world, in Thurman, includes the universe, nature, human society, and the state. In his discussion of the world, his primary thesis is that life is itself alive and that it seeks to manifest itself in a qualitative pattern of order that makes for wholeness, harmony and integration. Of particular interest, for the purpose of this study, is his understanding of society and the state. The historic struggle of black Americans within the context of American society as the objects of racism and segregation sanctioned by the state is a major concern in his thinking regarding the meaning and potential of human community.

The Totality

The three elements that comprise the triadic nature of community—the individual, God, and the world—have been examined separately for purposes of analysis. In Thurman's understanding of community, however, the three principals are dynamically interrelated. Each interacts with the other in a creative unity which proceeds toward a common purpose which he understands to be the Mind of God coming to Itself in time and space.[79] The totality of the interaction between the individual, God, and the world is seen most clearly in the religious experience which he refers to as "the creative encounter." In the religious experience, the individual and God are the primary principals, while the world is secondary. As stated, the world is not illusory, but is positive and reflects the same qualitative urge towards community as the rest of life. Its secondary status, therefore, does not reflect its significance or value, rather it proceeds from his emphasis on the primary relationship between God and the individual. In *The Creative Encounter*, Thurman treats the nature of religious experience. Following the distinctions between the inner and outer dimensions of experience, he examines "the inwardness of religion" and "outwardness of religion." The former categorization refers to the encounter between the individual and God; the latter, to the individual's encounter with the world. This distinction is essential for Thurman because he believes that one cannot authentically move toward the actualization of community in her/his external environment until harmony and integration are sought within. It is in the creative encounter that the individual discovers the integral relationship between the inner life and "world-mindedness."

> The concept of world-mindedness has to do with the development of the logic of the primary discoveries of the inner life in the external relationships between the multiple manifestations of life...world-mindedness is the outer expression among men of an awareness of the individual's sense of being a child of God, being rooted and grounded in the life of God.[80]

In the religious experience, therefore, although the individual and God are primary, the world is not a separate, insignificant element, but a salient and dynamic part of the total experience.[81] Because of Thurman's emphasis on the primacy of the individual and God in the religious experience, it is important to explicate the components of their interaction. In the next chapter the implications of the "creative encounter" for the actualization of community will be addressed.

The Religious Experience

Thurman defines religious experience as "the conscious and direct exposure of the individual to God." He says, "Such an exposure seems to the individual to be inclusive of all the meaning of life—there is nothing that is not involved."[82] The encounter between God and the individual is a cooperative affair; it is a double search: "Religious experience in its profoundest dimension is the finding of man by God and the finding of God by man."[83]

For the individual, there are two demands of the religious experience. The experience must first give the individual a sense of *ultimate security*. This sense of being ultimately cared for and affirmed identifies the individual with all of existence as one created being among many others and establishes an ultimate or transcendent point of reference. The second demand of the religious experience is that the encounter with God must give the individual *personal assurance*, i.e., s/he is dealt with at her/his most private and intimate center. This gives the individual a basis for understanding his/her own value and inherent worth as a child of God.[84]

The nature of the religious experience is not casual, rather there is always a volitional element involved. The self actively and consciously participates in the experience.[85] The context of the experience may be casual or random, but the individual must make a conscious decision to participate in the encounter with God. This is part of an individual's freedom and serves as the ground for the moral quality of the will.[86]

Disciplines for Preparation

Religious experience, therefore, involves preparation or spiritual discipline by the individual for the creative encounter. The central discipline is prayer. Prayer, in this sense, is a *method* by which the individual prepares or "readies" her/his spirit for the divine encounter. Thurman refers to this form of prayer as meditation. In the experience of meditation, the individual quiets the stirring of the inner self so that the Presence of God residing within the person may be realized. In meditation, "the self moves toward God" and "God touches the spirit and the will and a wholly new character in terms of dimension enters the experience."[87] The individual is both participant and observer in the encounter, which means that s/he enters the experience with her/his own facticity or "residue of God-meaning."[88] It is in the Presence of God that one sees oneself as one is seen by God, and it is there that one is both enabled and required to seek community within oneself and in the world.[89] This is the crux of commitment.[90]

The other discipline that may prepare the individual for encounter with God is suffering. Suffering "is a physical pain or its equivalent with reference to which the individual may be inspired to protect himself, so that despite its effects he may carry on the functioning of his life."[91] There are two spiritual problems that surface in the individual's experience of suffering: *the personalizing of the problem of evil* and *hostility towards God*. First, in the personalizing of evil, the suffering is seen as an invasion of the individual's privacy or a violation of the orderliness of personality; it is, in essence, a denial of the good.[92] Evil cannot be treated as a detached, abstract thing but as a part of personal experience. The individual must, therefore, search for some rational basis for the experience as it affects her/his person. A rational explanation is sought by the sufferer in the context of ultimacy. This need often expresses itself in hostility towards God (or whatever is one's view of ultimate meaning).[93] But in the individual's hostility and personalization of evil, the inner resources are brought to an acute focus that prepares her/him for an encounter with God. He writes:

> The two spiritual problems created by suffering—the personalizing of the problem of evil, and the hostility against God that is inspired—may become handmaidens or guides in the very midst of the encounter which is at the heart of the religious experience.[94]

The totality of the interaction between the individual, God, and the world is seen most clearly in religious experience. It is in the creative encounter that the individual discovers the integral relationship between the inner and outer dimensions of life which provide the basis for the actualization of community. The encounter between God and the individual is not casual, but always involves consciousness and a volitional element. Therefore, the individual can make preparations for the encounter with God. Prayer and suffering are disciplines of the spirit which may bring the individual into the Presence of God where s/he is ultimately confirmed and personally assured that s/he is a child of God. There, one is both enabled and required to seek community within oneself and in the world. The person who makes the commitment to community in the Presence of God "is dedicated therefore to the removing of all barriers which block or frustrate this possibility in the world."[95]

In the analysis of the nature of community in the thought of Howard Thurman, his conception of community and the triadic character of community have been examined. He defines community as "actualized potential" which is rooted in the dynamic, teleological nature of life. The inherent quality of community is discernible at microcosmic and macrocosmic levels of existence. The sources of his search for community include creation accounts, living structures, utopias, common consciousness, and identity. These sources reveal the fundamental nature of community as an inalienable pattern in life which seeks wholeness, integration, and harmony.

The second section of this chapter was concerned with the triadic character of community represented in his understanding of the individual, God, and the world. These three elements are integrally related and form the basic analytical construct for the dynamic character of community. It has been demonstrated how community is a cooperative project involving all three elements. The individual and God are the primary principals, while the world, though positive and salient, remains secondary in relation to the centrality of religious experience. Thurman's vision of reality is theocentric and this understanding informs his thinking regarding the relationship of the individual to the world or the moral life. The basic questions raised in this chapter have been, What is the nature of community? How is it conceived? and What are its characteristics? The following chapter explores the actualization of community, i.e., How is community achieved? and What are the personal and social barriers that must be overcome in the realization of community?

Chapter 3

A Heavenly View

All around us worlds are dying and new worlds are being born;
All around us life is dying and life is being born,
The fruit ripens on the tree;
The roots are silently at work in the darkness of the earth
Against the time when there shall be new leaves, fresh blossoms, green fruit,
Such is the growing edge!
It is the extra breath from the exhausted lung,
The one more thing to try when all else has failed,
The upward reach of life when weariness closes in upon all endeavor.
This is the basis of all hope in moments of despair,
The incentive to carry on when times are out of joint and men have lost their
    reason;
The source of confidence when worlds crash and dreams whiten into ash.
The birth of a child—life's most dramatic answer to death—
This is the growing edge incarnate.
Look well to the growing edge!

—Howard Thurman

Wait a little while,
Then we'll sing a new song.
Wait a little while,
Then we'll sing a new song.
Sometimes I get a heavenly view,
Then we'll sing a new song.
And then my trials are so few,
Then we'll sing a new song.

—Negro Spiritual

The following chapter is concerned with the actualization of community in the thought of Howard Thurman. Specifically, this analysis will include Thurman's treatment of *the barriers to community* and his recommendations for *overcoming the barriers to community*. The discussion of the former involves his understanding of 1) the nature and role of evil; 2) the personal and social dimensions of sin; and 3) the individual's response to the barriers to community.

The analysis of Thurman's recommendations for *overcoming the barriers to community* will explore 1) community as the norm and goal of the moral life; 2) community, religion, and social action; and 3) community as an empirical reality.

Barriers to Community

The Nature and Role of Evil[1]

For Thurman, evil is the *positive* and *destructive* principle inherent in life which works against harmony, wholeness, and integration.[2] Evil manifests itself "in terms of pain, suffering, and in varying degrees of frustration."[3] Evil is included in life; it is rooted in the very fiber of life and feeds on the abundance of its vitality for nourishment and growth. It is not an intruder, but a constituent part of life. "Life is good," says Thurman, "in the sense that it contains both good and evil."[4] Because evil is a part of life, it also exhibits an orderly, rational structure of cause and effect.[5] This perspective of evil as being an orderly, rational principle is important for understanding Thurman's method for removing barriers that impede self-realization and the actualization of community. Analysis of a particular expression of evil provides insight into the way the phenomenon can be eradicated or transformed. "Naming" the evil thing places the individual in a new relationship to it; knowledge of its conception, growth, birth, and development gives the individual a sense of authority over evil. Such knowledge, *per se*, does not assure the defeat of evil, but it does enable the individual to maintain a sense of dignity and self-worth. Consider Thurman's respective treatments of segregation and hate in *The Luminous Darkness* and *Jesus and the Disinherited*. In each case, he first attempts to demonstrate the genesis and development of the phenomenon by formulating its anatomy. Second, based on the facts of a particular phenomenon, he renders his interpretation of the findings. And third, he offers the solution he deems most commensurate with the religious experience.[6]

Thurman recognizes three types of evil or suffering: natural, punitive, and moral. *Natural evil* has to do with suffering as a natural consequence of being a creature among other created beings which are a part of the impersonal, logical order of the universe. Natural evil is part of the course of existence. The human agent bears no responsibility for its reality or presence in the world. Nonetheless, the individual's experience of suffering is always private and personal.[7] Second, there is *punitive* suffering. There is a retributive dimension of evil that is a consequence of the logic of reward and punishment. "The moral law," says Thurman, "is binding."[8] In his exposition of *Habbakuk*, he suggests that the fate of Judah at the hands of the Chaldeans is indicative of the retributive judgment that comes to individuals and nations for their breach of the moral order.[9]

Third, there is *moral evil*. Much of the suffering present in the world is due to human initiative and persistence in evil.

> It is of immeasurable comfort to remember that much of the chaos and disorder of our lives is rooted in causes that are understandable; much of the evil in life is reasonable, in the sense that the roots can be traced and it is not necessary to place blame on the devil or some blind, senseless process. The naked responsibility for human misery, you and I and ordinary human beings like us must accept.[10]

Evil has a purpose in the process and evolution of life. The destructive, disintegrating presence of the demonic in life is to upset the balances in order to insure that the dynamic, creative quality of life does not become static and arrested.

> Whenever life seems to be in any sense complete or rounded out, there is a movement that upsets and upends. Another way of saying this is, Life itself seems to be against anything that has arrived, that has established equilibrium or even maturity. Life seems always to be on the side of that which is trying to arrive at a balance, equilibrium and maturity. Perhaps, this is one of the reasons why so many of the church fathers regarded pride as the chief of sins.[11]

The view of evil as an upender of life is helpful in understanding Thurman's theodicy. He argues that since evil is a dynamic part of life, then like all of life, it must be interpreted within the divine context. The divine context refers to the sovereignty of God.[12] As indicated earlier, God is transcendent and omnipotent; there is nothing outside the divine power and purpose. God is also immanent in history as Sustainer, Judge, and Redeemer. Therefore, all events in the individual's life or in the movement of human history must be regarded as part of the divine context. God's will is "a sovereign intent on making even the selfish and most anti-social ends of all the peoples of the earth serve his holy purpose."[13]

Given Thurman's understanding of the nature and role of evil in life and its instrumentality in the purposes and ends of God, it can be inferred that all suffering is potentially redemptive. It is important to note again that evil is not an intruder in the universe, but a vital, integral part of life.[14] For Thurman, the suffering of the innocent must be viewed from this perspective. There are two ways in which the suffering of the innocent is redemptive. One way involves the innocent person who is simply caught in the onslaught and perplexities of existence. This suffering of the innocent minority is propitiatory in that it restores the balance or equilibrium in humanity which is offset by moral evil. "Their shoulders hold the sky suspended. They stand, and earth's foundations stay."[15] Although the innocent sufferer, in this sense, is not conscious of her/his redemptive role, s/he still participates in the broader purposes of a creative, harmonious universe. This notion has significant implications for Thurman's understanding of America and the redemptive suffering of black people. For him America is more than an historical project, it is a divine-human experiment in the evolutionary processes of life. Despite the undue ravages and unmerited suffering of black Americans, his theodicy would suggest that their affliction has been a salvific element in an otherwise destructive destiny.[16]

The other form of redemptive suffering of the innocent is a conscious, deliberate act on the part of the individual.[17] Here the suffering is characterized by the discovery of ultimate confirmation the individual experiences in the Presence of God. In the Presence of God, the individual understands her/his life as being a part of the very rhythm and flow of life itself, which includes good and evil. Therefore, all the vissicitudes of existence, including death (the ultimate logic of suffering), have inherent meaning and value in the purposes of God. The fundamental experience which the individual realizes in her/his self-validation is love. The individual not only experiences love, but is moved to love; and it is in her/his response to the love of God that s/he is enabled to suffer willingly for others in light of a higher cause (value). "It is only for love of someone or something that a man knows that because of the confirmation of life in him, he can make death an instrument in his hands,"[18] Thurman says.

Redemptive suffering in love, therefore, becomes the means of removing barriers that inhibit the actualization of community.[19] Unlike the former dimension where the redemptive suffering of the innocent is unconscious, in this dimension it is a moral action involving the will and freedom. The moral agent consciously participates in the collective destiny of the human community. S/he acknowledges the dynamic tensions and crises wrought in life by evil, but refuses to ascribe normalcy to this state of affairs. The individual's vision is set rather to an ideal of harmony, integration, and wholeness that is always in the future. S/he never accepts "the absence of community as his destiny."[20] In redemptive suffering, therefore, the individual is driven by her/his identification with the movement of life towards community. For such a person, "To be confirmed in life is to make even of death a little thing."[21]

Unmerited suffering, in this sense, gives valuable insight into the power and miracle of love in creating human community. Thurman argued that the lives of great historical personages (Jesus, Socrates, John Brown, Galileo, etc.) attest to this fact. The loving, sacrificial death of Jesus is but one illustration of the profound truth that the contradictions of life are not final.[22] The contradictions of life are not final because while evil feeds on life and gains its validity from the same source as goodness, the weight of the universe is ultimately against any on-going dualism.[23] This is the "growing edge" of hope for the individual who chooses to suffer redemptively for the actualization of human community.[24]

The Personal and Social Dimensions of Sin

For Thurman, sin is disobedience to God's will; it is essentially human cooperation with evil. Sin is volitional and involves freedom and responsibility. Although there is in Thurman's thought a suggestion of original sin, it is not developed beyond his fundamental claim that within the human spirit there are both creative and destructive possibilities rooted in the will and human freedom.[25]

The root of sin is pride or egosim,[26] which creates disharmony within the self and in relations with others. Pride is manifested as an "ill will" or a "stubborn will" that rebels against the purpose and intent of the God of life.[27] Fear, deception, hate and all forms of violence have their basis in pride. Egoism is the fatal spiritual malady of all oppressors and insures their downfall because ultimately life will not support the evil enterprise.[28] The greatest expression of arrogance is idolatry, in which a bad thing is called "good" or a good thing is called "bad." The judgment of idolatry is in the act itself. When a person continually calls a good thing "bad" or a bad thing "good," moral discrimination is eventually lost so that the arrogant cannot distinguish good from evil.[29]

Although sin is fundamentally a private and personal affair between God and the individual its consequences have profound social implications. The social dynamics of sin are evident in political, economic, and cultural patterns and arrangements that are detrimental to the well-being or inner harmony of individuals. The person who seeks harmony within discovers that s/he cannot achieve self-realization in a society that is antithetical to her/his pursuit. Therefore, the quest for personal salvation inevitably leads to the need for social transformation. "Social sin and personal sin are bound together in an inexorable relationship so that it is literally true that no man can expect to have his soul saved alone."[30]

Thurman holds that an "individual-centered" or "personality-centered" culture is the most desirable form of society for the self-realization of persons. He perceives democracy as being the ideal political arrangement in this respect.[31] He believes that the central concerns any society must address are the intrinsic worth and the moral inviolability of the individual. Therefore, any political or economic arrangement that treats persons as *means* to an *end* and denies the fundamental equality of all persons is evil; and to cooperate with evil policies is to commit sin.[32] Racism, as it is reflected in segregated statutes, is but one example of social sin that is against the self-realization of persons, in sum, against community.[33]

The Individual's Response to the Barriers to Community

Thurman's basic concern with evil is where it "touches" the individual. This does not mean that the complex social implications of evil are not important. His emphasis, however, is on the individual because he believed that the will is the seat of pride or the ground for creative and constructive transformation of the self and society. Thurman insists that the barrier erected by pride in the individual's personal center must be the point of departure for the actualization of community. The internal dimensions of the self are the citadels that must be confronted before external circumstances are challenged. The operative assumption is that the individual is a microcosm of the greater society, and that the same dynamics of pride that destroy the soul of the individual are at work in society, only at a greater scale. Therefore, the place to begin in removing barriers which impede the actualization of community in the world is within the self.

Sin is encountered and removed only through confession and self-surrender, which involve the inner consent of the will.[34] In the act of surrender, the willful, egoistic elements of the self, which are the results of of inordinate strivings wrought by the inner need for love and self-confirmation, are transformed by the love of God. The individual is reconciled with God and is enabled and required to live authentically in the world.[35] What one has discovered within propels one into society as an agent of reconciliation. S/He is dedicated to "the removing of all barriers which block or frustrate this possibility in the world."[36]

The major question in regard to overcoming evil is not the traditional formulation of theodicy.[37] The critical concern, rather, is what the individual does with the evil that touches the personal and private places of her/his existence and how one keeps evil from destroying all meaning in human life.[38] The underlying rationale in this position is expressed in Thurman's understanding of the nature and role of evil as being an essential ingredient in the dynamic and creative pattern of existence. Implied in this perspective is the argument that while the individual must struggle against evil, its total eradication is not the primary concern because of the overwhelming magnitude of its reality.[39] Nevertheless, the individual is called upon to do all within her/his power to arrest the development and consequence of evil. While an individual initiative may seem minuscule given the multitudinous social complexities that shape and form society, Thurman argued that when a solitary individual chooses not to cooperate with evil, but places his or her life on the side of goodness, that person anticipates community at the level of her/his functioning.[40]

It is not sufficient simply to remove an evil thing; it must be replaced with something good. The dynamic nature of evil is such that it grows with greater intensity and rapidity than goodness. Although life is ultimately against evil and will sustain the good, the principle of goodness tends to be slower, less organized, and concentrated. Consequently, when evil is "plucked out" it grows back unless good is cultivated in its stead. This tends to be true in nature, in personality, and in human relations.[41] In society, says Thurman, those who are involved in evil designs tend to proceed on a basis of a clearly defined plan and a structure of orderliness that draws upon all the available resources to fulfill their diabolical schemes. He suggests that in a sense, there is an understanding that the directiveness of life is against their designs, therefore they work with greater effort and concentration. It is paramount, therefore, that those who work towards community realize that goodness must be achieved through careful planning, deliberate effort, and hard work.[42] "It is not enough to evict the devil, but something else must be put in his place and maintained there, or else he returns, refreshed and recharged, to deliver greater tyranny,"[43] he writes.

The replacement of evil with good begins with the internalization of the virtues of love and truth at the personal level and by working nonviolently for their actualization in the greater society.[44] Conflict between good and evil is inevitable. Conflict is an essential part of the experience of growth and maturity for the individual and the basis for the transformation of society. In the individual's spiritual growth, there is a dialectical tension at work. There is a force which "pushes forward" to the new and an opposing force which "pulls back" toward the old. The resolution of these two forces is a creative synthesis in the dynamic development of personality. Personality, as such, is always an unfinished project.[45] The dialectical tension that undergirds conflict in personality is also apparent in cellular behavior in the organism. The aggressive urges to maintain and to change are the dialectical elements which lead to conflict and to transformation.

> Aggression cannot be separated from the urge for and to community. It may be that we get a grand and awesome preview of these two in the incipient ground of human behavior in what has been discovered about the behavior of the cell in seeking its own nourishment and rejecting, by an uncanny directed spontaneity, any intruder that is sensed as a threat to the inner cohesiveness of the structure of the cell. *No understanding of the significance of community can escape the place and significance of aggression.*[46]

The individual who is committed to the actualization of community must acknowledge the role of conflict as an essential element in the creation of a just and loving society. The ground of resolution for conflict begins with the presupposition that life is on the side of goodness, and that the contradictions of life are not final. Because the one devoted to community refuses to accept the contradictions of life as ultimate, this does not mean that s/he acquiesces or retreats from struggle or conflict. To the contrary, s/he anticipates protest and indignation because the structures of experience guarantee their presence in any creative adventure.

> The structure of human experience consists of tensions and releases, of veritable contradictions and paradoxes, of trial balances between affirmations and negations; in time, there seems to be a de-focalized but conscious dialectic at the very core of experience which may have only a secondary reference to reflective thought. It is a salutary fact, however, that the human spirit is reluctant to give to this tension an ultimate significance of reality.[47]

The struggle against evil is always directed towards a higher synthesis which approximates the good, community. This creative synthesis, however, is not a compromise with evil. The individual is under an absolute moral imperative to say "no" to evil.[48] The synthesis is achieved only when good is victorious over evil. Embodied in the synthesis is a greater revelation of love and truth, in essence, a greater understanding of God. The individual who seeks to remove the barriers of evil which militate against community discovers that s/he has divine companionship, and is assured of ultimate victory. Thurman says, "He who places his life completely at the disposal of the highest ethical end, God, to him will not be denied the wine of creative livingness."[49] For the work of community is the work of God coming to God's Self in the world. The human-divine interrelatedness is tightly interwoven in such a way that the oppressed's struggle for liberation against evil systems of dominance, is also God's struggle. In a revealing personal statement, Thurman says:

> As a religious man, I feel that God cannot be what God is destined to be in the world as long as any man is held back and held down. I think that whenever a man is in prison, God is in prison. And in the things that work for his release, life is on their side. The things that work to hold them there, life is against... It doesn't matter how high the odds are, because the things that work for bigotry and discrimination—all these things—life is against and they cannot abide. With absolute confidence I work, and knowing that my responsibility is to do everything I can not to be the one to keep the key in the lock of the prison house. That is my job![50]

54

In this analysis, Thurman's understanding of the nature and role of evil in life and his treatment of the question of theodicy have been examined. The primary concern in his treatment of evil is its significance for the individual. His understanding of sin and its relationship to the individual is similar. However sin is not simply a private matter between the individual and God, rather sin has profound social consequences which demand self-surrender on the part of the individual and a commitment to social transformation. Conflict is an inevitable product of the work of community; it is indigenous to the structure of human existence. The creative resolution of good and evil is guaranteed by the logic of life. The contradictions of life, therefore, are not final. This is the ground of hope for the person who works to overcome the barriers of evil and sin in her/himself and the world. While this discussion has, at points, anticipated Thurman's recommendations for overcoming the barriers, the following section will deal more extensively with this important element.

Overcoming the Barriers

Community as the Norm and Goal of the Moral Life

It has been stated that the ideal of community refers to community as the norm for ethical reflection and the goal toward which all life strives.[51] It is important to note that for Thurman the normative character of community is not an external imposition upon life, but a disclosure of what life is about as it seeks to realize itself in myriad time-space manifestations. Community is inherent in the process of life and is the expression of the will or "intent" of God. Therefore, community as the norm for the moral life proceeds from an ethical theory that is theocentric.[52] His construal of the world begins with the God of life who is ultimately and actively engaged in all of existence.[53] According to James Gustafson, theocentric ethics raises the practical moral question, "What is God enabling and requiring us to be and do?" His general answer to the question is that we are to relate ourselves and all things in a manner appropriate to their relation to God.[54]

Thurman's answer to the theocentric moral question is found in his exposition of the nature of religious experience. As it has been presented, in the creative encounter with God the individual is *enabled* and *required* to realize harmony within her/himself and to actualize community in the world.[55] Therefore, faith precedes morality. The content and structure of the moral life is founded upon the individual's experience of God, who is conceived in terms of supreme worthfulness. God is the source and goal of the moral life. He argued that "the guarantee of the ethical ground is to be found in the underlying vitality of the universe as expressed in the aliveness of life, which in turn, is sustained by the God of life."[56]

Fundamental to the moral life is the act of *commitment*. Commitment involves volition, which may be a radical, self-conscious yielding on the part of the individual, or a systematic, disciplined effort over a period of time.[57] The result of the commitment of the individual is a new, integrated basis for moral action; a new value content and center of loyalty inform her/his actions in the world.[58] The person's loyalty to God, which proceeds from the personal assurance of being loved by God, forms the ground of the moral life. What is discovered in private must be witnessed to in the world. Thurman comments on the nature of the individual's religious experience and its relationship to moral action:

> His experience is personal, private, but in no sense exclusive. All of the vision of God and holiness which he experiences, he must achieve in the context of the social situation by which day-to-day life is defined. What is disclosed in his religious experience he must define in community. That which God shareth with him, he must inspire his fellows to seek for themselves. He is dedicated therefore to the removing of all barriers which block or frustrate this possibility in the world.[59]

The Means of Actualization: Love and Truth

The two ethical principles which undergird the moral life and serve as the means for the actualization of community are love and truth. They are integrally related and provide the basis for ethical reflection and praxis.[60] Love and truth, as ethical principles, arise from a theocentric perspective which is decidedly relational. Unlike prescriptive or descriptive ethical formulations, the basis for moral judgment is relational. Thurman's relational ethics, however, differs from the contextualist or situationalist stance, which emphasizes principle in relation to context.[61] He is more properly located within the relational motif that accentuates "virtue" or what Edward Long terms "response to divine initiative."[62] The emphasis in this position is on the internalization of love and truth discovered in divine encounter, which disposes the moral agent to make the "fitting decision."[63] The disciplines of the spirit which Thurman emphasizes (commitment, growth, prayer, suffering, and reconciliation)[64] are means of creating virtue. Careful disciplining of the moral life disposes the individual to discernment of proper moral action and realization of the good. The good deed is done, consequently, without hypothetical motives or deontological decrees, but because the virtuous individual deems it good.

The virtuous act may or may not pay dividends. In the last analysis, men cannot be persuaded to be good because of reward either here or beyond this "vale of tears." Men must finally come to the place in their maturity which makes them do the good because it is good. Not because it is a command, even a divine command, but because the good deed...is itself good.[65]

Love

The ethical principle of love is central for understanding Thurman's method for the actualization of community. He believed that all love is of God, and therefore, to love is the most profound act of life and that only in a secondary sense is it an act of religion or morality.[66] Love is the fruit of the presence of God and is the power that overcomes barriers that divide and separate individuals, groups, and nations from one another.[67] Thurman defines love as "the experience through which an individual passes when he is able to deal with another human being at a point in that human being beyond all good and evil." The experience of being loved "is to have the sense of being dealt with at a point in one's self that is beyond all good and beyond all evil."[68]

First, Thurman makes a distinction between love as interest in another person and love as intrinsic interest.[69] Love as interest is an expression of interest in another person for ulterior motives, and as such the other person is not addressed as a subject, but is seen as an object to be manipulated. Love as intrinsic interest in another person goes beyond all of the dimensions and aspects of the personality and moves to the central core of the individual. There the person is dealt with intimately and personally, concretely, as a subject. "To love," says Thurman, "means dealing with persons in the concrete rather than the abstract. In the presence of love, there are no types or stereotypes, no classes and no masses."[70]

Second, love also includes truth.[71] At the core of love there is a real body of facts which must be dealt with. Love is always seasoned with intelligence and understanding.[72] Love devoid of rationality becomes sentimental and potentially destructive. Thurman illustrates the relationship between love and reason with the case of a person who gives chocolate to a friend who is allergic to it. Such an act is unloving because it disregards the facts of the situation, and is therefore potentially destructive.[73]

Third, love transcends justice. Justice, according to Thurman, is normally understood as "the artificial equalization of unequals—the restoration of balance, of equilibrium, in a situation in which the balance has been upset."[74] It operates on the inherent relationship between deed and conse-

57

quence, reward and punishment as expressed in *lex talionis*. Central to the notion of justice is power. Although Thurman does not define power *per se*, there is operative in his thinking about justice the assumption that power includes both the *will* and *ability* to effect change in a given situation.

Thurman examines two expressions of justice.[75] One type is the justice to which persons appeal when they are dealing with one another from within a context of equality of will, when neither has the ability to inflict her/his will upon the other. This he refers to as "blind-folded justice" or the justice of the law. Here the notion of justice as the "artificial equalization of unequals" is operative. Justice as such is *external* to the individual and beyond her/his power to effect.

The other idea of justice is expressed in structures when individuals are unequal in terms of power. If the person who has the advantage wields power over the other s/he strips that person of selfhood, of her/his "private, autonomous existence" and reduces her/him to a thing. But if the individual who has the advantage refrains from exercising her/his power over the other, that individual establishes voluntary distance between his/her ability and will. In this instance, the idea of justice is not *external* to the individual, but *internal*. When one refrains from executing power over the other in such a context, s/he shows mercy or love. Thurman argues that love in this sense fulfills justice by recognizing the inherent worth and equality of the other as a child of God.

Love and justice[76] are part of the moral integrity of life. The moral order operates on the logic of cause and effect, deed and consequence. Therefore, the unrighteous deed will not go unpunished, but the wronged individual is never the avenger. Judgment for the evil deed is inherent in life itself. "The moral law is abiding," Thurman writes. "There is no escape from the relentless logic of antecedent and consequence."[77] The individual, therefore, who shows love, even to her/his enemy, will ultimately be vindicated. But the exercise of vengeance or retaliation is not the individual's, but God's. This is true at both personal and social levels:

> There is a judgment which presides over the private and collective destiny of man. It is a judgment that establishes itself in human history as well as in human character. God is the Creator of life, and the ultimate responsibility of life is to God. If there be any government or social institution...that operates among men in a manner that makes for human misery...to the extent that it is so, it cannot survive, because it is against life and carries within itself the seeds of its own destruction.[78]

Fourth, love includes imagination. Imagination is a constituent part of the individual's nature as a self-transcendent being. Imagination can be an *angelos*, a messenger of God, when the individual through self-transcendence puts her/himself in another's place. Imagination, in this sense, is synonymous with "sympathy." Through the use of imagination, the individual is enabled to transcend her/himself and reach the other at the core of their being, at the seat of "common consciousness." In doing so, the other is addressed at a place beyond all good and evil. This is the experience of love. When an individual is addressed at the centermost place of personality, s/he experiences wholeness and harmony with the one who loves him/her. This is the "common ground" of our relations with others:

> I see you where you are striving and struggling and in light of the highest possibility of your personality, I deal with you there. My religious faith is insistent that this can be done only out of a life of devotion. I must cultivate the inner spiritual resources of my life to such a point that I can bring you to my sanctuary before his presence, until, at last, I do not know you from myself.[79]

Fifth, the experience of love involves redemptive suffering. To love one another is to expose ourselves in such a way that the other may have free access to our inner self. This involves vulnerability and the potential for suffering, but it is only through our willingness to risk suffering that redemption of the other is achieved. Redemption occurs when one person becomes for the other what is needed at the time when the need is most urgent and acutely felt.[80] The act of love as redemptive suffering is not contingent on the other's response; love, rather, is unsolicited and self-giving. It transcends merit and demerit. It simply loves. Ultimately, love is victorious over any defenses, even hate, because it is the creative power of God creating community, the very essence and vitality of all being.[81]

Finally, love is synonymous with reconciliation.[82] Reconciliation occurs within the individual when her/his inner need to be cared for and understood is met in encounter with God. The experience of reconciliation with God becomes the ground and moral mandate for sharing one's experience in relations with others and in society. Whatever impedes the actualization of community at either personal or social levels must be confronted. Thurman believed that the way to the reconciliation of society is through redemptive suffering rooted in love. Meaningful experiences of love shared among individuals would accomplish that end. "Experiences of meaning which people share are more compelling than the barriers that separate them," he writes. "If such experiences can be multiplied over a time interval of sufficient duration, then any barrier between men, whatever kind, can be undermined."[83] For him, this was the central ethical imperative of religion, to love and to be reconciled.[84]

In summary, love is the experience through which one passes when s/he is able to deal with another human being at a point in that person beyond all good and evil. Likewise, to *be loved* is to have the sense of being dealt with in one's self at a point beyond all good and evil. Love is intrinsic interest in the other; it goes beyond abstract generalizations and expresses itself *in concreto*. Love and reason are not opposed, rather the head and the heart must work together in the actualization of community. Love transcends and fulfills justice. Included in the experience of love is the role of the imagination, which allows the individual to identify with the other at the centermost place of their being. Finally, through the exposure of one's self to the other, love issues forth in redemptive suffering, the creative power that reconciles and restores community.

Truth

The other ethical principle operative in the actualization of community is truth. At one level, truth is the rational element that is always present in love. Throughout his writings and meditations, Thurman insists that the head and the heart are one.[85] The rational nature of truth is predicated upon the inherent order or logic in life. There is a natural affinity between the order in life and the activity of the human mind which makes knowledge of the world possible.[86] As stated, Thurman uses life as a hermeneutical principle. He claims that an empirical analysis of the movement and activity of life will yield principles of interpretation which are helpful in understanding human experience. An example of his method is found in his interpretation of Negro spirituals as sources of reflection for universal human experience. In his analysis of the spiritual, "Wade in the Water,"[87] the slave's experience of the troubled waters discloses a more profound meaning of God's activity in human suffering. The following passage illustrates his method:

> Here is an insistence that one must look deep within the churning waters to find the clue to their meaning... Let us examine as an illustration one phase of human experience, human illness or sickness. Consider the study of cancer... With great versatility, men apply in myriad ways the scientific method to the malignant growth of cells in hope that the rational principle in man may make contact with the rational principle in malignancy, and result in understanding, insight and healing. All the research says that inherently cancer has a logic and rational principle operative within it. When one discovers what the rational principle is, then the resources of knowledge and wisdom and techniques can be

put at the disposal of the immunizing of the organism against the ravages of the malignancy, or reduce the malignancy to manageable units of control and understanding... The aim is to make available to the sufferer the deep inner resources of an ordered organism at the point of the malignancy... God is troubling the waters when we are sick. Not in the sense that he causes illness, not in punishing us with sickness; but rather God is troubling the waters in human illness because inherent in the illness something rational is active, and if it is understood, its secret can be revealed so that all the overtones and creative possibilities that result from the radical interruption of one's normal processes can be turned into glorious and redemptive account.[88]

Thurman's conception of truth is also sentient; it incorporates and transcends rationality. He emphasizes the intuitive nature of truth. He defines intuitive knowledge as "immediate, direct, and not an inference from logic... It is an awareness of literal truth directly perceived."[89] Intuition is a constituent part of personality. It is not spontaneous, but always deeply rooted in the data with reference to which the process of intuition is related. Thurman compares intuition to doing a broad jump: the runner dashes down the path until s/he comes to the threshold of the pit, and is carried forward by the momentum created by the speed and drive in her/his path. He says further:

There is in all intuition the element of revelation which may be characterized as the leaping element. This aspect of intuition makes it throw light on known materials; and the thing that makes it an intuition is the fact that it establishes clearly and definitively what was known peripherally, vaguely, or merely dimly sensed. The intuition says that I bring you knowledge which has been there and in you all along.[90]

Intuition is involved in moral judgment.[91] Through intuitive understanding, the individual becomes aware of her/his proper moral response to given situations. In an article entitled "Mysticism and Ethics," Thurman illustrates the intuitive nature of moral decision making. He refers to Leo Tolstoy's response to an execution at the Public Square:

When I saw the head separate from the body and how they both thumped into the box at the same moment, I understood, not with my mind, but with my whole being, that no theory of reasonableness of any present progress can justify this deed; and that though everybody from the creation of the world, on whatever theory, had held it to be necessary, I knew it to be unnecessary and bad.[92]

61

As truth is found in the external world, it is also resident within the individual. It is "the quality or dimension of personality which has an element in it beyond thought and interpretation."[93] It is part of the "givenness of God" which is available to the individual by virtue of being a child of God. Yet truth or "the inner light" is not the distinct property of any person. The inner light is discovered both through encounter with the external world and in the inner sanctuary of the self.[94] Thurman acknowledges the inherent danger of subjectivism and privatization of the truth in this regard. He maintains, however, that the community provides a safeguard against this temptation. In the gathering of the community, as in worship or common prayer, the common ground of truth becomes available to all. In the act of "centering down," that which is indigenous to all moves from a common ground and the truth is given. He relates how once in a Quaker meeting, he was invited to give "the Word." He went to the meeting purposefully unprepared—without a manuscript or thoughts about what he would say. During the moment of quietness, as he and the awaiting congregation "centered down," there was given to him the passage of Scripture he was to preach. To his surprise, as his mind began to engage the thought and prepare it for the presentation, throughout the congregation the same Scripture was quoted *verbatim* by others.[95]

The individual is also responsible for guarding against self-deception. This is a major concern for Thurman and the theme arises throughout his writings. Always the individual is called upon to test her/his perspective against the facts of her/his own experience and the experiences of others.[96] He says, "You may have a glass of water out of the ocean, but all the water in your glass is not the ocean."[97]

Finally, his view of the truth as an ethical principle is theonomous and absolutist.[98] In all circumstances or situations, truth-telling is the only proper response. He quotes Jesus, "Let your conversation be Yea, yea; Nay, nay: whatsoever is more than these cometh of evil."[99] Honesty and sincerity are demanded in relation to self, to God, and others.[100] Truth-telling underscores the fundamental dignity and worth of human persons. It highlights the equality of all persons regardless of color, class, status or social advantage. This is an important observation embodying radical implications for the oppressed's understanding of themselves and their relationship to oppressors. Deception or lying are never viable moral alternatives because they destroy the value structure of the one who deceives and lies. "The penalty of deception," Thurman suggests, "is to become a deception, with all sense of moral discrimination vitiated."[101] But if the disinherited individual adheres to the truth, s/he equalizes the relationship between her/himself and the one who has the advantage. Deception perpetuates the relationship of the powerful and the powerless.[102] Truth understood thusly liberates the individual from any form of external bondage. For within the person who internalizes the truth, there is an inner authority which allows her/him to say "no" even at the threat of violence and death. This is the essence of the freedom of the individual and her/his birthright as a child of God.[103]

Truth is intuitively discerned. Intuition involves a process of "knowing" which includes both sentinence and reason. Truth, understood in this manner, informs moral judgments and demands honesty and sincerity in all contexts. It is the rational/cognitive counterpart of love, but in its transcendence of rationality it is indistinguishable from love. Truth, like love, is "that which makes for wholeness, for integration, for inner togetherness, for a sense of being present and accounted for in one's life."[104] It is not the distinct property of any individual; it is ultimately the common ground of our being, which is God. The individual is called to be a "high priest of truth," an agent in the creation of community.[105]

In summary, the internalization of love and truth enables the individual to work for harmonious relations in the world. The realization of love and truth at the core of the individual's being creates an awareness of the need to work for the actualization of community. "Neither a man nor an institution can embrace an ethical imperative without either becoming more and more expressive of it in the common life or developing a kind of enmity to it,"[106] Thurman writes. The work of community involves volition, the disciplining and tutoring of the will. When the will is yielded to the divine initiative and purpose, the individual becomes a participant in the realization of community.

Overcoming the Internal Barriers to Community

There are internal barriers that must be overcome before the work of community can be actualized in the world. These obstacles are fear, deception, and hatred. Since deception has already been referred to, the following discussion will focus upon fear and hate.[107]

Fear is rooted in violence or the threat of violence to which the individual is exposed. Violence, physical and psychological, is an attack against the victim's sense of self. Fear, therefore, is a defense mechanism of the weak and powerless. In order to maintain self-respect and self-worth, the individual develops behavioral patterns that minimize the onslaught of violence.[108] But when fear is internalized, it becomes a spiritual strait-jacket that destroys the creative potential of the self. That which originally served as a means of self-protection from a hostile environment becomes destructive to the personality. The result is death to the personality. "The power that saves [fear] becomes the executioner."[109]

The individual is enabled to overcome the power of fear through the realization that s/he is a child of God. To know that one is a child of God assures oneself of her/his inherent self-worth and fulfills the inner need for love. Once a person comes to this realization, fear loses its power over her/him. The love of God gives the oppressed "the faith and the awareness that overcome fear and transforms it into the power to strive, to achieve, and not to yield."[110]

Hate is another internal barrier that a person must surmount who seeks community within her/himself and the world. Hate is born in unsympathetic climates characterized by "contact without fellowship," where the individual is not recognized as a subject, but as an object which does not belong in a "magnetic field of morality."[111] Hate, asserts Thurman, ultimately manifests itself as "ill will" toward others, which in time grows into a willing for the non-existence of others. In the case of the oppressed, hatred is

> born out of great bitterness—a bitterness that is made possible by sustained resentment which is bottled up until it distills an essence of vitality, giving to the individual in whom this is happening a radical and fundamental basis for self-realization.[112]

Hate, however, like deception and fear, ultimately destroys the one who hates. Jesus rejected hatred because it "meant death to the mind, death to the spirit, death to communion with the Father."[113]

Deception, fear, and hate are internal barriers to the actualization of community within the self. Truth and love, as internalized ethical principles, create the value content and inner authority which allow the individual to overcome these destructive personal obstacles and to perform the work of community in the world. The emphasis, again, is on the individual and what the individual discovers in personal encounter with God as the center of her/his loyalty. There can be no genuine commitment to harmonious relations in the external world until there is a surrender of the self to the God of life who both *requires* and *enables* the individual to realize wholeness and integration within her/himself and the world. The discussion below will show how these ethical principles are employed in encounter with forces that are antithetical to community. The method of nonviolence will be discussed as an ethical imperative in the actualization of community.

Nonviolence as Ethical Imperative in the Actualization of Community

Central to the religious experience, Thurman argues, is the ethical imperative to be reconciled, to create the kind of nurturing and caring environment in which the individual can realize her/his innate potential. He refers to this quality of existence as "the climate of love."[114] The creation of a climate of love in society involves more than a situation of practical equality imposed from without by the state, which reserves the right to inflict violence upon perpetrators. Rather, a truly just society is one in which mercy or love predominates.[115] The method by which such a society is created and ordered is nonviolence. Nonviolence is an expression of truth and love, and is synonymous with reconciliation.[116]

Nonviolence is a creative, life-affirming response to a violent act towards oneself in a manner that meets the need of the perpetrator to be cared for, to be understood—in sum, to be loved.[117] Violence, on the other hand, "is the imperious demand of a person to be cared for, to be understood."[118] Violence is quick and seemingly efficient; it inspires panic in the human spirit so that it makes capitulation possible without moral compromise; its purpose is to force one's will upon another.[119] Ultimately, it is a need to be cared for, to be loved. It fails, however, in its real intention because it succeeds only in driving the victim's will underground where it waits for a more propitious moment to retaliate. A climate of violence is therefore created which is characterized by fear, deception, and hate.[120] As indicated, these are internal barriers that impede the actualization of community. The only viable way to overcome the destructive quality of the climate of violence is through nonviolence.

> There is but one place for refuge for any man on this planet and that is another man's heart. And what the nonviolent man does, he makes his heart a swinging door and the violent man seals his door against intrusion and thereby becomes a prisoner in his own house.[121]

Nonviolence not only creates a climate in which harmony can exist between individuals, it is also a *technique* or *discipline* that seeks to confront the violent person or system in a way that effects change in attitudes and social policies working against community, e.g., through sit-ins, boycotts, pray-ins and other techniques. This is accomplished through spiritual discipline and commitment to God. It is important to note that nonviolence is not simply a tool of tactical significance, but is primarily a moral demand which arises from religious commitment. Nonviolent resistance as a method divorced from spiritual and moral substance can be used as a weapon of violence. Nonviolence used in this way is counterproductive and ultimately destructive because it fails to address the opponent at the level of personal worth and to call for a change in values. The locus of nonviolent encounter is the human will. Unlike violence,

> nonviolence insulates itself into the will. It is often slow—its most creative dimension is the way in which it activates the imagination of the individual or individuals so that it makes it possible for them to project themselves into another man's place and thereby opens the way for him to do something for them.[122]

Nonviolence therefore rejects violence in both its physical and non-physical expressions. To refrain from physical violence and to employ psychological means of violence is inconsistent with the logic of nonviolence. *The purpose of nonviolence is always the redemption of the other.* It seeks to create the conditions in which opponents may realize their personal worth and dignity as children of God. This approach demands that "nonphysical tools" of nonviolence be used: 1) always to refrain from automatic response to violence, i.e., to fight or flee; and 2) to overcome the spirit of retaliation.[123] The source of the individual's power to fulfill these requirements is found in life itself. "When a man is able to bring to bear upon a single purpose all the powers of his being, his whole life is energized and vitalized."[124]

The ultimate goal of nonviolence is the creation of human community based on truth and love. As a means it is consistent with its goal. Violence, on the other hand, can never bring about wholeness and harmony. It is antithetical to the genius of community. Only love and truth can ultimately overcome the forces that work against the creation of "a world of friendly men underneath a friendly sky."[125]

Luther Smith criticizes Thurman's understanding of love and the role of nonviolence as a means of effecting social change. He suggests that Thurman's vision of nonviolence as a method of social transformation is noble, but unrealistic. Using the Niebuhrian analysis of love and justice, Smith argues that Thurman's ethical theory fails to take into account the moral impotency of love in the creation and ordering of society.[126] Smith argues that, in Thurman, the efficacy of the nonviolent method as an avenue for social change is predicated on Thurman's understanding of redemption. Smith says that Thurman believes nonviolence is moral when it is redemptive, i.e., when it is able to "find a way to honor what is deepest in one person and to have that person honor what is deepest in the other."[127] Therefore, the key issue that Thurman fails to resolve is whether violence can ever be redemptive.[128] Smith suggests that there are instances when perhaps nonviolence is immoral and non-redemptive in confronting exploitive systems that lack the cultural values to support nonviolent resistance. Oppressive situations like pre-Maoist China and the present conditions in South Africa, according to Smith, are convincing examples for the alternative of revolutionary violence as a means of social change. He insists, however, that revolutionary violence is not an end itself, but sometimes it is the only means to achieve justice.[129]

Although, as Smith indicates, there are instances in which Thurman is unclear as to his own actions in life-threatening situations,[130] he still embraces nonviolence as his fundamental philosophy of action. The temptation to compromise ethical ideals is acknowledged by Thurman,[131] but there are some issues where compromise is inappropriate and where the individual "must draw the line."[132] In such instances, compromise is a denial of the ideal.[133] Nonviolence, as an ethical ideal, is non-negotiable for Thurman because it is rooted in the very nature of love and truth. To deny it in praxis, therefore, is to deny the redemptive possibilities of life itself.[134] Therefore, those instances in which Thurman was or would be tempted to use violent means must be viewed as personal conflicts of loyalties between the God of life and himself. Thurman did not consider them as grounds for establishing violence as a viable alternative for social change.

Smith's major contention centers upon Thurman's synonymy of nonviolence and redemption and whether violence can ever be an expression of redemptive love. As indicated, violence and redemption, for Thurman, are antithetical and cannot work in concert in creating a nurturing and caring society. Nonviolence is the only viable method of creating harmonious relations among persons and actualizing world community. Three important facets of Thurman's thought are crucial for understanding his view of the relationship between nonviolence and redemption. They are, respectively: 1) his theocentric vision of reality; 2) the role of the creative individual as a redemptive sufferer in the collective destiny of the human race; and 3) patience and social change.

In respect to Thurman's theocentric vision of reality, it is important to note that divine activity is not concerned primarily with human initiative or human benefits as it is presupposed in an anthropocentric construal of reality. The emphasis, rather, is on the sovereign and cosmic purposes of God. The moral life is a response to the divine initiative. Human freedom means that humankind can choose to cooperate with or reject God's will for community. He remarks that even if human beings were to destroy themselves through their own devices, God is infinitely more resourceful and creative than any expression of life. He agrees with Arnold Toynbee that "if we are so foolish to destroy our entire civilization and our own lives, then the creator of life could very easily make an ideal culture out of the ant."[135] Although the individual is free to participate in or to reject God's plan for community, God has chosen to entrust the Kingdom of values with human beings.[136]

Second, as mentioned, the theme of the role of the creative individual in the collective destiny of the human race is persistent in Thurman's works.[137] Throughout history the committed individual as a creative agent has had far-reaching redemptive significance. The solitary individual who works for community is not a lone voice; rather, her/his voice is the voice of God.[138] The good deed or the redemptive act carries within itself its own creative seed which bears fruit beyond its time. "All of life," says Thurman, "is a planting and harvesting. No man gathers merely the crop that he himself has planted."[139] Therefore, when one places one's life at the disposal of divine purposes, that person becomes a veritable incarnation of the Presence of God in history. That individual's life becomes a pedagogical instrument in the hands of God to show the way of community.[140]

The great challenge and genius of redemptive suffering for the individual is to demonstrate in her/his own life the "community-making" power of suffering love so that others might follow the path s/he has shown. Thurman firmly believed that if these experiences could be multiplied over a time interval of sufficient duration they would be able to undermine all barriers that separate and divide individuals, groups, and nations from one another.[141]

> When the ideal is brought into focus in the mind of the individual or the people of a state and held there with sufficient intensity over a time interval of sufficient duration, the ideal tends to realize itself in the very life of the people.[142]

This is the essential message in *A Track to the Water's Edge*.[143] In an excerpt from Olive Schreiner's "Three Dreams in the Desert," the story is told of a woman who is seeking the land of freedom. In her quest, she meets an aged man who personifies Reason. Reason points her to the land of freedom which is beyond a "dark, flowing river." He informs her that the journey will involve great suffering and sacrifice. The woman has to sacrifice her child whom she has concealed beneath her clothing before she makes her "track to the water's edge." Finally, when she reaches the bank of the river, she says to Reason:

> "For what do I go to this far land which no one has ever reached? *Oh, I am alone! I am utterly alone!*"
> And Reason, that old man, said to her, "Silence! what do you hear?"
> And she listened intently, and she said, "I hear a sound of feet, a thousand times ten thousand and thousands of thousands, and they beat this way!"
> He said, "They are the feet of those that shall follow you. Lead on! make a track to the water's edge! Where you stand now, the ground will be beaten flat by ten thousand times ten thousand feet." And he said, "Have you seen the locusts how they cross a stream? First one comes down to the water-edge, and it is swept away, and then another comes and then another, and then another, and at last with their bodies piled up a bridge is built and the rest pass over."
> She said, "And, of those that come first, some are swept away, and are heard of no more; their bodies do not even build the bridge?" "And are swept away, and are heard of no more—and what of that?" he said.
> "They make a track to the water's edge."

"They make a track to the water's edge—" And she said, "Over that bridge which shall be built with our bodies, who will pass?"

He said, *"The entire human race."*

And the woman grasped her staff.

And I saw her turn down that dark path to the river.[144]

Again, it is important to remember that for Thurman, God in divine sovereignty wills to actualize community through individuals who freely choose to cooperate with the divine purposes. Redemptive suffering, or suffering love, is the means through which community is achieved. This truth, argues Thurman, is fundamental to the dignity and worth inherent in human personality. Redemption must of necessity be nonviolent, for violence merely perpetuates the climate of violence which is characterized by deception, hate, and fear. The purpose of nonviolence is to demonstrate the power of love and reconciliation in human relations. Redemptive suffering has its own creative power to reach the inner dimensions of personality where society has its basis. The key to the problem is "a time interval of sufficient duration" in which the multiplication of spiritual experiences of unity have opportunity to undermine the barriers which separate and divide. The achievement of community through redemptive suffering demands "revolutionary patience."[145]

This "revolutionary patience," so intimately connected with social change, is the third consideration for Thurman. The need for patience at all levels of one's existence is fundamental for growth.[146] Patience to him does not mean inactivity or resignation. It is, rather, a dynamic process only partially concerned with time or waiting, one which also includes a quality of steadfastness.[147] While he is not unaware of the potentially negative implications of such a doctrine for the oppressed who must struggle against evil, exploitation, poverty and other negative forces, Thurman insists that there are some things, including social change, that demand patience. "Sometimes things cannot be forced but they must unfold, sending their tendrils deep into the heart of life, gathering strength and power with the unfolding days."[148] While there are some situations in which radical change through swift and concise action is possible, others demand a slower process of constant resistance. "Some things can be removed only by allowing them to *soak*,"[149] he writes. The reason why individuals, groups and nations opt for violence as a means for social change is because violence tends to be quick, decisive, and efficient,[150] whereas nonviolence tends to be slow and creative as it seeks to insulate itself into the other's will and perform the redemptive work of love.[151] Nonviolence demands "revolutionary patience," a patience which does not simply accept or tolerate evil, but which adopts a method of creative change rooted in the very processes of life as they work toward community. This, says Thurman, is a point of crucial identification with the Mind and Will of God. "Sometimes I think that patience is one of the great characteristics that distinguishes God from man. God knows how to wait, dynamically; everybody else is in a hurry."[152]

For Thurman, then, nonviolence is the only viable moral method for bringing about the social transformation of society. Revolutionary violence, as a temporary solution or as a means of confronting and changing exploitive systems, is not acceptable as a philosophy of action, because it perpetuates the very reality it seeks to destroy. A climate of love is the basis of a just and merciful society. Its actualization is brought about through the internalization of truth and love. The role of the creative individual as a redemptive sufferer is primary in the development of a society in which truth and love are operative. This ideal state of existence can become a reality only if spiritual experiences of unity can be multiplied over a time interval of sufficient duration so that the barriers which separate and divide can be undermined. This requires "revolutionary patience," which arises from a theocentric perspective of time and history. In the following discussion on the role of religion and the church in the actualization of community, it will be seen how Thurman perceives the church as a center where spiritual experiences of unity occur.

Community, Religion, and Social Action

Thus far, this examination of Thurman's understanding of the actualization of community has dealt with community as the norm and goal of the moral life, love and truth as ethical principles that serve as the means for actualization of community, overcoming internal barriers, and the role of nonviolence in the actualization of community. Two other important elements in Thurman's thinking regarding the actualization of community remain for discussion: the role of religion and the church in social action, and community as an empirical reality.

The discussion of Thurman's view of religion and social action involves two foci: 1) the individual (moral agent) and social action; and 2) the nature and role of the church in the creation of community.

The Individual and Social Action

Thurman's mystical interpretation of life informs his treatment of the individual and social action. Although he seldom referred to himself as a "mystic," he was deeply rooted in the American mystical tradition.[153] His early experiences as a boy growing up in Daytona Beach were mystical in the profoundest sense. Later, as part of his formal education, he studied with Rufus Jones, who made a singular impact upon his formulation of mysticism and its relatedness to social action.[154] Thurman defines mysticism in the manner of his former teacher. Mysticism is "the type of religion which puts the emphasis on the immediate awareness of the relation with God, on direct and intimate consciousness of...'divine presence'... This definition includes not only a personal attitude toward God, but a recognition of the primary experience of God with the inner core of the individual."[155] For Thurman and Jones, it is central to the mystic's claim that in the creative encounter, s/he experiences that which is perceived as "vital, total, and absolute" at a profoundly personal level while s/he remains a creature involved in all the perplexities of finitude and limitation.[156] Also with Jones, Thurman makes the distinction between the "negation mystic" and the "affirmation mystic."[157] The affirmation mystic's *raison d'etre* is the transformation of society because as s/he experiences it, the social world "ensnares the human spirit in a maze of particulars so that the One cannot be sensed or the good realized."[158] Mysticism is not "life-denying" in the sense of detachment and withdrawal from the world; rather, it is "life-affirming." That which the mystic discovers within is also inherent in all of life. The outer world, like the inner world, is pregnant with truth and meaning. The Infinite is discoverable in the finite, transitory world of nature, people, and other living things. Therefore, engagement with the world is not opposed to union with God, but the beatific vision, ultimate meaning, and truth are found in all dimensions of life.

The individual who experiences God in personal encounter must seek to share her/his experience of the love of God in community with others. The committed individual is dedicated to the removal of all barriers which impede the possibility of becoming whole in the world. "He is under judgment," Thurman writes, "to make a highway for the Lord in the hearts and market place of his fellows."[159] This involves creative confrontation and transformation of the cultural pattern in which one finds oneself.[160] While the basic ethical significance of mysticism is individualistic, the vision of unity experienced in the divine Presence impels the individual into the world.

Thurman recognizes that the overwhelming problems of human relations cannot be solved by the radical transformation of individuals in society.[161] His contention, however, is that two personal concerns demand the involvement of the mystic in society. One is the concern that grows out of the individual's own limitations and corruptions inherent in belonging to a community of people, and the concomitant interests which perpetuate the social barriers preventing one from achieving union with God. Second, in an individual's effort to realize the good, the individual finds it necessary to be responsive to the human needs by which her/his life is surrounded.[162] The mystic, therefore, is driven to service in society among her/his fellows, primarily because of a personal religious commitment. While economic and political arrangements are significant variables in the individual's quest for the actualization of community, religious and moral grounds are the bases for her/his creative engagement with the world. Personal piety, in such an endeavor, is central but it is not an end in itself. Piety must be expressed in positive and life-affirming service in society.[163]

Thus the mystic is one who has a personal encounter with God within her or his own soul. The mystical experience demands that the individual authenticate in the world what was received in the divine Presence. The individual's personal piety is not grounds for detachment from society, which is shaped and molded by political and economic forces, but rather it is the basis for creative confrontation and transformation of any social barrier that impedes the individual's personal quest, and the quests of her/his fellows, for community.

The Nature and Role of the Church In Social Action

The church is the social institution entrusted with "the Jesus idea."[164] It is an inclusive religious fellowship in which the individual seeks communion with those who share the common encounter with divine Presence. Moreover, it is "the organism fed by the springs of individual and collective religious experience through which the Christian works in society."[165] The ministry of the church is twofold: it should provide for an environment of worship in which experiences of spiritual unity are achieved, and it should serve a pedagogical function by teaching and interpreting the religious and moral implications of political, economic, and social arrangements in which the church finds itself.

A basic theme of Thurman's ecclesiology is that experiences of unity and fellowship are more compelling than the fears, dogmas, and prejudices that separate people. As noted, he believed that if spiritual experiences of unity could be multiplied over a time interval of sufficient duration, they should be able to undermine any barrier that separates one person from another.[166] The collective worship of God is the primary locus where experiences of inner unity are achieved. In worship individuals are stripped to their literal substances and enabled to realize their "common ground" as children of God.

> In the act of worship, one sees himself as being in the presence of God. In His presence the worshipper is neither male nor female, black nor white, Protestant nor Catholic nor Buddhist nor Hindu, but a human spirit laid bare, stripped to whatever there is that is literal and irreducible. This kind of worship inspires a quality of life that makes barriers of separateness among men increasingly and finally untenable. Worship, therefore, is central in the church.[167]

72

Jesus is the central figure of the Christian church.[168] Jesus placed before humankind three great truths with which the church is entrusted.[169] First, Jesus gave to humankind the vision of a great creative ideal, community. The ideal of community affirmed that the normal characterization of all human relations is in terms of inclusiveness. It maintains that the family of humankind is the family of God, and therefore, all persons are inextricably bound to one another. Jesus proclaimed community as the Will of God, the intent of life at its most profound level—the kingdom of God that is coming to itself in the world: Second, Jesus taught that the method by which community is achieved is love. For Jesus love transcended and gave meaning to all organic relationships and is the only means available to overcome divisions between human beings. The love of the enemy is the ultimate test of love. The ethic of love is the *modus operandi* for the ideal of community. Third, Jesus gave the resource by which men and women can achieve community and are empowered to love. Jesus called the resource God. The life of Jesus is an example of unrelenting loyalty and dependence upon God. He demonstrated in his living that the love of God is present as "an immediate available resource upon which man may draw in order to implement the ideal which is set before man."[170]

These three great truths form the essential construct of "the Jesus idea." The church, as a social institution, is the custodian of this idea and has the moral responsibility to practice the message embodied in its revelation within its own fellowship and in society. A major difficulty for the church, however, is its parochial character as a religious institution. The truth that the church is called to practice is universal, but its institutional arrangements are ultimately separatist and divisive. Thurman argues poignantly that a parochial religious institution cannot sustain the demand of a universal ethic.[171] He maintains that this indictment against the institutionalized church has implications for understanding its impotency in relation to the problems that plague society in general and that prevent the actualization of community within the church itself.

The inclusive nature of the church demands that the "Jesus idea" be practiced within its own fellowship. The greatest obstacle to Christianity is its tragic identification with the cultural norms and practices that work against harmonious relations among people in society. Racism and classism within the church are flagrant contradictions to the ideal of community which Jesus lived and taught. Unless these barriers are addressed and eradicated within the institutional church, its social witness will continue to be severely limited.[172] The church stands under the same judgment of God as other social institutions that are against the will and intent of life. Any institution that is against the goal and purpose of life is "evil and a diabolical perversion" and carries within itself its own seeds of destruction.[173] Thurman considered the eradication of racism and classism within the Christian fellowship as primary to its social witness.

The church must also transcend denominationalism.[174] The "adjectival" character of Christian institutions (i.e., "Baptist" church, "Methodist" church) works against the performance of the ethical mandate of inclusiveness. Denominationalism is inconsistent with the genius of "the Jesus idea." He says "the separate vision of a denomination *tends* to give the one who embraces it an ultimate particularized status, even before God."[175] This assertion against denominationalism, however, does not mean that Thurman sees no merit in different views and approaches to God. In fact, the ecumenical nature of the church is celebrated by him.[176] His concern, rather, is with hardened and calcified creeds and dogma which prevent mutual dialogue and exchange.[177] When a denominational perspective is viewed as ultimate, it contradicts the dynamic and creative nature of truth that is inherent in life.[178] Therefore, when dogmatists and denominationalists argue for the sole truth of one perspective against another, they behave "like dogs that fight over bones in the backyard."[179] Creeds and dogma are but frames of reference through which God is perceived; they can never claim ultimate truth.[180]

Finally, the "Jesus idea" with which the church is entrusted is universal, and therefore demands an inclusiveness that is open to intimate fellowship with others of different religious faiths. Religious loyalties are primarily accidents of birth and culture.[181] God, not Jesus, is the primary subject involved in the religious experience of the individual. If Jesus is considered the primary subject in the religious experience, then the ground is set for the exclusiveness and superiority of the Christian faith. But if in a religious fellowship, the worship of God is central, different orientations and cultural loyalties are transcended. In such an inclusive fellowship, religious claims and perspectives need not serve as bases for division, but can be complementary in ascertaining greater truth. A common, universal faith which embraces truth in any religious expression can become the leaven which redeems and transforms society.[182]

The church also has a social pedagogical function. The Christian minister is responsible for teaching and interpreting the significance of various political, economic, and social arrangements as they impinge upon the spirituality of individuals.[183] Thurman does not counsel the church as an *institution* to confront unjust social structures. His primary emphasis remains the spiritual cultivation of individuals who are enabled through the worship/teaching ministry of the church to confront the powers that oppose the realization of community. This does not mean that the individual *per se* is left alone to challenge injustice in society; he or she may represent other organizations or institutions within society that struggle for social change. His ministry at the Fellowship Church included such notable personalities as Alan Paton, Eleanor Roosevelt, and Josephine Baker.[184] Thurman, however, perceived his role as minister and the role of the church as an *interpreter* and *enabler* for those involved in the quest for social justice.

> It was my conviction and determination that the church would be a resource for activists—a mission fundamentally perceived. To me it was important that the individual who was in the thick of the struggle for social change would be able to find renewal and fresh courage in the spiritual resources of the church. There must be provided a place, a moment, when a person could declare, 'I choose!'[185]

In summary, the church, as the social institution entrusted with "the Jesus idea," is called to actualize the vision of community within its own fellowship and in the world. Any division within the church (including racism, classism, sexism, denominationalism, religious exclusivism) that militates against inclusiveness is also against the will and intent of life, and comes under the judgment of God. The ministry of the church is twofold: it should provide for an environment for worship in which experiences of spiritual unity are achieved; and it should serve as a pedagogical function by teaching and interpreting the religious and ethical implications of political, economic, and social arrangements in which the church finds itself. The church as an institution is not counseled to confront unjust systems and practices. The emphasis in Thurman is on the church as an interpreter and enabler of the individual who works for community in the world.

Community as an Empirical Reality

Thurman's understanding of the nature and role of the church is a product of both theory and practice. His pastoral experience, which embraced over thirty- six years, gave him empirical bases for his theoretical claims.[186] His parishes and university chaplaincies served as laboratories where he had unique opportunities to experiment with his ideas in concrete situations and to test his major hypothesis that *the worship of God is the central and most significant act of the human spirit, and that in the presence of God, all classifications by which human beings define themselves, though meaningful, are ultimately artificial.*[187]

The Fellowship Church is perhaps the best model of his experiences in community building. He served the church for over nine years, from 1944 to 1953. It was there that Thurman experimented with the power of religious experience to remove racial, cultural, and religious barriers that impede the actualization of human community. The church began with less than fifty members of various denominational, ethnic, and cultural backgrounds, primarily Caucasian, Black, and Asian American. Before he resigned in 1953, the congregation had grown to over 200 resident members and over 1,000 members-at- large.[188]

Thurman incorporated the arts, special music, sacred dance, and meditation into the worship services as he had done in earlier settings. At the Fellowship Church, however, meditation and prayer became more prominent in the worship experience.[189] The church's religious education program stressed intercultural and interreligious understanding, with particular interest in the development of common grounds of unity. The church's role in society was not the primary focus of the fellowship. The social mission of the Fellowship Church was one of an exemplar of community and a resource for those engaged in the creation of a loving and just society.

> The true genius of the church was revealed by what it symbolized as a beachhead in society in terms of community, and as an inspiration to the solitary individual to put his weight on the side of a society in which no man need be afraid.[190]

One incident that illustrates the social witness of the church grew out of Thurman's indignation at a window display in a prominent downtown department store in San Francisco. It was a display of a black woman and children which expressed the stereotype of "Black Mammy and Pickaninnies." Thurman, without describing the scene or sharing his feelings, asked members to view the display. He says that by noon on the following Monday, the entire display had been removed.[191]

Smith suggests that Thurman's ecclesiology can be interpreted as providing a "lemonade stand" where individual parishioners are refreshed and empowered to do battle with unjust forces in society, while the church as an institution wields no power in the social arena. Smith says that although this argument is not without merit, it fails to address the real issue which concerned Thurman. It was not Thurman's intention, Smith argues, to build a *model* for social action involvement, rather, he was concerned with the creation of a model for inclusive religious fellowship. The church, like Thurman, "made a specific witness which fits its character and mission for its time and place."[192]

While it cannot be denied that the time and context of Thurman's ministry in the San Francisco area must be considered in any accounting of his ministry there, it is instructive to challenge his position on the social witness of the church.[193] Smith's response to the criticism fails to deal with the central issue involved in the question of the church's role as an institution in the affairs of society. The fundamental issue raised by the criticism is not the distinction between religious inclusiveness or social involvement of the church as an institution. These ideas are not mutually exclusive; rather, the latter follows from the former as a logical corollary.

The quest for religious inclusiveness in Thurman necessarily leads one into engagement with society and demands that the church as a social institution entrusted with "the Jesus idea" make a formal stand against what it perceives as being antithetical to its witness in the world. Therefore, the question that must be raised with Thurman's understanding of the church's social witness is whether the church can afford not to become engaged as an institution in the affairs of society. Or is the "lemonade stand" approach sufficient for the type of witness Thurman suggests must be effected in society to combat the evils that operate against human community? This view represents an important difference between himself and the perspective of his younger visionary, Martin Luther King, Jr., which will be treated in chapters 7 and 8.

This chapter has been concerned with the actualization of community in the thought of Howard Thurman. His treatment of the barriers to community and his recommendations for overcoming the barriers to community were examined. The analysis of the barriers to community focused on evil as barrier to community, the personal and social dimensions of sin, and the individual's response to the barriers of community. The analysis of Thurman's recommendations for overcoming the barriers to community included his understanding of community as the norm and goal of the moral life; the means of actualization of community; community, religion, and social action; and community as an empirical reality.

Part II

The Search for the Beloved Community:
The Ideal of Community in Martin Luther King, Jr.

And I saw the holy city, New Jerusalem, coming down out of heaven from God...

Revelation 21:2

Chapter 4

Bound for Canaan Land

There are...periods in the history of the race, mysterious times of gestation, when something new is coming to be, however dimly the age itself comprehends the significance of its travail. These racial 'budding periods,' like the others, have organic connection with the past. They are life-events which the previous history of humanity has made possible, and so they cannot be understood by themselves.

The most notable characteristic of such times is the simultaneous outbreaking of new aspects of truth in sundered places and through diverse lives, as though the breath of a new Pentecost were abroad. This dawning time is generally followed by the appearance of some person who proves to be able to be the exponent of what others have dimly or subconsciously felt, and yet could not explicitly set forth. Such a person becomes by certain divine right the prophet of the period because he knows how to interpret its ideas with such compelling force that he organizes men, either for action or for perpetuating the truth.

−Rufus M. Jones

I grew up in the church... My father is a preacher, my grandfather was a preacher, my great grandfather was a preacher, my only brother is a preacher, my daddy's brother is a preacher, so I didn't have much of a choice I guess.

—Martin Luther King, Jr.

O Canaan, sweet Canaan,
I am bound for the land of Canaan,
O Canaan, sweet Canaan,
I am bound for the land of Canaan.

—Negro Spiritual

The search for community was the defining motif of Martin Luther King, Jr.'s life and thought. From his early childhood until his death, there is a progression in his personal and intellectual understanding of the nature and goal of human existence which he refers to as "the beloved community."[1] King's search for community was characterized by an insatiable thirst for truth and a deep-seated religious faith that began in his early years in the intimate contexts of his family, the black church, and the larger black community of Atlanta, Georgia. The development of the ideal in King is discernible in his educational pursuits at Morehouse College, Crozer Theological Seminary, and later Boston University. After his formal education and training, his experiences as pastor and spokesman for the black community in Montgomery served as a "proving ground" for his embryonic, theoretical formulation of community that would be refined in the praxis of the Civil Rights Movement. The early development of the ideal of community in King reaches its zenith in the March on Washington in 1963, but the following four and a half years proved to be a period in which his vision of community received its severest criticisms and challenges. These final years of his life and ministry, although beleaguered with controversy and sabotage, are the most crucial in understanding the maturation of his personal and intellectual growth in respect to community. It is in this period that one sees most clearly King's wrestling with nonviolence as a means of achieving human community, his increased realization of the international implications of his vision of community, and his understanding of the nature and role of conflict in the realization of human community.

The first part of this chapter will follow the unfolding pattern of King's search for "the beloved community": 1) early years; 2) education; 3) Montgomery; 4) the American Dream; and 5) the World House. The latter part will examine the intellectual sources of his ideal of community.

The Experiential Sources
The Early Years

The Family Context

Martin Luther King, Jr.'s earliest understanding of community began in the contexts of his family environment, the fellowship of the black church, and in the larger context of the black community of Atlanta, Georgia. In these interrelated environs one sees most clearly the genesis of his search for community and the developing sense of mission that accompanied his vision.

Martin Luther King, Jr. was born into a family heritage deeply steeped in the tradition of black protest and struggle against the ravages of white racism. Born on January 15, 1929, in Atlanta, he was the second child of the Reverend and Mrs. Martin Luther King, Sr. (the former Alberta Christine Williams). His maternal grandfather, the Reverend A.D. Williams, who pastored Ebenezer Baptist Church from 1894 to 1931, was well known for his valiant campaigns against racial injustice.[2]

Martin Luther King, Sr., who succeeded his father-in-law as pastor of Ebenezer Baptist Church in 1931, continued the legacy of protest against segregation in Atlanta. He led boycotts, a voting rights march, and fought for full arrest rights of black policemen.[3] The young King, an inquisitive and sensitive child, was deeply affected by his father's struggle against the segregationist policies in Atlanta. In his book, *Stride Toward Freedom*, he comments on his father's legacy of protest:

> From before I was born, my father refused to ride the city buses, after witnessing a brutal attack on a load of Negro passengers. He had led the fight in Atlanta to equalize teachers' salaries, and had been instrumental in the elimination of Jim Crow elevators in the courthouse. As pastor of the Ebenezer Baptist Church...he had wielded great influence in the Negro community, and had perhaps won the grudging respect of the whites. At any rate, they had never attacked him physically, *a fact that filled my brother and sister and me with wonder as we grew up in this tension-packed atmosphere.*[4]

King, reflecting upon the examples of his father and grandfather, writes, "With this heritage, it is not surprising that I had also learned to abhor segregation, considering it both rationally inexplicable and morally unjustifiable."[5]

There were also strong black women in his family who contributed greatly to his sense of self-worth and growing sense of mission. His mother, a quiet, dignified, and well-educated woman, was a source of comfort and strength for her young son, who had to deal with the devastating consequences of racism at an early age. When he was six years old, his white playmates' parents informed him that he could no longer play with their children. Perplexed by this sudden change in relations, he questioned his mother. He remembered how she explained to him the history of slavery, emancipation and the Civil War, and the divided system of segregation. She helped him to understand that this was a social condition and not the natural order. "Then she said the words that almost every Negro hears before he can yet understand the injustice that makes them necessary: 'You are as good as anyone.'"[6] King was also very close to his maternal grandmother, who lived with the family after the death of her husband. Grandmother Williams helped to raise the children and spent many evenings telling them interesting stories. [7]

The influences of his family environment gave Martin a sense of personal worth and a basis for belief in a "friendly universe." These two interrelated themes were fundamental to his emerging vision of community and in the coming years they would be given greater conceptual clarity.

The Black Church Experience

Young King's family life was inseparable from his religious development. He was bred and nurtured in the rich and powerful religious idiom of the black church.[8] He joined Ebenezer Baptist Church when he was five years old. He never recalled having an "abrupt" conversion experience; he says, rather, that "religion has just been something I grew up in." He comments further: "Conversion for me has been the gradual intaking of the noble ideals set forth in my family environment, and I must admit that this intaking has been highly unconscious."[9]

His early religious development, however, was not without questions, despite his young age. King had great difficulty accepting what he perceived as the excessive emotionalism and fundamentalism in his church experience. When he was twelve or thirteen years old, he shocked his Sunday School teacher by denying the bodily resurrection of Jesus.[10] His skepticism continued through college. In fact, he despaired of the role of the black church as a creative agent for change in society because of its emotionalism and fundamentalist interpretation of Scriptures. It was not until he met well-educated and articulate preachers like Dr. George D. Kelsey and Dr. Benjamin E. Mays at Morehouse College that he was able to make a decision for Christian ministry.[11]

Nevertheless, it was in the black religious experience at Ebenezer Baptist Church that King first discovered the deep-rooted spirituality that sustained him in his struggles to create human community, and also where he received a sense of mission and purpose that led him to accept the call to Christian ministry at the age of seventeen. In a revealing statement in his "Autobiography of Religious Development," written while he was a student at Boston University School of Theology, King reflects on his reasons for entering ministry and his early childhood experiences with his family and the church:

> At present I still feel the effects of the noble moral and ethical ideals that I grew up under. They have been real and precious to me, and even in moments of theological doubt I could never turn away from them. Even though I never had an abrupt conversion experience, religion has been real to me and closely knitted to life. In fact the two cannot be separated; religion for me is life.[12]

The Black Community

King's early development in the contexts of his family and the church were complemented by the larger black community of Atlanta. A product of the black middle-class community of Atlanta, he was raised in the

84

relative comfort of a materially successful household.[13] The black community of Atlanta during his early years boasted of a large and varied black middle-class comprised of college professors, contractors, real estate agents, insurance executives, bankers, businessmen, physicians, dentists, and morticians.[14] Throughout his early years, King was surrounded by these symbols of success and progress, which reinforced the sense of self-worth and mission he experienced in the contexts of his family and the church. Of central significance was the priority placed on education and cultural sophistication. The pioneer black sociologist, E. Franklin Frazier, in his book, *Black Bourgeoisie*, contended that among the Negro middle-class there was a quest for social status that developed from an "inferiority complex" engendered by slavery and segregation. This fixation with status and prestige was manifested in the aspirations of the middle-class Negro in puritanical family and sexual mores, which set them apart from the black masses. "But the chief compensation for their inferior status in American society," writes Franklin, "was found in education."

> While their racial heritage and conventional standards of morality only gave them a privileged position in the Negro community, education gave them access to a world of ideas that provided an intellectual escape from their physical and social segregation in American life. Therefore, they placed an exaggerated importance upon academic degrees, especially if they were secured from white colleges in the North. If one secured the degree of doctor of philosophy in a northern university, he was regarded as a sort of genius. Consequently, for the relatively small group of educated Negroes, education was an indication of their 'superior culture' and a mark of 'refinement.'[15]

Martin King was reared in the intellectual and cultural streams of the black community reflected in this analysis. James Cone argues that King's black middle- class social origins informed his integrationist philosophy and his method of nonviolent protest. He claims that King followed in the tradition of accommodation and protest wielded by Frederick Douglass, Booker T. Washington, and the N.A.A.C.P., which held that black progress was measured in terms of economic advantage and appeals to the constitutional rights of Negroes with the ultimate aim of assimilation into the dominant white culture.[16]

However one interprets the influence of Atlanta's black middle-class community on the developing personality of King, it must also be acknowledged that class distinctions among black people did not immunize them from the indignities and impersonal logic of segregation. King's early experiences of segregation had an equal effect on shaping his understanding of community and caused him to search for a method to overcome the barriers that separate human beings from one another. In *Stride Toward Freedom*, he writes:

> I had grown up abhorring not only segregation but also the oppressive and barbarous acts that grew out of it. I had passed spots where Negroes had been savagely lynched, and had watched the Ku Klux Klan on its rides at night. I had seen police brutality with my own eyes, and watched Negroes receive the most tragic injustice in the courts. All of these things had done something to my growing personality. I had come perilously close to resenting all white people.[17]

These and other atrocities which he witnessed and experienced during his early years in the Deep South brought King to the realization that he must dedicate his life to the eradication of the evil system of segregation.[18] It would not be until his first year at Crozer Theological Seminary in 1948, however, that he would "begin a serious intellectual quest for a method to eliminate social evil."[19]

In summary, the formative influences in King's early years from his family environment, the black church experience at Ebenezer Baptist Church, and the black community in Atlanta instilled in him a sense of personal worth and a growing sense of mission. These positive influences helped to lay the groundwork for an emerging vision of unity among human beings. The negative force of segregation which opposed the communal ties and orientation King experienced in his family, church, and the black Atlanta community convinced him of the inner necessity to dedicate his life to the creation of a just society in which black people could live freely and with dignity among whites. While his middle-class origins may have helped to shape his developing theoretical and strategic concerns, the ever-present reality of segregation and its assaults against his sense of personal dignity equally informed his developing world view and quest for a method of creative social change.

Education

Early Educational Experience

King's formal education began in the segregated black public schools of Atlanta. In 1935 he entered the Yonge Street Elementary School and three years later transferred to the David T. Howard Colored Elementary School. In 1941, when his family moved, he entered the Atlanta University Laboratory School, an experimental secondary school for gifted black youth, but at the end of his second year there the school closed for economic reasons. He transferred to Booker T. Washington High School where he was allowed to skip the ninth grade. While at Booker T. Washington, King compiled a B+ average. His favorite subjects were history and English. His love for the English language and his sweeping breadth of history would reap high dividends in his role as spokesman and interpreter of the history of the black struggle for freedom. In the eleventh grade, he won an oratorical contest sponsored by the Negro Elks in a neighboring Georgia town. His topic was "The Negro and the Constitution," a theme that would remain a major focus of his thought throughout his life.[20]

Morehouse College

In 1944, Morehouse College started a program for exceptional high school students. The program was designed, in part, to fill the depleting enrollment of students because of wartime conscription.[21] After completing a battery of entrance examinations, King again skipped a grade and entered Morehouse College when he was only fifteen years old. At Morehouse, he found a robust fraternal atmosphere well-tailored for his intellectual pursuits. As stated, the venerable Benjamin E. Mays continued in the rich legacy set forth by John Hope and Samuel Archer.[22] Among the other outstanding faculty were Samuel Williams, Professor of Philosophy, George D. Kelsey, Professor of Religion and Philosophy, Gladstone L. Chandler, Professor of English, and Walter Chivers, Professor of Sociology.

The Morehouse experience was also beneficial for his understanding of the potential for wholesome relations with white people. King's resentment of white people, which began early in his youth, continued to grow through his college years until he reached a point where he was determined to hate all white people. It was not until he began to serve on the Atlanta Intercollegiate Council, an interracial student group, that he was able to conquer this "anti-white feeling."[23] His professors at Morehouse also aided him by holding frank discussions about race and encouraging the young Morehouse men to seek positive solutions to the race problem.[24]

While a student at Morehouse College, King acknowledged his call to ministry.[25] Licensed to preach in 1947, he became assistant to his father at Ebenezer Baptist Church. In February of the following year, he was ordained to the Baptist ministry. That same year, at the tender age of nineteen, King was graduated from Morehouse College with a Bachelor of Arts degree in Sociology. His ordination to ministry and his graduation represented a closing chapter in his early development.

The experiences of racial dialogue and exchange which began at Morehouse College prepared him for the coming years in which his faith in the inherent worth of personality would be severely tested in the crucible of struggle in the heartlands of the Deep South and in the ghettos of the urban North. The formative influences upon his intellectual development at Morehouse College also provided him with the confidence and heightened sense of mission that would enable him to excel in the academic environments of Crozer Theological Seminary and Boston University. He had written earlier that year in the Morehouse student journal, *The Maroon Tiger*, that:

> The function of education...is to teach one to think intensively and to think critically. But education which stops with efficiency may prove the greatest menace to society. The most dangerous criminal may be the man gifted with reason, but with no morals.[26]

The remainder of his educational and public careers is a bold testimony to this belief.

Crozer Theological Seminary and Boston University

When King began his studies at Crozer Theological Seminary in the Fall of 1948, a new stage in his personal and intellectual development began. He found himself in an overwhelmingly white academic environment which made him painfully aware of his "blackness" and his self-imposed mission to overcome white stereotypes of "the Negro."[27] No doubt, for this reason as well as his superior intellectual gifts, he excelled at Crozer, earning an "A" in every course he took in the curriculum. He was valedictorian of his class.

The teacher at Crozer who contributed most to the young scholar's theological and philosophical underpinnings of community was George W. Davis, Professor of Christian Theology from 1938 to 1960. King began his formal study of personalism with Davis. The theological personalism that informed many of the evangelical liberal doctrines taught by Davis would find its fruition in King's doctoral studies at Boston University.[28] Other important intellectual sources that he would engage while at Crozer were the works of Walter Rauschenbusch, Karl Marx, Mahatma Gandhi, and Reinhold Niebuhr. His theological and ethical formulations of the beloved community owe much to these sources.[29]

King was graduated from Crozer in June 1951 and entered Boston University during the fall of the same year. His major philosophical and theological studies at Boston University were with Edgar Sheffield Brightman and L. Harold DeWolf. Brightman, his major professor, died during his second year at Boston University and DeWolf, a protege of Brightman, became his adviser. King acknowledges that both men greatly stimulated his thinking.[30] It was mainly under these thinkers that he studied personalism. Others whom he acknowledged as making significant contributions to his intellectual pilgrimage while at Boston University were Walter Muelder and Allen Knight Chalmers. According to King, these renowned pacifists provided examples of the inherent potential of human beings to create a just and loving society through cooperation with God.[31]

While he was a student at Boston University, he met a young woman who was to become his life-long companion in the struggle to create human community. The daughter of Bernice McMurray and Obadiah Scott, who had triumphed over the many obstacles of race and class, Coretta Scott was well acquainted with the rigors of life in the segregated South. Though her family did not bear the social prestige of the Kings, the Scotts had successfully carved a position of economic stability in the hopeless setting of Marion, Alabama.[32] Coretta was a graduate of Oberlin College in Ohio and a student at the New England Conservatory of Music when she and King met.[33] The young couple were married on June 18, 1953.

During King's last year at Boston University, Howard Thurman was appointed as Dean of Marsh Chapel. On at least one occasion during that period, he was a guest at the Thurman's home. Both being sports enthusiasts, they watched the World Series together.[34] In an interview with Lewis Baldwin, Phillip Lenud, King's roommate in Boston, indicated that he and the young scholar and orator attended some of the services at Marsh Chapel and were enamored by Thurman's preaching style and the profundity of his moral and spiritual thought.[35] Obviously, the appreciation was mutual. Thurman acknowledged that Mrs. Thurman and King seriously discussed the possibility of his assuming the pastorate of the Fellowship Church, but he had already decided to go to Montgomery.[36]

Montgomery: "The Proving Ground for Community"

Montgomery, Alabama, was "the proving ground" for King's early vision of community. His keen intellectual abilities and his eclectic appropriation of thought from a variety of philosophical, theological, historical, and social sources had well equipped him for the mission which lay ahead. His entire life from early childhood through the higher echelons of academia seemed to follow a direct path that converged on the kairotic moment in Montgomery. Not to be overlooked is the underlying idiom of the black religious experience from which King was never divorced. His long years of academic pursuit were undergirded by a deep spirituality and an understanding of life which informed his decision to return to the South. He and his wife felt that they had a moral obligation to return.[37]

On October 31, 1954, Martin Luther King, Sr. installed his 25-year-old son as the twentieth pastor of the Dexter Avenue Baptist Church in Montgomery, Alabama. The following June King received his Ph.D. in Systematic Theology from Boston University. Just five months prior to his installation, another significant event which would greatly affect his life and ministry also took place. On May 17, 1954, the Supreme Court of the United States ruled unanimously in *Brown vs. Board of Education* that racial segregation in public schools was unconstitutional. The high court's ruling precipitated a climate of "interposition," "nullification," economic reprisals, and violence against black people led by White Citizens Councils and the Ku Klux Klan from Virginia to Texas.[38] In December of that same year, King became the spokesperson for the Montgomery Improvement Association, a position that placed him in the practical arena of social action where his developing understanding of the nature of community and the method for its actualization would be tested in the praxis of struggle. His able leadership as spokesman for the Montgomery Improvement Association, which came into being after Rosa Parks refused to relinquish her bus seat to a white man, ushered in a new era not only for the Montgomery black community, but for the continuing civil rights movement throughout the country. King felt that the movement in Montgomery was divinely inspired and that God was using Montgomery "as the proving ground for the struggle and triumph of freedom and justice in America."[39]

King's ministry in the Montgomery Movement was characterized by two significant realizations that became working hypotheses in his future campaigns to achieve the beloved community: his practical realization of the method of nonviolent resistance as the means to achieve his vision of community and the power of the federal government to combat the barriers to community imposed by segregated statutes and unjust laws.[40]

Nonviolent Direct Action as the Method

In Montgomery, King realized the power of nonviolent resistance to achieve his vision of community; the black church was the place which served as the source of its inspiration. Lerone Bennett contends that his great achievement in reference to nonviolent resistance was to turn the Negro's rooted faith in the church to social and political account by melding the image of Gandhi and the image of the Negro preacher and by overlaying all with Negro songs and symbols that bypassed cerebral centers and exploded in the well of the Negro psyche.[41]

Before Montgomery, his understanding of nonviolence was confined to an abstract association of ideas and readings from his intellectual pursuits, but in the midst of the struggle he came to understand its power to effect change, both in society and within the votary him/herself. It is also important to understand that nonviolent resistance as a viable alternative for social change had been debated and attempted by the black leadership long before King emerged as a proponent of the method.[42] Initially, the method of the movement which came to be called nonviolent resistance was conceived in the hearts of the black people of Montgomery as "Christian love." King writes that:

> From the beginning a basic philosophy guided the movement.... It was the Sermon on the Mount rather than a doctrine of passive resistance, that initially inspired the Negroes of Montgomery to dignified social action. It was Jesus of Nazareth that stirred the Negroes to protest with the creative weapon of love.[43]

The inspiration of Gandhi was to exert its influence through the letter of Miss Juliette Morgan to the Montgomery *Advertiser*, and later through the help of several Christian socialists and pacifists who collaborated with King as he fashioned a philosophy of nonviolence for the Montgomery Improvement Association.[44] He says:

> Nonviolent resistance had emerged as the technique of the movement, while love stood out as the regulating ideal. In other words, Christ furnished the spirit and motivation, while Gandhi furnished the method.[45]

The philosophy of nonviolent resistance was disseminated in the mass meetings held in the black churches throughout the city. King felt that the black church was the natural place for this idea to be taught because of the long history of redemptive suffering that black people had endured. After Montgomery, he believed that American Negroes had been chosen by history to become "instruments of a great idea," the idea of nonviolent resistance.[46]

The other important lesson King learned in Montgomery was the place of the democratic principles inherent in the Constitution and the power of the federal government to combat the barriers to community imposed by segregated statutes and unjust laws. Early in his ministry at Dexter Avenue Baptist Church, he formed a Social and Political Action Committee. The purpose of the committee was to educate the church and community on the importance of the NAACP and to uplift the necessity of being registered voters. During local, state and national elections, the committee sponsored forums and mass meetings to discuss the major issues affecting the Negro community.[47] Later, in the bus boycott, he came to realize that the battle for political and economic justice in the South would have to be fought beyond the local and state courts. The insidious tactics of the local and state courts and lawmakers in Montgomery convinced him that the federal government would have to take strong and aggressive leadership to create the political environment in which integration could become a reality.[48] The two strategic cases which determined the outcome of the Montgomery boycott were those in which the federal courts overruled the local courts. On June 4, 1956, a United States district court ruled that racial segregation on city bus lines was unconstitutional. Later, on November 13, 1956, the United States Supreme Court affirmed the decision of the three-judge district court in declaring unconstitutional Alabama's state and local laws requiring segregation on buses. He was well aware, however, that politics alone could not legislate morality, but it could insure the opportunity for the dispossessed and disenfranchised to have an equal voice in their destinies and the destiny of the country. He remarked at the end of the Montgomery movement:

> Government is not the whole answer to the present crisis, but it is an important partial answer. Morals cannot be legislated, but behavior can be required. The law cannot make an employer love me, but it can keep him from refusing to hire me because of the color of my skin.[49]

In summary, Montgomery was a proving ground for King's ideal of community. The road which lay ahead for him would be filled with many lessons, but two significant elements emerged in this campaign which would become integral to his evolving understanding of the conception, character, and actualization of the beloved community: his realization of the *method* of nonviolent resistance as the means to achieve his vision of community, and the power of the federal government to combat the barriers to community imposed by segregated statutes and unjust laws.

The American Dream
Montgomery to Washington

The years of 1957-1963 represent the period of King's development referred to as his quest for the American Dream. Here one sees an intense focus on the role of the federal government and the place of the Declaration of Independence, the Emancipation Proclamation, and the Constitution in his articulation of the beloved community. In 1960, in an address entitled, "The Negro and the American Dream," King says:

> In a real sense, America is essentially a dream—a dream yet unfulfilled. It is the dream of a land where men of all races, colors and creeds will live together as brothers. The substance of the dream is expressed in these sublime words: 'We hold these truths to be self-evident, that all men are created equal, that they are endowed by their Creator with certain unalienable rights, that among these are life, liberty and the pursuit of happiness.'[50]

As he was to speak later to the national conscience about his dream, which was "deeply rooted in the American dream," King, at this point in his development, tends almost naively to identify the beloved community with the American dream, which for him was centered around enfranchisement of the American Negro, desegregation and integration through legislation, and economic empowerment of black people.[51] It is also significant that during this period King took two trips abroad in which he was exposed to the international scene of poverty and the struggle of colonized nations against crumbling European power. In March 1960, the Reverend and Mrs. King took their first trip abroad as part of an American contingent to celebrate the independence of the Gold Coast. The entourage included such notables as A. Philip Randolph, Adam Clayton Powell, and Ralph Bunche. Vice-President Richard Nixon was the official U.S. representative, but Kwame Nkrumah had invited black leaders as well. King, who had just reached his twenty-eighth year, was included in this distinguished company. On March 9, he and his wife were among the thousands of people gathered to hear Nkrumah shout, "The battle is ended. Ghana, our beloved country, is free forever."[52] This experience made a momentous impact upon King's understanding of the liberation struggles of colonized nations and their role in the creation of world community.[53] From February 2 through March 19, 1959, King and his wife spent a month in India as guests of Prime Minister Nehru where they studied Gandhi's techniques of nonviolence. After India, they visited Israel, Cairo and Athens. Upon his return, King was even more determined to bring his vision of community in America into actualization. After his visit to the

93

land of Gandhi, nonviolence became more than just a philosophy or technique for social change for King, it became a way of life.[54]

The bus boycott had catapulted King into national and international prominence, but despite his popularity, Montgomery would remain his base of operation until January 1960. He would later move to Atlanta and serve as co- pastor with his father at Ebenezer Baptist Church so that he could devote more time to the movement. The successful campaign in Montgomery culminated in the founding of the Southern Christian Leadership Conference (SCLC) on January 10, 1957. With SCLC, King became president of a larger organization to coordinate nonviolent protest movements that were appearing in various parts of the South. SCLC's activity centered upon two main foci: the use of nonviolent philosophy as a means of protest and securing the right of the ballot for every citizen, particularly black southerners. The new organization's ultimate goal was "to foster and create 'the beloved community' in America where brotherhood is a reality."[55]

King's optimism in the realization of the American Dream of equality and justice for all people was fueled by successful projects such as the Prayer Pilgrimage (1957),[56] the Crusade for Citizenship (1958),[57] and the election of John Fitzgerald Kennedy to the presidency of the United States. Kennedy's intervention in King's release from a Georgia jail won the critical black votes he needed to defeat Richard Nixon.[58] For King, Kennedy's action underscored his fundamental premise that the Negro franchisement was the most powerful tool at the Negro's disposal to foster "the beloved community" in America. King also saw the symbolic significance of Kennedy's presidency for the historical movement of America toward real community.[59] In an article entitled "Equality Now," he compared the new Kennedy administration with the Lincoln presidency one hundred years earlier. He felt that Kennedy, like Lincoln, stood at a unique place in history wherein he had an opportunity to adopt a radically new approach to race relations and to determine the moral destiny of the nation. He encouraged Kennedy to take the offensive in the passage of a civil rights bill that would safeguard voting rights and other long-overdue benefits entitled to citizens of color. He also called upon Kennedy to abolish segregation by executive order, a move which, like the Emancipation Proclamation of Lincoln, would set the legal tone for the moral course of the nation.[60]

The years of 1961-1963 continued for King in the same pattern toward the realization of community in America. His optimism was severely tested during this period by the overt violence and disunity within the movement associated with the Freedom Rides[61] and later by his unsuccessful campaign in Albany, Georgia in 1961-62.[62] He learned invaluable lessons, however, from both these episodes, lessons that uniquely prepared him for "the Battle of Birmingham" that would take place from March through May of 1963.[63]

The Birmingham campaign brought the Negro's struggle before the national conscience. In his "Letter From A Birmingham Jail," King illustrates how his willingness to suffer nonviolently for justice was rooted in the principles of democracy and a greater vision of community. In response to his clerical critics who accused him of being an outside agitator, he wrote:

> I cannot sit idly by in Atlanta and not be concerned about what happens in Birmingham. Injustice anywhere is a threat against justice everywhere. We are caught in an inescapable network of mutuality tied in a single garment of destiny. Whatever affects one directly affects all indirectly. Never again can we afford to live with the narrow, provincial 'outside agitator' idea. Anyone who lives inside the United States can never be considered an outsider anywhere in this country.[64]

The March on Washington

The success of the Birmingham campaign created public sympathy and support which forced the vacillating Kennedy administration to take an affirmative stance in behalf of the repeated appeals of King and other civil rights leaders to submit a civil rights bill to Congress that would open public accommodations to Negroes across Dixie. On June 19, Kennedy submitted his new civil rights package to Congress. In order to create the pressure on Congress to pass the proposed legislation, the heads of the five civil rights organizations, King (SCLC), A. Philip Randolph (Brotherhood of Sleeping Car Porters), Roy Wilkins (NAACP), Whitney Young (Urban League), and James Farmer (CORE) met with President Kennedy, Attorney General Robert Kennedy, and Walter Reuther (UAW) to discuss a march on the nation's capital. Although the President initially disagreed, he later lent his support to the rally. On August 28, 1963, thousands of pilgrims from every social class, religion, and race gathered at the foot of the Lincoln Memorial to hear a long list of speakers address the theme of the march, "Jobs and Freedom." But by far, the most eloquent and memorable address was King's articulation of his dream of community in America. In his speech, he referred to the theme that he had been rehearsing since Montgomery: the democratic principles inherent in the Declaration of Independence and the Constitution had been grossly ignored in regard to America's citizens of color. The Emancipation Proclamation of Lincoln, said King, had come "as a great beacon light of hope to millions of Negro slaves who had been seared in the flames of withering injustice," but "one hundred years later" the Negro was still not free. In fact, "the Negro is still languished in the corners of American society and finds himself in exile in his own land." America had written the Negro a "bad check" by reneging on the sacred promises written in the Declaration of Independence and the Constitution which guaranteed to all its citizens the unalienable rights of life, liberty, and the pursuit of happiness. The dream of which he spoke was rooted in the American dream that "one day this nation will rise up and live out the true meaning of its creed, 'We hold these truths to be self-evident, that all men are created equal.'" The vision King enunciated in this speech was at once communitarian and eschatological, for it called into community persons from every class, religion, and race and suggested that the freedom of humanity is bound to the sacred destiny of America:

> When we allow freedom to ring, when we let it ring from every village and every hamlet, from every state and every city, we will be able to speed up the day when all God's children, black men and white men, Jews and Gentiles, Protestants and Catholics, will be able to join hands and sing in the words of the old Negro spiritual, 'Free at last! Free at last! Thank God Almighty, we are free at last.'[65]

The March on Washington had a profound impact on King's sense of mission and his self-perception as an "historical individual" entrusted with the message of community. After the assassination of President Kennedy in November, 1963, President Lyndon Johnson signed the Civil Rights Act into law on July 2, 1964. During that same year in Oslo, Norway, King was awarded the Nobel Peace Prize for his role in the Civil Rights Movement in the United States. In accepting the international honor, King said:

> The tortuous road which has led from Montgomery, Alabama to Oslo bears witness to this truth (nonviolent resistance is redemptive). This is the road over which millions of Negroes are traveling to find a new sense of dignity. This same road has opened for all Americans a new era of progress and hope. It has led to a new civil rights bill, and it will, I am convinced, be widened and lengthened into a super-highway of justice as the Negro and white men in increasing numbers create alliances to overcome their common problems.
>
> I accept this award today with an abiding faith in America and an audacious faith in the future of mankind.[66]

King's optimism concerning the actualization of the beloved community in America was tried by the increasing number of violent eruptions in black communities across the nation and by fiery denunciations of nonviolent direct action as ineffective and ultimately demeaning to black Americans' sense of dignity and self-respect. The most articulate and formidable opponent of King at this juncture was Malcolm X, the spokesperson for the Honorable Elijah Muhammad, founder and leader of the Nation of Islam.[67] Malcolm accused King of succumbing to the wiles and enticements of the "white devil" by teaching black people to adhere to nonviolence. He castigated King as a coward for his use of children in Birmingham and referred to the March on Washington as "a sellout" and "a takeover" by the white power establishment.[68] King would later encounter similar criticisms from the Student Nonviolent Coordinating Committee and other black groups and intellectuals. The criticism from SNCC had been a growing concern for King since the Freedom Rides. SNCC's mounting criticisms of his nonviolent method reached divisive levels in the "March Against Fear" through Mississippi in 1966. He rejected these criticisms on moral and practical grounds and maintained that "If every Negro in the States turns to violence, I will be the one lone voice preaching that this is the wrong way."[69]

King's nonviolent campaigns in St. Augustine (1964) and in Chicago (1966) confronted myriad problems in terms of strategy, organization, and timing, all of which added to the already declining acceptance of nonviolence as a method for bringing about creative social change. St. Augustine was considered a failure by most observers,[70] and Chicago, at best, only a partial victory.[71] Even the Selma campaign (1965), though it led to the passage of the Voting Rights Act of 1965, was seen by some as a symbol of King's weakness as a leader and a sharp blow to nonviolence.[72]

King responded to his critics by emphasizing the ultimate ineffectiveness and impracticality of violent resistance within the context of American society. His argument was that violence, even in self-defense, fails to address the real issues that affect the quality of life of black Americans and the poor. Moreover, violence does not eradicate the structural problems of economic injustice and racism but actually contributes to the vicious cycle of fear and hatred which create the climate of violence that works against the realization of community. Nonviolence, on the other hand, gives black Americans the moral offensive necessary to reveal the underlying causes of the exploited conditions of the poor and disenfranchised and creates an environment in which love and justice may flourish. He wrote in 1966:

> I must continue by faith or it is too great a burden to bear and violence, even in self-defense, creates more problems than it

solves. Only a refusal to hate and kill can put an end to the chain of violence in the world and lead us toward a community where men can live together without fear. Our goal is to create a beloved community and this will require a qualitative change in our souls as well as a quantitative change in our lives.[73]

During the latter years of King's life, there was also an increased appreciation of the international implications of his vision of community. As indicated earlier, King had from the beginning been aware of the international scope of his struggle for civil rights in America. As early as 1956, there is evidence in his speeches of the relationship between the struggles abroad and the black struggle for civil rights in America.[74] In the years following his receipt of the Nobel Peace Prize, however, his public remarks regarding international events became more pronounced.[75] His most critical commentary on international events was his bold excoriation of the Vietnam War. Despite the scathing attacks of black and white critics, King maintained that his opposition to the war in Vietnam was consistent with his fundamental vision of world community. Responding to the criticism that his stand against the Vietnam War was a tactical mistake that fused civil rights with the peace movement, King said:

> I have always insisted on justice for all the world over, because justice is indivisible and injustice anywhere is a threat against justice everywhere. I will not stand idly by when I see an unjust war taking place and fail to take a stand against it. I will continue to express my opposition to this wrong policy without in any way diminishing my activity in civil rights....[76]

As noted, the role of conflict is an important theme in King's conception of human community[77] and nowhere is it more clearly illustrated than in his decision to speak out against Vietnam. His outspoken position against the war earned for him the disfavor of other civil rights organizations and key supporters of SCLC. He nevertheless insisted that justice is universal and that the mandate of justice arises out of a fundamental conception of the interrelatedness of all life. Caught in the fires of controversy and sabotage,[78] King's understanding of human community was forged into a conceptual and ethical framework which allowed him to see the American struggle within the context of an international perspective he called the "world house."[79]

The World House

The personal and intellectual odyssey that began in the context of the black American experience (i.e., family, church, community, and education), his eclectic search through the corridors of higher education at Crozer Seminary and Boston University, and his practical engagement within the Civil Rights Movement provided the essentials from which King formulated his mature thinking regarding the conception, character, and actualization of world community.[80] His maturing vision of community is, therefore, a product of reflective thought and practical engagement which emerged from struggle and conflict. At the time of his death, his vision had become international in scope and he had raised the fundamental problems of militarism, poverty, and racism as the major impediments to the actualization of human community. His recommendation for creative change that would culminate in world community was a call for a "revolution of values and priorities" that would be both national and international in scope. He called upon America, because of its unique democratic heritage and its great resources of wealth and technology, to be the leader in this revolution. King stressed, however, that a true "revolution of values and priorities" would issue forth in structural changes within the American economic and political system and in its foreign policy.

> I am convinced that if we are to get on the right side of the world revolution we as a nation must undergo a radical revolution of values. A true revolution of values will soon cause us to question the fairness and justice of many of our present and past policies. A true revolution of values will look uneasy on the glaring contrast between poverty and wealth. With righteous indignation, it will look across the seas and see individual capitalists of the West investing huge sums of money in Africa, Asia, and South America only to take the profits out with no concern for the social betterment of the countries, and say 'This is unjust.' It will look at our alliances with the landed gentry of Latin America and say: 'This is not just.' The Western arrogance of feeling that it has everything to teach others and nothing to learn from them is not just.[81]

King had also come to a place in his thinking in which he understood more clearly the dynamic tensions at work between poverty, racism, and war within the American society and their relationship to the exploitation of the poor and powerless abroad.[82] Shortly before his death in Memphis, SCLC had planned a "Poor Peoples Campaign" to converge upon Washington, D.C. in April of 1968 and demonstrate nonviolently in massive civil

99

disobedience until Congress acted to help alleviate the abject poverty across the nation. King felt that such a national confrontation with the federal government by an interracial coalition of 3,000 poor whites, Native Americans, Hispanic Americans, and blacks (who would comprise the majority) would symbolically demonstrate the class-based economic and social discrimination inherent in the national policy.[83] He also argued that the national policy of discrimination against the poor and ethnic minorities was but a microcosm of the nation's foreign policy which was most dramatically illustrated in the Vietnam War. In his words, "The war in Vietnam is but a symptom of a far deeper malady within the America spirit."[84] It was King's position that the problems of poverty and race within the United States are international in scope and therefore "inseparable from an international emergency which involves the poor, the dispossessed, and the exploited of the whole world."[85]

King's personal and intellectual struggle to realize the vision of a world house in which sectionalism would give place to ecumenicity, and loyalties to race, class, and religion would be overcome by a greater loyalty to the interrelatedness of all life, came to an abrupt end in Memphis, Tennessee, where he had joined sanitation workers in a strike for improved wages and working conditions. This campaign, like the many others in which he had been involved, symbolized his life-long quest to bring to realization his ideal of the beloved community. His closing words in his book, *Where Do We Go from Here?*, captures King's forthright and urgent appeal to create world community and frames the story of his life and ministry: "We still have a choice today: nonviolent coexistence or violent coannihilation. This may well be mankind's last chance to choose between chaos and community."[86]

The Intellectual Sources

King was a highly eclectic thinker who appropriated knowledge from a variety of sources in the shaping and molding of his ideal of community.[87] This brief accounting of the intellectual sources which contributed to the development of his thought will be concerned primarily with the intellectual foundations at Morehouse College, Crozer Seminary, and Boston University.

Morehouse College

As stated, the stimulating intellectual atmosphere of Morehouse College was well suited for the budding young preacher and theologian. The two men who were most responsible for King's early intellectual appreciation of religious life were Professor George Kelsey and Dr. Benjamin E.

Mays. Kelsey was Professor of Religion and Philosophy and Director of the School of Religion at Morehouse College from 1945 to 1948. He challenged King "to see that behind the legends and myths of the book were many profound truths which one could not escape."[88] Kelsey also condemned the excessive emotionalism of churches as obsolete and useless and convinced King of the need for a more intellectual and social approach to the question of Biblical faith. King credits Kelsey with challenging him to reformulate his attitudes toward religion and the church.[89]

Benjamin Mays, the stalwart and scholarly President of Morehouse College from 1940 to 1967, had also served as mentor and friend to Howard Thurman when he was a student at Morehouse. Through his weekly chapel messages and personal counseling, he made a singular impact on the religious and intellectual development of King.[90] In men like Mays and Kelsey, he saw models of black preachers with keen intellectual skills and heightened social consciousness which he felt were necessary to address the overwhelming social problems confronting his people.

King's first formal introduction to philosophy was in the classroom of Professor Samuel Williams. At Morehouse, each student was required to take Williams's two-semester course in Philosophy. In Williams's class, he was introduced to some of the great thinkers who would serve as intellectual companions and resources throughout his career. Among these were Socrates, Plato, Niccolo Machiavelli, Rene Descartes, Immanuel Kant, G.W.F. Hegel, Karl Marx, and most notably, Henry David Thoreau. King was to remark later:

> During my student days at Morehouse I read Thoreau's *Essay on Civil Disobedience* for the first time. Fascinated by the idea of refusing to cooperate with an evil system, I was so deeply moved that I reread the work several times. This was my first intellectual contact with the theory of nonviolent resistance.[91]

Another professor who made a lasting contribution to the intellectual formation of King during his college career was Gladstone Lewis Chandler, Professor of English. Chandler helped the young student to master the art of elucidating ideas in the powerful oratorical fashion he had first encountered in the black church experience. In his sophomore year, under the able supervision of Chandler, he won second place in the Webb Oratorical Contest.[92]

Perhaps the most penetrating and lasting contribution at this stage of his intellectual development came from Walter Chivers, who supervised King in his major in Sociology. Chivers, who had done extensive investigations into lynchings in the South,[93] taught his students that racial injustice and economic injustice were inseparable allies in the exploitation of black people. He pointed out, "Money is not only the root of evil; it is also the root of this particular evil—racism."[94] Chivers's analysis was confirmed for King during summer breaks when he worked as a laborer in order to identify more intimately with the plight of his underprivileged black brothers and sisters. Chivers was helpful, therefore, in enabling him to understand that racism was not simply a personal phenomenon, but that it had its sources and vitality in the indigenous economic and political systems which conspired against black people.

Crozer Theological Seminary

George Davis

The major professor at Crozer who contributed to King's theological and philosophical underpinnings of community was George W. Davis, Professor of Christian Theology from 1938 to 1960.[95] Davis was a representative of the evangelical liberal tradition which stressed a personality-centered Christianity, reason and experience, witness to moral and social issues, theological personalism, and an evolutionary revelation of faith.[96]

Smith and Zepp identified five major themes in Davis's writings which influenced King: 1) the existence of a moral order in the universe; 2) the activity of God in history; 3) the value of the personal; 4) the social character of human existence; and 5) the ethical nature of the Christian faith.[97] Ansbro claims that Davis's influence can be seen most clearly in respect to King's conception of the necessity of *agape*, which reveals the inherent worth of human personality,[98] and his understanding of divine providence and history.[99]

Rauschenbusch, Marx, Gandhi, and Niebuhr

While at Crozer, King also read major religious, theological, and philosophical thinkers who would serve as significant intellectual sources in his conception of community. King acknowledged his indebtedness to Walter Rauschenbusch for giving him a theological basis for the social concern with which he had grown up. Although he felt that the social gospeler had "fallen victim to the nineteenth-century 'cult of inevitable progress' which led him to a superficial optimism concerning man's nature,"[100] he agreed with Rauschenbusch's insistence that the gospel is holistic, i.e., it deals with both the person's spiritual and physical well-being:

> It has been my conviction ever since reading Rauschenbusch that any religion which professes to be concerned about the souls of men and is not concerned about the social and economic condi-

102

tions that scar the soul is a spiritually moribund religion only waiting for the day to be buried.[101]

King was deeply impressed by Rauschenbusch's treatment of the Kingdom of God. For Rauschenbusch, the Kingdom of God is the interpretive paradigm by which one exegetes history.[102] The Kingdom of God functions both as an ideal to attain and the source of hope in human history. It is "the progressive social incarnation of God" which is manifested in association and cohesion implanted by the Spirit of God. [103]

After reading Rauschenbush, King began a serious study of the social and ethical theories of philosophers such as Plato, Aristotle, Rousseau, Hobbes, Bentham, Mill, and Locke. While these thinkers taught him a great deal about the nature of the self and social reality, it was Karl Marx who challenged him to take a more critical look at the economic determinants in the history and development of human society and the concomitant need for social justice.[104] After studying Marx's theory of history and the evolution of the State outlined in *Das Kapital* and *The Communist Manifesto* and other interpretive works on Lenin and Marx, King ultimately rejected Marx's materialistic interpretation of history, his ethical relativism, and the political totalitarianism of the state.[105] He argued, however, that there were notable points in the Marxist analysis of society which he found challenging. Despite communism's "false assumptions" regarding the nature of human persons, the destiny of human history, and its "evil methods," King felt that its emphasis on a classless society and its concern for social justice were truths that Christians ought to accept.[106] His reading of Marx reinforced his early concern for the gulf of inequity that existed between the "superfluous wealth and abject poverty" he had witnessed in his youth. His dialectical analysis of Marx led him to respond:

> In so far as Marx posited a metaphysical materialism, an ethical relativism, and a strangulating totalitarianism, I responded with an unambiguous 'no'; but in so far as he pointed to weaknesses of traditional capitalism, contributed to the growth of a definite self-consciousness in the masses, and challenged the social conscience of the Christian churches, I responded with a definite 'yes.'[107]

Another formidable challenge to King's positive view of Christian faith to effect change in society came from Friedrich Nietzsche. Nietzsche's scathing criticism of Judeo-Christian morality as a glorification of weakness and his exultation of the will-to-power represented in a new breed of "supermen" disheartened King to the point that he despaired of the power of redemptive love to address the momentous concerns of social justice. In the midst of this personal and intellectual struggle, a beam of hope fell on his darkened and clouded mental skies when he heard a powerful sermon by Dr. Mordecai Johnson, who had recently returned from a pilgrimage to India to see Gandhi.[109] In the sermon, he extolled the message of nonviolent resistance taught by Mahatma Gandhi. King was so moved by Johnson's "profound and electrifying" message that he left the meeting and purchased a half-dozen books on Gandhi's life and works.[110]

Several scholars have made a connection between Thurman's earlier trip to India in 1936 and its indirect influence on King's interest in Gandhi's method of nonviolent resistance after hearing Johnson's message. S.P. Fullwinder suggests that Thurman may have been the first person to plant the "seed of nonviolent suffering" in the Negro mind. He credits Thurman with having interested Johnson in the significance of Gandhi's philosophy for the black struggle in America. After Johnson's trip to India to see Gandhi, he began a campaign to spread the philosophy of nonviolent resistance which King heard at the Fellowship House of Philadelphia.[111]

King was deeply fascinated by the campaigns of nonviolent resistance by which Gandhi challenged the moral conscience of the British through the power of "Satyagraha." Before reading Gandhi, he had despaired of the ethics of Jesus as being a viable means of transforming social evil. But after reading Gandhi, he saw the redemptive possibilities inherent in the method of nonviolent resistance which enabled persons to strive toward the actualization of human community.[112]

> It was in this Gandhian emphasis on love and nonviolence that I discovered the method for social reform that I had been seeking for so many months... I came to feel that this was the only morally and practically sound method opened to oppressed people in their struggle for freedom.[113]

King's intellectual pilgrimage to nonviolence continued with his reading of Reinhold Niebuhr. He notes that there was a period in his development in which he became so enamored by Niebuhr that he almost "fell into the trap of accepting uncritically everything he wrote."[114] James P. Hanigan observed that "King's class notes and papers reveal more work on Niebuhr than on any other author, except the personalist philosophers with whom he dealt at Boston University."[115] These statements are but small indicators of the impact of Reinhold Niebuhr upon the future leader's understanding of human community.

King's indebtedness to Gandhi and the love ethic of the Sermon on the Mount provided the basis for his formulation of nonviolent resistance. Niebuhr, however, played an equally important role in "purging" King of any sentimentalistic, romantic attachment he might have had to nonviolent resistance. Niebuhr contended, as King indicates, "that there was no intrinsic moral difference between violent and nonviolent resistance."[116] Niebuhr argued that nonviolence, like violence, also coerces and destroys because "it enters the field of social and physical relations and places physical restraints upon the desires and activities of others."[117] The basic distinction between violence and nonviolence for Niebuhr, is not in degree, but in the aggressive character of one and the negative character of the other.[118]

The absolutizing of nonviolent resistance as an ethical ideal or imperative was rejected by Niebuhr. His dialectical interpretation of human nature, sin, and history would not allow him to locate grace in time.[119] This was the essence of King's criticism of Niebuhr's position:

> Niebuhr's ultimate rejection of pacifism was based primarily on the doctrine of man. He argued that pacifism failed to do justice to the reformation doctrine of justification by faith, substituting for it a sectarian perfectionism which believes 'that divine grace actually lifts men out of the sinful contradictions of history and establishes him above the sins of the world.'[120]

Niebuhr, however, did see nonviolent resistance as the most viable social strategy for black Americans, and this may very well have had an understandable impact upon King. In *Moral Man and Immoral Society*, Niebuhr wrote that the "emancipation of the Negro race in America probably waits upon the adequate development of this kind of social and political strategy."[121]

King acknowledged the contributions of Niebuhr's thought upon his own development at several significant points: 1) Niebuhr's refutation of false optimism in segments of Protestant liberalism; 2) his insight into human nature, i.e., individuals as well as groups and nations; 3) the relationship between sin and power; and 4) the reality of social evil.[122]

Boston University

When King graduated from Crozer in June 1951, he was still grappling with Niebuhr's critique of nonviolent resistance. It was at Boston University, however, that he was able to resolve intellectually the question of the possibility of *agape* as a means of creating human community.[123] Although King was deeply influenced by Niebuhr's critique of nonviolent resistance, he finally rejected Niebuhr's "pessimism concerning human nature" under the influence of the personalists with whom he studied at Boston University.[124] He rejected Niebuhr's theological presupposition regarding the imperfectability of human nature in history. In a research paper written later while he was a student at Boston University, King appealed to the immanence of *agape* in human nature and history as being concretely conceived. He argued with Walter Muelder that Niebuhr had failed to appreciate the historical effectiveness of *agape*.[125] Muelder had written:

> There is a Christian perfectionism which may be called a prophetic meliorism, which, while it does not presume to guarantee future willing, does not bog down in pessimistic imperfectionism. Niebuhr's treatment of much historical perfectionism is well-founded criticism from an abstract ethical viewpoint, but it hardly does justice to the constructive historical contributions of the perfectionist sects within the Christian fellowship and even within the secular order. There is a kind of Christian assurance which releases creative energy into the world and which in actual fellowship rises above the conflicts of the individual or collective egoism.[126]

King's major philosophical and theological studies at Boston University were with Edgar Sheffield Brightman and L. Harold DeWolf. It was mainly under these thinkers that King studied personalism.[127] Under Brightman's tutelage, he began studying the philosophy of Hegel. Although the study was primarily concerned with Hegel's *Phenomenology of Mind*, he also read his *Philosophy of Right* and *Philosophy of History*.[128] King rejected Hegel's "absolute idealism" because he felt it tended to converge the One and the many, but he was deeply influenced by the Hegelian contention that "truth is the whole." This contention led King to a philosophical method of rational coherence, which is a key personalistic doctrine.[129] The Hegelian dialectic enabled King to develop a methodology for dealing with conflict and struggle, both in the intellectual and practical social arenas. He maintained that the dialectical process enables one to see how growth comes through conflict and struggle.[130] The dialectical method also gave him a keen analytical tool with which he could exegete the inner tensions of the human psyche and life.[131]

After the death of Brightman, L. Harold DeWolf, who was the dominant influence upon King's theistic personalism, became his major professor. He was deeply influenced by DeWolf's treatment of a personal God of love and power.[132] Unlike his predecessor, Brightman, who maintained that God is limited in power by a "nonrational Given,"[133] DeWolf held an absolutist view of God which maintained that the loving purposes of God will ultimately be victorious over evil, and that any limitations on God's power were self-imposed for the sake of human freedom and perfection. Every evil, according to DeWolf, has a positive place in the ultimate purposes of God.[134]

106

King's philosophical appetite was not confined to Boston University; he also studied at Harvard University where he read existentialists like Karl Jaspers, Soren Kierkegaard, and Jean-Paul Sartre.[135] His qualifying examinations at Boston University reveal that he was well acquainted with the Milesian, Pythagorean, Eleatic, and Atomist philosophers of Greece.[136]

In summary, the experiential and intellectual sources of King's understanding of the beloved community are rooted in an existential quest for a method to overcome the barriers to community which he ultimately identified as racism, poverty, and militarism. But it should be noted that his initial search began in the context of the black community of Atlanta, Georgia, where he struggled with the ominous presence of racism and segregation. Therefore, the intellectual probings at Morehouse, Crozer, and Boston University cannot be separated from his personal search to find a way to overcome these obstacles which he felt impeded human community.

Chapter 5

O What a Beautiful City!

There are three dimensions to any complete life...length, breadth, and height...and without the three being correlated, working harmoniously together, life is incomplete. Life is something of a great triangle. At one angle stands an individual person, at the other angle stands other persons, and at the top stands the Supreme, Infinite Person, God. These three must meet in every individual life that is to be complete.

—*Martin Luther King, Jr.*

My Lord built a dat city,
De city was jes' a four square,
Said He wanna all o you sinners,
To meet Him in a de air,
'Cause He built a twelve gates to de city,
Hallelujah!

O what a beautiful city,
O what a beautiful city,
O what a beautiful city,
'Cause He built a twelve gates to de city,
Hallelujah!

—*Negro Spiritual*

Human community ordered by love (*agape*) is the central category of Martin Luther King, Jr.'s thinking and provides the basis for understanding his view of persons, God, and the world. This ideal is rooted in the interrelatedness of all life and in the unity of human existence under the guidance of a personal God of love and reason who works for universal wholeness.[1] For him, the ideal of community, which he called "the beloved community," was also the Christian social eschatological ideal which served as the ground and the norm for ethical judgment. In the following chapter, the nature of community in the thought of Martin Luther King, Jr. is examined in reference to his conception of community and his interpretation of the triadic character of community.

The Conception of Community

King's conception of the beloved community draws upon several significant theological and philosophical sources. Most notable among these sources are the personal idealism of Edgar S. Brightman and L. Harold DeWolf, Protestant liberalism as represented by Walter Rauschenbusch, and "the black Christian tradition."[2]

The term "the beloved community" has its origins in the philosophical writings of Josiah Royce and R.H. Lotze,[3] both of whom were influential in the development of the philosophy of "personal idealism" or "personalism," King's basic philosophical position.[4] In this view, God is disclosed as Person in history. Human relations have their grounding and validity in the Person of God, manifested in love for the neighbor. His positive view of the potentialities of human persons, and consequently, human history, is a fundamental theme in personal idealism. E.S. Brightman, perhaps its most articulate spokesman, observed:

> The world of shared values can reach such levels of cooperation that man is liberated from his selfishness and is empowered to give himself to his neighbor. On the level of cooperation the Kingdom of God is realized—where "all races and creeds meet, learn, and respect each other in religious liberty."[5]

In King's thinking, the beloved community was synonymous with the Kingdom of God, and his understanding of the latter was deeply influenced by Walter Rauschenbusch. John Cartwright has shown that Rauschenbusch is indebted to Josiah Royce, who introduced the term "beloved community" as a solidaristic view of human society.[6] Rauschenbusch contended that the Kingdom of God was the central theological theme around which all other doctrines found their meaning.[7] In *A Theology for the Social Gospel*, he writes:

> If theology is to offer an adequate doctrinal basis for the social gospel, it must not only make room for the doctrine of the Kingdom of God, but give it a central place and revise all other doctrines so that they will articulate organically with it.[8]

King, like Rauschenbusch, held that the Kingdom of God referred to a transformed and regenerated human society:

> The Kingdom of God will be a society in which men and women live as children of God should live. It will be a kingdom controlled by the law of love.... Many have attempted to say that the ideal of a better world will be worked out in the next world. But Jesus

taught men to say, 'Thy will be done in earth, as it is in heaven.' Although the world seems to be in bad shape today, we must never lose faith in the power of God to achieve his purpose.[9]

Concretely expressed, then, the beloved community is "the mutually cooperative and voluntary venture" of persons in which they realize the solidarity of the human family by assuming responsibility for one another as children of God.[10] This is the basis for King's ethical argument for integration.[11] King contends that civilization, the development of human community, began when the Cro-magnon man put aside his stone ax and decided mutually to cooperate with his neighbor. He believed that this critical moment in the development of human community marked the most creative turn of events in human existence. He maintained that:

> The universe is so structured that things do not quite work out rightly if men are not diligent in their concern for others. The self cannot be self without other selves. I cannot reach fulfillment without thou... All life is interrelated. All men are caught in an inescapable network of mutuality, tied in a single garment of destiny.[12]

King's early development and active participation in the black church experience was also the major force in his conception and articulation of the beloved community.[13] In his article "Black Christians in Antebellum America: In Quest of the Beloved Community,"[14] Lawrence Jones writes, "Ever since blacks have been in America, they have been in search of 'the beloved community'," a community which is grounded in an unshakable confidence in a theology of history. Jones argues that black churches sought to actualize on earth the vision of the "'beloved community' embodied in the Declaration of Independence and explicit in the Bible. They longed to see the kingdom made concrete in history."[15] The intellectual influences of protestant liberalism and personalism that contributed to King's conception of the beloved community found their practical application in the black religious experience to which King was a most noble heir.

Finally, the influence of Thurman on King's conception of community is suggested by Lewis V. Baldwin,[16] Larry Murphy,[17] Vincent Harding, and Ansbro.[18] In an interview with Harding, a co-laborer with King in the civil rights movement, Murphy reports that Harding claims that Thurman's writings, particularly, *Jesus and the Disinherited*, had a substantial impact on the kinds of ideas that had been germinating in King's mind.[19] Baldwin suggests that the themes of love, forgiveness, and reconciliation in Thurman are powerful expressions of what King came to believe after reading the writings of Thurman. This influence is apparent, according to Baldwin, from sermons King preached in black churches.[20] Ansbro also refers to Thurman's treatment of forgiveness as having had a significant influence on King.[21]

While the influence of Thurman on King's conception of community should not be dismissed, it is difficult to make a case for Thurman as a *primary* influence on King since, 1) neither thinker acknowledges any direct exchange of philosophies; and 2) King was a highly eclectic thinker who appropriated ideas from a variety of sources, including Thurman. King does not mention the influence of Thurman upon his thinking at any place in his writings, sermons, or speeches, although there are places, particularly in extemporaneous preaching, where he clearly appropriates ideas and even entire statements from Thurman's works.[22] While this does suggest some level of influence of Thurman upon King, a better case could be made for King's creative synthesis of the parallel themes in the respective traditions of protestant liberal theology, personal idealism, and the black church experience in America. Both Thurman and King were influenced by these traditions, and though the complementarity between the two thinkers could possibly suggest the direct influence of the former on the latter, this is not necessarily the most fruitful interpretation for our purposes. It seems that a more productive method of interpretation would be to explore the continuities between these traditions and their contributions to the conception, character, and actualization of community and their impact upon the two men.

As stated, the black experience of community is fundamental in understanding the conception of community in both Thurman and King. However, it is equally important to see how this common experience of the struggle to achieve universal community out of the particularity of the black religious experience found creative affinity in the intellectual traditions of liberal protestant theology and personal idealism. Thurman's mentors, Cross, Moelhman, Robins, and Jones, were located squarely within the American liberal protestant tradition. Cross, in particular, was influenced by the evangelical liberal tradition which had its roots in personal idealism.[23] Smith also indicates that Rufus Jones, like Cross and Robins, can be located within the theological stream of evangelical liberalism, and as Cross and Robins were concerned respectively with the essence of Christian faith and religion, Jones's concern was with the essence of Christian mysticism.[24] Smith places Thurman within the modernistic liberal tradition under the heading of "metaphysical or rationalistic modernism," which is the same designation Kenneth Cauthen gives to E.S. Brightman.[25]

King acknowledged his indebtedness to the protestant liberal theology of Rauschenbusch and personal idealism of Boston University. King's vision of the beloved community, however, was bred and nurtured in the black church tradition, which has historically seen its particular struggle for the liberation of black people through the prism of universal liberation of all peoples. The universal themes of forgiveness, reconciliation and hope that characterized King's vision of the beloved community have always been fundamental to the black community in general, and the black church in particular.[26] Timothy Smith writes, "The touchstones of the personal religious experience of Black Christians in nineteenth-century America...seem to me to have been first, forgiveness, awe and ecstacy, then self-respect, ethical awareness and hope."[27] This is not to suggest that King's studies in personalism with George Davis, E.S. Brightman, L. Harold DeWolf, Peter Bertocci, and Walter Muelder were not of equal significance in influencing his understanding of community, but his initial problematic was rooted in the black experience of oppression and segregation in the Deep South and the historical struggle of the black Americans to create and fashion a human community despite the overwhelming opposition of the dominant culture. In fact, evangelical liberalism and personalism bear striking continuities which easily accommodated the developing thought of King in his "serious intellectual quest for a method to eliminate social evil."[28] Smith and Zepp state that evangelical liberalism as it was represented by George Davis had the most impact of the two upon King. They insist that "most of the major themes of Martin Luther King were the themes of evangelical liberalism."[29] It should be noted, however, that in King's rendering of his intellectual odyssey, he does not refer directly to evangelical liberalism as a primary molder of his thought (though he does mention the influence of Rauschenbusch during his studies at Crozer).[30] Personalism, however, receives a notable treatment and is expressed as his basic *philosophical* position.[31] It is also significant that Smith and Zepp make the statement that "the personalism of Brightman was by far the single most important philosophical influence upon Davis's theology."[32] It can be argued that while evangelical liberalism provided the theological content and personalism the coherent methodology and philosophical formulation for King, the black church tradition of protest for equality and justice provided the source and the social context in which he worked out his conception of community and the method for its actualization.[33]

Summary

King's conception of the beloved community, then, is the Christian eschatological ideal which serves as the goal of human existence and the norm for ethical judgment. Concretely expressed, it is "the mutually cooperative and voluntary venture" of persons in which they realize the solidarity of the human family by assuming responsibility for one another as children of God. For him, the beloved community is synonymous with the Kingdom of God. He draws upon several significant sources for his understanding of community. Most notable among these are personal idealism, evangelical liberal theology, and "the black Christian tradition."

The Triadic Character of Community

In King's understanding of the nature of community, there is a triadic relationship between persons, God, and the world. These three elements are integrally related and form the basic analytical construct for the dynamic character of community. For the purpose of later comparison, this discussion will follow basically the same pattern utilized in the analysis of Thurman's understanding of the character of community: 1) the nature of persons: the sacredness of human personality, human freedom and responsibility, the moral law, the rational nature of persons, the dialectical nature of persons, and the communitarian nature of persons; 2) the nature of God: the personal God of reason and love, and God as creator and sustainer of community; 3) the world: the moral order of the universe, the theological theme of creation, human history, nature, human society, and the state; and 4) the totality: God and persons, God and the world, persons and the world.

The Nature of Persons

The sacredness of human personality is the major theme of King's anthropology. According to him, all persons are created in the image of God and, therefore, have inherent worth and dignity. Philosophically, this view is rooted in his personalistic interpretation of human persons. Personalism claims that personality is the clue to reality. Brightman wrote, "Personalism is the belief that conscious personality is both the supreme value and the supreme reality in the universe."[34] For personalists, personality is not only the key to reality, it also has ontological status, i.e., the process that creates persons is also personal. God is the Supreme Person and the Supreme Valuer in the universe. The sacredness of human personality, therefore, has its ground and being in the Person of God.[35]

King's understanding of the sacredness of human personality also had deep theological roots in the Biblical theme of creation.[36] His emphasis on the creation motif had strong implications for his treatment of sin and reconciliation and for his understanding of the potential goodness of persons.[37] According to King, the sacredness of human personality demands that "All men must be treated as ends and never as means."[38] The evils of segregation, economic injustice, and war fail to recognize the inherent worth of persons which is their birthright as children of God.[39]

114

King credits the black religious experience with uplifting the sacredness of human personality. This belief was the basis for self-respect and the bedrock of the spirit of protest in the black struggle for civil rights. In reflection on the "New Negro" involved in the Montgomery campaign, he wrote:

> Once plagued with a tragic sense of inferiority resulting from the crippling effects of slavery and segregation, the Negro has now been driven to re- evaluate himself. He has come to feel that he is somebody. His religion reveals to him that God loves all His children and that the important things about a man is not "his specificity but his fundamentum"—not the texture of his hair or the color of his skin but his eternal worth to God.[40]

He also maintained that because persons are created in the image of God, they are free. He understood freedom to be the very essence of human personality. Freedom, however, is always within destiny, i.e., it is not limitless nor is it the mere function of the will. Rather freedom, properly understood, includes the whole person.

> The very phrase, 'freedom of the will,' abstracts freedom from the person to make it an object; and an object by definition is not free. But freedom cannot thus be abstracted from the person, who is always subject as well as object and who himself still does the abstracting. So I am speaking of the freedom of man, the whole man, and not the freedom of a function called the will.[41]

King defines freedom in three ways: 1) freedom is the capacity to deliberate or weigh alternatives; 2) freedom expresses itself in decision; and 3) freedom is always wedded to responsibility.[42] "The immorality of segregation," King argues, "is that it is a selfishly contrived system which cuts off one's capacity to deliberate, decide and respond."[43] The denial of freedom relegates the person to a level of a thing by treating her/him as a means and not an end. King's understanding of freedom is essential for understanding moral agency. Moral choice cannot be postulated without the capacity of deliberation, decision, and responsibility. Closely related to his conception of human persons as being free is the rational nature of persons and his belief in the moral law. The moral law is a key doctrine in his anthropology. The moral law is rooted in the nature of God and can be objectively known.[44] For the philosophical treatment of the moral law, King is indebted to personalism.[45] However, as Ansbro correctly notes, he did not need personalism to provide him with the passion to oppose segregation, but it did help him to formulate principles for his attack on this and other injustices.[46]

115

His belief in the moral law enabled him to maintain an optimism in the ultimate victory of good over evil as persons ultimately choose to become co-workers with God in fulfilling God's purposes in human history. King believed that God "has placed within the very structure of the universe certain absolute moral laws. We can neither defy them or break them. If we disobey them, they will break us."[47] This belief in the moral law was the basis for his attack upon unjust structures and laws that desacralized human personality. Segregation and other forms of oppression should be abolished not only because they are against the principles of democracy, but because they are ultimately against the moral law of the cosmos. An unjust law is a human code that is out of harmony with the moral law. Therefore, it is the person's moral responsibility to break unjust laws. Just laws, on the other hand, are laws which uplift human personality and should be obeyed because they are in harmony with the moral law.[48]

Another theme in his understanding of persons is his view of the dialectical nature of the self. The dialectical nature of persons is rooted in their spiritual and physical existences. While we share our physical existence with other forms of nature, persons are also rational beings. For King, this is our crucial link with God. Human beings are not only biological creatures, they are also spiritual beings with the capacity for reason and self-transcendence. Rationality distinguishes persons from the lower animals, opines King.

> Somehow man is in nature, and yet he is above nature; he is in time, and yet he is above time; he is in space, and yet he is above space. This means that man can do things lower animals could never do. He can think a poem and write it; he can think a symphony and compose it; he can think up a great civilization and create it.[49]

The person is both a child of nature and a child of spirit, who lives in two realms, the internal and external.

> The internal is that realm of spiritual ends expressed in art, literature, morals, and religion. The external is that complex of devices, techniques, mechanisms, and instrumentalities by means of which we live.[50]

The existential problem of persons is the struggle to live a balanced existence in which the *means* by which we live do not out-distance the *ends* for which we live. This is the ongoing struggle for each person and whenever one allows the "means" to predominate the "ends," the occasion for sin is present.[51] This creates a "persistent civil war" within, "a tragic schizophrenic personality divided against ourselves."[52] The resolu-

116

tion of this inner conflict is brought about by the grace of God. The inherent potential for goodness within persons and the intervening grace of God were the basis for King's optimism in respect to the actualization of human community.[53]

Finally, King's view of the nature of persons is decidedly communitarian. He maintained that by definition a person is a social being whose ground of existence is rooted in the sociability of the cosmos, which is ultimately personal. King said, "God has a great plan for this world. His purpose is to achieve a world where all men live together as brothers, and where every man recognizes the dignity and worth of all personality." God is the Person who both creates and enjoys other persons. Although God's existence is not predicated on the existence of other persons, the nature of God is love, and love requires companionship.[54] To be a self (person)[55] means to live in a spiritual society of mutual cooperation and responsibility with other selves.[56]

An inclusive human community, in which persons are able to develop and realize their potential, is the goal of life. As political and economic systems reflect the social nature of persons and their interdependency, they contribute to the development of human personality.[57] As they work against the enhancement of spiritual values of cooperation and responsibility, they impede the development of human personality, and hence the actualization of human community.[58] In his sermon, "On Being a Good Neighbor," he raises the questions of interdependency and interrelatedness of persons to a spiritual level. "Neighborliness" transcends racial, national, and religious boundaries in loyalty to a spiritual goal of inclusiveness.[59]

In summary, the nature of persons includes the sacredness of human personality, human freedom and responsibility, the moral law, the dialectical nature of persons, and the communitarian nature of persons. This understanding of persons is important for the following discussion of his view of God and the world.

God

For King, the second principal in the triadic relationship involved in the actualization of community is God. This part of the discussion is concerned with the following foci: the personal God of reason and love, and God as the creator and sustainer of community. God is disclosed as Person in history. Human relations have their grounding and being in the Person of God who is manifested in love (*agape*) and reason (*logos*).[60] King's doctrines of the sacredness of human personality, the moral law, and the ultimate goodness of the universe are based on his belief that God is both loving and rational. Love is not simply an attribute of God, but is fundamental to God's nature, and the only way to know and experience God is through love for one another.[61] King's understanding of God as rational refers to God as a Purposer. God's rational nature is manifested in the orderliness and purposefulness of the cosmos.[62]

As noted, this understanding of God is a direct inheritance from personalism. Both Brightman and DeWolf maintained the nature of God is rooted in Divine love and reason.[63] This personalistic understanding of the nature of God was the basis upon which King rejected the "impersonal" conceptions of God in Henry Nelson Wieman and Paul Tillich in his doctoral dissertation at Boston University.[64] In what is perhaps his most definitive statement regarding his conception of God, King writes:

> I am convinced that the universe is under the control of a loving purpose, and that in the struggle for righteousness man has cosmic companionship. Behind the harsh appearances of the world there is a benign power. To say that this God is personal is not to make him a finite object beside other objects or attribute to him the limitations of human personality; it is to take what is finest and noblest in our consciousness and affirm its perfect existence in him. It is certainly true that human personality is limited, but personality as such involves no necessary limitations. It means simply self-consciousness and self-direction. So in the truest sense of the word, God is a living God. In him there is feeling and will responsive to the deepest yearnings of the human heart: this God both evokes and answers prayer.[65]

The personal God of love and reason is the creator of existence; all life has its origin and purpose in the creative activity of God. God is not like the Aristotelian "unmoved mover," but a creative force who is intimately engaged in history and in the lives of persons working to bring about universal wholeness.[66] The ultimate goal of God's creativity in persons and the world is the realization of community ordered by love.[67]

God is also the sustainer of community. This divine sustaining of community comes through God's loving purposes in cooperation with persons. The concepts of the power and the justice of God are important for understanding God's relationship to persons and the world. King was an absolutist in respect to his understanding of the power of God. He rejected Brightman's conception of a finite God and maintained, along with DeWolf, the traditional theological doctrine of omnipotence.[68] The power of God refers to God's ability to achieve purpose.[69] He understood the power of God in reference to God's ability to sustain the vastness of the physical universe:

> When we behold the illimitable expanse of space, in which we are compelled to measure stellar distance in light years and in which

heavenly bodies travel at incredible speeds, we are forced to look beyond man and affirm anew that God is able.[70]

God's power is also manifested in the divine ability to overcome the forces of evil within human history and individuals. History is replete, King argued, with the wreckages of civilizations that wielded great power, but were ultimately defeated by the forces of good that work for universal wholeness. The invisible, silent moral law of the cosmos ultimately triumphs over evil because it is rooted in the being and purposes of God.[71] Human beings are not able to subdue evil by their own ingenuity and powers, but as they willingly cooperate with the divine purposes for creation, they are granted the inner resources to overcome any obstacle that impedes community.[72]

Finally, God is a God of justice. Although King perceived the primary nature of God to be in the divine goodness expressed in *agape*, he made a critical distinction between the love of God and the justice of God. In a sermon entitled "A Tough Mind and a Tender Heart," he holds the two concepts in dialectical tension. God's relationship to persons is presented as a creative synthesis between the wrath and justice of God and God's love and grace. He claims that "God has two outstretched arms. One is strong enough to surround us with justice, and one is gentle enough to embrace us with grace."[73] The justice of God is manifested in the moral law of the cosmos, which is an imperative for persons to struggle against all forms of injustice working against the actualization of human community. The power of God furnishes those who struggle for justice with the inner resources to bring about creative change that leads to loving human relations.[74]

As stated, King's philosophical and theological ideas about the nature of God were confirmed in the context of religious experience.[75] In the heart of the Civil Rights struggle, King found the personal God of love and reason to be a dear companion and guide and the source of power to work for the realization of the beloved community. The interrelated concepts of the love, power, and justice of God, therefore, were not simply abstract notions from his intellectual explorations about God, but they were tested by the experience of faith and struggle.

In summary, King understood God as Person disclosed in history, who works through human agency to achieve the divine purpose for creation. The personal God of love and reason is also creator and sustainer of community. The power and the justice of God are two central concepts in King's formulation of the nature of God and God's relationship to persons and the world.

The third element in the triadic relationship which is involved in the creation of community is the world. The world refers to the vast totality of the cosmos, nature, human history, human society, and the state.

King's view of the world is sacramental, i.e., the world is the creation of God and a manifestation of divine handiwork. All reality is sacred and therefore bears the indelible signature of God. In this view, God's relationship to creation is not to be confused with pantheism, where "God is all"; rather, God is understood to be ontologically distinct, perhaps similar to the way an artist is related to his or her creation, but more.[76] Since God is irreducibly personal, God is not a cosmic force diffused throughout creation, but God's Presence in nature and human history is characterized by loving, reasoned, and totally self-determined activity. God continually sustains and creates the world; the world has its being in God, who is the ultimate ground of all being.[77] King believed that the universe was a manifestation of the creative activity of the Mind of God coming to itself in time.[78] In his sermons, he often referred to the magnificent orderliness of the universe as evidence for the existence of God.[79] While he acknowledged the marvelous human achievements through science and technology, he contrasted the limited ability of human efforts against the matchless power of God to create and sustain the universe.[80] The world, because it is the creation of God, is fundamentally benevolent and rational. King affirmed that the universe is friendly because God is love and that "at the heart of the universe, there is a Heart."[81] The orderliness of the cosmos allows persons to live and create in accordance with universal truths or principles that are discoverable by the human mind. However, the inherent order or rationality in the universe ultimately points to the moral law of the cosmos. "Reality," according to King, "hinges on moral foundations."[82] This suggests the inadequacy of science and human thought alone to create community. Science and religion share a complementary relationship.[83] Only as persons choose to become co-workers with God can the realization of the order in the universe come to fruition.[84]

Human history is the arena of the dramatic interaction between God and persons in the creation of the beloved community. A major theme of King's sacramentalistic view of the world is that of creation. Because of his strong conviction of the centrality of the divine creative act, King refused to equate creation with the fall.[85] King, rather, in the language of H. Richard Niebuhr, "distinguishes the fall very sharply from creation, interpreting the former as humanity's good nature becoming corrupted."[86] He does not allow his understanding of the sacredness of human personality and the sacramental character of the world to overpower nor to be overpowered by the act of atonement. This distinction is most essential for comprehending King's view of human persons as unique creations of God and their place in the realization of human community. This is not to suggest, in the least, that the estrangement of persons from God is not of significance. He was well aware that all human progress is precarious and that the struggle within history to achieve the ideal of community is perpetually confronted with new and more formidable obstacles. His notion of human progress, therefore, is not to be understood as a type of social Darwinism. For King, "Human progress is never automatic or inevitable."[87] The glaring reality of evil and human sin qualified his optimism in the redemption of history through human efforts alone. In several places he acknowledges that the realization of the Kingdom ideal is proleptic.[88] He insists, however, that the goal of community must be continuously pursued in cooperation with God. He writes, "Human progress never rolls in on the wheels of inevitability; it comes through the tireless efforts of men willing to be co-workers with God."[89]

King's conception of the world includes human society. Human society is rooted in personalism's recognition of the solidarity of the human family. Personalism affirms that the universe is a society of persons in which God is the Supreme Person. All persons have their ground and being in the nature of the Divine Person. Although God does not need persons for God's existence, God's "moral nature is love, and love needs comradeship. God is not a solitary, self-enjoying mind. He is love; He is...the Great Companion."[90] Human society is a response to the person's need to be cared for and fulfilled in community.[91] Such a society is necessarily inclusive and is rooted in neighborly concern for others. King saw the integration of blacks into the mainstream of American society as an expression of the becoming of human community. His understanding of integration, however, went beyond national, racial, and religious boundaries. True human society for King is pluralistic and international in scope and is based ultimately on moral foundations.[92] He, therefore, makes a distinction between integration and desegregation in reference to the actualization of authentic human society. Desegregation is essentially negative because it only eliminates discrimination in those areas of social life that can be regulated by law. It is an enforceable demand. Integration, on the other hand, cannot be enforced or legislated, rather it demands a moral commitment. Desegregation will only create

> a society where men are physically desegregated and spiritually segregated, where elbows are together and hearts are apart. It gives us special togetherness and spiritual apartness. It leaves us with a stagnant equality of sameness rather than a constructive equality of oneness.[93]

121

King's conception of the state is closely related to his view of society. The two, however, are analytically distinct. The state represents the politico-economic entity which nurtures and maintains human society. His view of the state was decidedly positive. He constantly called upon the state to fulfill its moral obligation to intervene on behalf of the powerless and oppressed of society. His political recommendations can be categorized as follows: recommendations to increase the political power and participation of black Americans; recommendations for blacks to form more intra-political alliances and more effective coalitions with other oppressed groups within society; recommendations for a greater role for the federal government on the side of the poor and minorities seeking basic constitutional and human rights; and recommendations of international cooperation in which America would take a leading role.[94]

King's understanding of the nature and the role of the state is rooted in his belief in the universal, democratic ideal which upholds the dignity and worth of human personality and the solidarity of human existence.[95] His view of the state evolved into a type of democratic socialism that maintained the primacy of the individual while advocating the abolition of poverty through the redistribution of wealth.[96] His critique of American capitalism called for radical reform. He believed that it is possible to "work within the framework of democracy to bring about a better distribution of wealth."[97] During the latter years of his life, he called for a guaranteed income for all citizens. He recommended that the relationships between production, distribution, and the consumer receive more careful attention in order to avoid national catastrophe.[98]

> The contemporary tendency in our society is to base our distribution on scarcity, which has vanished, and to compress our abundance into the overfed mouths of middle and upper classes until they gag with superfluity. If democracy is to have breadth of meaning, it is necessary to adjust this inequity. It is not only moral, but it is also intelligent. We are wasting and degrading human life by clinging to archaic thinking.[99]

King was keenly aware of the tendency to ascribe to the state a transcendent character which creates a conflict of loyalties between God and human institutions. In his sermon, "Paul's Letter to American Christians," he cautioned the church to maintain its dual citizenry as a people of faith and citizens of the state.[100] Although he was acutely aware of the potential conflict between loyalty to God and loyalty to the state, he still insisted that there is an intricate relationship between responsible citizenship (devotion to the democratic principles inherent in the Declaration of Independence and the Constitution) and responsibility to God. King believed that America is essentially a "dream unfulfilled."[101] It is an idea in the mind of God which is manifesting itself in time. The principles of democracy (inherent worth of the individual and equality of persons) were the basis of this loyalty to America.[102] Despite the "schizophrenic character" of the American experiment in democracy that resulted in slavery and segregation, the nation has a unique destiny in the history of human civilization.[103] Loyalty to God, therefore, demands that persons uplift the noble principles of democracy and work in cooperation with the purposes of God in fulfilling this destiny. The black American, though victimized by the shameful atrocities and blatant contradictions of the dream, must assume a responsible role in calling upon the nation to live out "the true meaning of its creed."[104] The civil rights movement is a manifestation of the love and justice of God operative within American society; its mission is to prick the conscience of America and to call it to repentance.He believed that the struggle of American blacks to fulfill the promises of democracy may be God's instrument to save the soul of America.[105] Ironically, King was perhaps the most articulate spokesperson for Robert Bellah's description of American civil religion as "the transcendent universal religion of the nation."[106] The irony is magnified in that King's prophetic denunciation of America's cultural xenophobia serves both as a critical and developmental principle in the American civil religion debate and has significant implications for the recovery and reinterpretation of authentic second languages posed by Bellah et al in *Habits of the Heart*.[107]

The idea of world, in King, includes the universe, nature, human history, human society, and the state. In his discussion of the world, the primary emphases are on the sacredness of human personality and the social nature of human existence. The Biblical theme of creation informs his sacramentalistic cosmology. Of particular interest is his understanding of society and the state. The historical struggle of black Americans as the objects of racism and segregation sanctioned by the state is a major concern. This is a prominent theme which will receive further treatment at relevant points throughout this discussion.

The Totality

The three elements comprising the triadic nature of community—persons, God, and the world—have been examined separately for purposes of analysis. In King's understanding of community, the three principals are integrally and dynamically interrelated. Each interacts with the other in a creative network of mutuality and cooperation. Persons cooperate with God as self-conscious, self-directed, and free participants in the creation of community; and God, as the Supreme Person and World

Ground, makes the divine purposes known in the created order and in human personality. In the following pages we shall discuss the totality of this interaction as follows: 1) God and persons; 2) God and the world; and 3) persons, the world, and God.

God and Persons

King understood God as Person disclosed in history, who works through human agency to achieve the divine purposes for creation. The personal God of love and reason is also creator and sustainer of community. God wills that persons cooperate with God in the creation of community. He contends that it is neither God nor persons alone who will bring about the world's salvation, but persons working with God.[108] He gives three ways in which persons can cooperate with God: through work, intelligence, and prayer.[109] The key ingredient, however, that undergirds these three ways of cooperating with God and which unleashes the power of God in the life of the person is faith. King makes a distinction between two types of faith, "mind faith" and "heart faith." "Mind faith" is giving intellectual assent to the belief that God exists. Such faith is inadequate by itself. "Heart faith," on the other hand, is the type of faith which allows the person truly to know God and to become a co-worker with God in the achievement of divine purpose.[110] "Heart faith" is the spiritual substance that is essential for the eradication of racism and other social ills that plague human society.

> This is the meaning of faith. If we want to solve the race problem, this is it. We can't do it alone. God will not do it alone. But let's go out and protest a little bit and he will change this thing and make America a better nation. Do you want peace in this world? Man cannot do it by himself. And God is not going to do it by himself. But let us cooperate with him and we will be able to build a world where men will beat their swords into plow shares and their spears into pruning hooks and nations will not study war anymore.[111]

God and the World

— For King, God is immanently involved in the world as creator and sustainer; all life has its origin and purpose in the creative activity of God. The rational order of the world makes possible the role of persons as co-creators and purposers with God. There is not a strict dichotomy between fact and value or science and religion; rather, both are complementary. Therefore the achievements of science and technology are not necessarily in conflict with the purposes of God as long as they are in harmony with

the moral order of the universe.[112] When persons choose
workers with God, the realization of the harmonious, crea
universe can come to fruition.[113]

King's understanding of the immanence of God is Ch
King, Jesus Christ is the supreme revelation of God in the world. Christ is
"the language of eternity translated into time," "the New Being," and "a
rock in a weary land."[114] In Christ we see the Person of God manifested in
history as a loving Parent who requires of persons the same self-giving
love.[115] In Christ we are called to the difficult task of loving even our
enemies in order to realize a unique relationship with God. Like Christ we
are "potential sons [and daughters] of God. Through love that potentiality
becomes actuality."[116] Christ is the source and norm of the beloved
community and the Cross is the symbol of God's redemptive love for
humanity.[117]

King's Christological formulation is largely indebted to the personal
theism of L. Harold DeWolf.[118] DeWolf understood Jesus to be the supreme manifestation of the will and purposes of God in the world. He
believed that through Jesus's life, teachings, and redemptive suffering on
the cross, the love, power, and forgiveness of God are demonstrated as the
act of reconciliation between persons and God. In DeWolf's book, *A
Theology for the Living Church*, he devotes a chapter to Christology, entitled
"The Son of God: Christological Reconstruction." Here he argues against
the identification of Jesus as God, the explanation of Jesus as a religious
genius or saint, and the Bultmannian and Barthian claims of "the Christ of
faith." DeWolf outlines the basic elements to be included in what he
perceives as essential to an adequate Christological reconstruction, beginning with the unique moral authority of Jesus. He says, "Other men of
history may shame us in this or that particular aspect of life, but only Jesus
has stood the test of being the norm of life itself, from its very center."[119]
DeWolf claims that Jesus's filial God-consciousness, his wisdom and
power, and the finding of God in Jesus Christ by other men and women
recommend him as the unique ideal of human personality.[120] He suggests
that while Jesus was indeed human, bearing in his physical and social
existence all the marks and weaknesses of human imperfection, his
mission as the supreme revelation of the purposes of God in history sets
him apart as the archetype of human personality toward which all humanity strives.

A lengthy but informative quote captures the basic thrust and import
of DeWolf's argument for the claim of Jesus's uniqueness as the Son of
God:

> While everyone is called to take a special, individual place in
> God's kingdom, Jesus was called to perform a particular task in
> one time and place and for certain people around him—though he

did that as a carpenter of Nazareth and as friend and minister to certain individuals. He was also to perform the universal task for all peoples who were yet to be in any age or nation, the task of living the total purpose and meaning of the reign of God. Jesus was called to be not only, before God, the subject to that reign, but also to be, before men, Lord of the Kingdom. He was to show in word and life the purpose, spirit, and power of God issuing forth in human life. He was thus not only to teach, but to be the highest of all teachers. He was not only to heal but to be the norm of true health. He was not only to lead in worship but to show in his own person, as no words nor ritual nor any impersonal symbol could possibly show, Him who is alone worthy of worship. He was not only to *speak* words concerning God, but to *be* the Word spoken of God.[121]

The redemptive love of God, revealed in Jesus Christ, is King's answer to the possibility of achieving community within history. While he did not believe that human efforts alone could bring the Kingdom of God into realization, he strongly believed that the power of God was sufficient to accomplish the eternal purposes. For King, this is a fact accomplished in the death and resurrection of Jesus Christ. He interpreted the Christian symbols of the Cross, the Resurrection, and the Holy Spirit as a trinitarian expression of God's immanence in the world.[122]

King found his Christocentric vision of community revealed in the Christian Scriptures. As indicated, he was a highly eclectic thinker, drawing upon a variety of intellectual sources for truth. The Scriptures served as the fount of revelation for him in which the person and work of Jesus Christ became the chief hermeneutical principle in translating the purposes of God in the creation of human community into the contemporary context of the black struggle for liberation. Carl H. Marbury makes this claim in an article entitled, "An Excursus on the Biblical and Theological Rhetoric of Martin Luther King, Jr.":

> The main question for any student with more than purely historical and/or objective concerns is, how does Jesus come to be contemporary with us, as early Christians believed him to be? The principle is basic for understanding the Biblical theology of Martin Luther King.[123]

In a number of King's published and unpublished sermons, this hermeneutical principle is operative.[124]

The reality of evil and human sin in the world makes salvation a human impossibility. This was the basis of King's critique of communism, humanism, secularism, and all anthropocentric efforts to redeem history without the intervention of grace.[125] This truth is illustrated most dramatically in the redemptive work of Christ.[126] "Christianity affirms," says King,

> that at the heart of reality is a Heart, a loving Father who works through history for the salvation of his children. Man cannot save himself, for man is not the measure of all things and humanity is not God. Bound by the chains of his own sin and finiteness, man needs a Savior.[127]

Persons, the World, and God

It has been stated that the totality represents the creative interaction of the three principals (persons, the world, and God) in a harmonious relationship that issues forth in the beloved community. At the beginning of this discussion, the question of John Cartwright regarding King's notion of the beloved community as a Christian eschatological ideal was utilized. He asked, "From a Christian perspective, what kind of society must human society be when human society truly becomes?"[128] In his favorite sermon, "The Dimensions of a Complete Life," King answers this question by stating that the ideal human society is the correlation of these three interrelated elements. The vision of the New Jerusalem which John sees on the isle of Patmos, according to King, is the "city of ideal humanity." It "is not an unbalanced entity but it is complete on all sides."[129] He suggests that life is like a great triangle: at one angle there is the individual person, at the other angle there are other persons, and at the top is the Supreme, Infinite Person, God. All three dimensions of life are fulfilled in love. The individual person represents the *length of life*. Here the primary concern is the cultivation of the internal life of the person; it is that dimension of life in which the person pursues personal ends and ambitions. Self-love and inner harmony between ends and means are essential for a proper understanding of the length of life. At the next angle, there is *the breadth of life*. This dimension represents social existence and is characterized by love for others and the broader concerns of all humanity. This is a horizontal relationship between persons. King uses the analogy of the Good Samaritan to illustrate the altruism that is essential to fulfill the social goal of human existence. Finally, there is the third and final dimension, which he refers to as *the height of life*. The height of life refers to the vertical relationship between persons, world, and God. The other two dimensions of life are incomplete without the vertical pole. King encourages the individual person to

> Love yourself, if that means rational, healthy and moral self-interest. You are commanded to do that. That is the length of life. Love your neighbor as you love yourself. You are commanded to

do that. That is the breadth of life. But never forget the first and even greater commandment, "Love the Lord your God with all thy heart and all thy soul and all thy mind." This is the height of life.[130]

In the discussion of the nature of community in King, the conception of community and the triadic character of community have been examined. The conception of community in the thought of King is rooted in his understanding of the interrelatedness of life, the sacredness of human personality, the moral order of the universe, the personal God of love and reason who is revealed in power, and the social nature of human existence. The beloved community, as it is articulated by King, is the social, eschatological Christian ideal which draws upon several significant theological and philosophical sources: the Protestant liberal tradition represented by Rauschenbusch, the personal idealism of E.S. Brightman and L. Harold DeWolf, and "the black Christian tradition." The influence of Thurman on King's conception of community has been noted, but with an important caveat, that the two thinkers are products of the black American religious experience and that the ideal of community which was inherited from this tradition found creative affinity with the respective traditions of protestant liberal theology and personal idealism. These three interrelated traditions emphasize the ideal of human community ordered by love, which provides a basis for understanding their respective views of persons, God, and the world.

King's conception of community is triadic in character. The elements comprising the triadic nature of community (persons, God, and the world) have been examined separately for purposes of analysis and viewed in relationship with one another as a totality. In King's understanding of community, the three principals are integrally and dynamically interrelated. His anthropology accentuates the social nature of the self. This emphasis has major implications for his understanding of the moral life and society's responsibility to the individual, which is the concern of the next chapter.

Chapter 6

Mine Eyes are Turned to the Heavenly Gate

Christianity clearly affirms that in the long struggle between good and evil, good will eventually emerge as the victor. Evil is ultimately doomed by the powerful, inexorable forces of good. Good Friday must give way to the triumphant music of Easter.

—Martin Luther King, Jr.

Stay in the field,
Stay in the field,
Until the war is ended.
Mine eyes are turned to the heavenly gate,
Till the war is ended.
I'll keep my way, or I'll be too late,
Till the war is ended.

—Negro Spiritual

This portion of the analysis of the thought of Martin Luther King, Jr. is devoted to *the actualization of community*. The chapter is divided into two parts. The first part is an examination of King's treatment of *the barriers to community*. It will proceed as follows: 1) the nature and role of evil; 2) the personal and social dimensions of sin; and 3) the individual's response to barriers to community. The second part will treat King's recommendations for *overcoming the barriers to community*. The analysis will proceed as follows: 1) community as the norm and goal of the moral life; and 2) community, religion, and social action.

Barriers to Community

The Nature and Role of Evil

King sees evil as a force in the world which works against wholeness and harmony in creation. Evil is real and is characterized by disorder, disruptiveness, intrusion, recalcitrance, and destruction.[1] It is not an illusion or error of the mind, rather it is rooted in life itself.[2] He believed that "there is a tension at the heart of the universe between good and evil."[3] Nevertheless, evil is not ultimately victorious over goodness, for it carries within itself its own seeds of destruction.[4] Goodness ultimately defeats evil because goodness is more fundamental than evil:

> Christianity clearly affirms that in the long struggle between good and evil, good eventually will emerge as victor. Evil is ultimately doomed by the powerful, inexorable forces of good. Good Friday must give way to the triumphant music of Easter.[5]

King does not offer an explanation for the origin of evil, but he emphasizes the biblical perception of evil as real and destructive.[6] He treats the question of theodicy by insisting that God placed a limitation on divine power to insure human freedom and responsibility. He maintained that if God's will were forced upon persons, then God would defeat the divine purpose and would "express weakness rather than power."[7] Human persons must be free to choose God's purpose and to cooperate with God in the creation of the beloved community. The question of the role of natural and moral evil and human suffering is understood as part of the creative purposes of God.[8] In his sermon, "The Death of Evil on the Seashore," King states:

> I do not pretend to understand the ways of God or his particular timetable for grappling with evil. Perhaps if God dealt with evil in the overbearing way we wish, he would defeat his ultimate purpose. [9]

Evil, however, is never caused by God, but is the by-product of God's self-imposed limitation on divine power. To suggest that God causes or ordains evil is to deny human freedom and to resign to fatalism. God permits evil in order to preserve human freedom, yet God does not cause it:

> A healthy religion rises above the idea that God wills evil. Although God permits evil to preserve the freedom of man, he does not cause evil. That which is willed is intended, and the thought that God intends for a child to be born blind or for a man to suffer the ravages of insanity is sheer heresy that pictures God as a devil rather than as a loving Father.[10]

King firmly believed that human suffering can be redemptive. In a revealing testimony on his perception of personal suffering, he emphasized how his trials had taught him the value of unmerited suffering.[11] He suggests that there are three ways in which one can deal with suffering:

one may react in bitterness, one may withdraw, or one may seek to transform the suffering into a creative force.[12] To choose the latter is to cooperate with the divine purposes of God who is revealed in the crucified Christ of Calvary.[13] In the experience of suffering, God gives the individual interior resources to sustain and enable him/her to transform the "spear of frustration" into "a shaft of light."[14] Human suffering is overcome as the person freely chooses to cooperate with God in the struggle against evil.[15] Evil is overcome, however, not only because of the individual's struggle against it, but because of God's power to defeat it.[16] When the individual chooses to become a co-sufferer with Christ, pain is transformed into a creative good.

> Almost anything that happens to us may be woven into the purposes of God. It may lengthen our cords of sympathy. It may break our self-centered pride. The cross, which was willed by wicked men, was woven by God into the tapestry of world redemption.[17]

The cross is the interpretive paradigm for redemptive suffering. It symbolizes the love of God in Christ that is expressed in redemptive suffering. "Every time I look at the cross," says King, "I am reminded of the greatness of God and the redemptive power of Jesus Christ."[18] He understood the suffering of black Americans in this theological framework. He believed that in the unmerited suffering of black Americans lay the redemption of America.[19] King felt that the redemptive suffering of black Americans could inject "a new meaning into the veins of history and civilization."[20] He often suggested that by virtue of their historical suffering and oppression, black Americans were naturally suited for the role of suffering servants in the American context.[21] Nonviolence is the method through which redemptive suffering of black Americans is most effectively expressed.[22] Black Americans are entrusted with the distinctive responsibility of loving, forgiving, and creating the environment in which reconciliation between the races can take place.[23]

The Nature of Sin

King also recognized the prevalence of sin in human existence. His treatment of sin is rooted in the existential struggle between freedom and finitude. Sin is a product of the "civil war of the soul" or the "tragic schizophrenic personality"[24] that wills righteousness but is unable to attain it.[25] This is a product of King's dialectical anthropology. He did not concentrate on the individual's struggle with sin, rather he stressed the social manifestations of sin in selfishness, pride, and ignorance. Sin is dis-

131

tinguished from evil in that it involves human volition, freedom, and responsibility.[26] Sin is related to evil in that egoism, selfishness, and ignorance lead one to cooperate with the enterprises of malevolence.

Sin, for King, is both *formal* and *material*. Formal sin refers to the willful act of choosing contrary to self-acknowledged obligations. Material sin, on the other hand, refers to choosing contrary to the actual will of God, whether or not that will is known. King inherited this distinction primarily from L. Harold DeWolf.[27] King uses the language of "sin" and "ignorance" to designate formal and material sin, respectively. When he refers to sin in the formal sense, he is speaking of consciously choosing to break self-acknowledged moral ideals. This understanding of sin has its roots in egoism and misdirected pride. This is the sin of Augustine when he cries out, "Lord make me pure, but not yet."[28] King suggests that

> In a real sense the "isness" of our present nature is out of harmony with the eternal "oughtness" that forever confronts us. We know how to love, and yet we hate. We take the precious lives that God has given us and throw them away in riotous living. We are unfaithful to those to whom we should be faithful. We are disloyal to those ideals to which we should be loyal.[29]

Ignorance, or material sin, refers to moral blindness.[30] Many of the tragic expressions of sin, such as war, racism, and economic injustice, are the products of moral blindness. His conviction that nonviolence or redemptive suffering for others is the only method for removing the barriers which impede community is related to this important distinction between formal and material sin.[31] King's technique of moral suasion arises out of this fundamental belief that sin as ignorance is a barrier that the moral agent must overcome to realize inner harmony and to struggle for creative change in the world.

Sin grows out of a fundamental need to be recognized and given attention.[32] The desire to be recognized and understood is fundamental to wholeness in human personality, but inordinate and misdirected goods issue forth in disharmony and destructiveness to the self and to others.[33] King agreed with the psychoanalyst, Alfred Adler, that the quest for recognition and distinction is the basic impulse of life. Adler referred to this impulse as "the drum major instinct." To King, the "drum major instinct" can be constructive or destructive; it depends ultimately on how the individual chooses to use it. If this basic instinct for recognition and gratification is not harnessed and disciplined, it is destructive to one's personality and to others.[34] But if it is given in genuine love for others, it becomes a powerful creative force in establishing wholesome and harmonious human relationships.[35]

Sin is both personal and social. In its social manifestation, sin is a breach in relationship – not only with God, but in relationships with others. The social nature of sin was King's dominant concern. He inherited much of his understanding of sin as a social phenomenon from Rauschenbusch, from Niebuhr, and from the glaring reality of segregation.[36] He especially agreed with Niebuhr that in our collective lives sin rises to greater heights and to greater levels of destructiveness.[37] He identified racism, economic injustice, and war as examples of collective sin and barriers to world community.[38]

While King's emphasis is essentially on the social manifestations of sin, it is important to note that he recognized personal sin as an internal barrier that the moral agent must overcome in order to realize inner harmony and to struggle for creative change in the world. At various places, he identifies these internal barriers as ignorance, fear, and hatred.

Ignorance is a major obstacle that must be overcome by the person who works for community. As indicated, ignorance refers to intellectual and spiritual blindness.[39] Ignorance is partly the cause of many of the great inhumane acts of history, i.e., the execution of Socrates by the citizens of Athens, the persecution of the early church by Paul, the church's rejection of the revolutionary insights of science and uncritical patriotism. The crucifixion of Jesus, says King, was not executed by evil persons, but by blind men who did not know what they were doing: "Blindness was their trouble; enlightenment was their need."[40]

It is important to note that King does not equate ignorance with sin as disobedience; nonetheless, it is treated as a sin against the will and purposes of God. His equation of ignorance with moral blindness is a crucial distinction in his nonviolent method of bringing truth to light on unjust situations where the conscience is addressed through moral suasion. The way of overcoming ignorance is by enlightenment. His understanding of the question of ignorance and the need for enlightenment in the making of moral judgments grew out of his fundamental allegiance to philosophical and theological idealism, and to moral suasion as a means of appealing to the conscience. It is a perspective which views situations of conflict and human striving in terms of the concepts of reason, truth, and meaning.[41] At the heart of nonviolent direct action is the belief that enlightenment is capable of transforming the enemy into friend, and winning the opponent's commitment to the truth of the cause.[42] The individual who works for community, therefore, is called upon to enrich his or her mind through education. Education, however, is not limited to academic achievement. Education is defined in broad terms by King, and it is his insistence that the pursuit of truth is available to all. He suggests that "the heart cannot be totally right if the head is totally wrong."[43] He maintained that we are commanded to love God not only with our hearts and souls, but also with our minds. Intelligence is the only remedy for ignorance. Intelligence is "a call for open mindedness, sound judgment, and a love for the truth. It is a call for men to rise above the stagnation of closemindedness and the paralysis of gullibility."[44] The "transformed nonconformist" is called upon to act out of informed conviction, not to social mores and customs which work against community.[45]

The second internal barrier that must be overcome is fear. King sees fear as essentially positive and creative. It is a natural physiological and psychological response to danger, but abnormal fear has a destructive quality that destroys both the individual and society. "Normal fear motivates us to improve our individual and collective welfare; abnormal fear constantly poisons and distorts our inner lives."[46] The problem of fear for the individual is not how to get rid of it, but how to master it. The mastery of fear involves honest confrontation (truth), courage, faith, and love.[47] Honest confrontation involves a rational analysis of fear. When most fears are analyzed in the light of reason, they are discovered to be more imaginary than real. Some of our fears are "snakes under the carpet."[48] Second, fears must be confronted courageously. Courage is the power of the mind to overcome fear; it is the "power of life to affirm itself in spite of life's ambiguities," pains, and disappointments.[49] Third, fears must be confronted in love. Racial hate and segregation are products of irrational fears based on ignorance and insecurities. Love, as understanding and organized goodwill, is the only remedy that overcomes the obstacle of racism. The irrational fears of many white persons, says King, could be absolved through education and redemptive suffering of black Americans. "The Negro must show them (white men) that they have nothing to fear, for the Negro forgives and is willing to forget the past. *The Negro must convince the white man that he seeks justice both for himself and the white man.*"[50] A mass movement exercising love and nonviolence is the best way to achieve this end. The external barriers to community (war, racism, and poverty) find their origin in fear.[51] Fourth, fear is mastered through faith. Faith refers to trust or confidence in the inherent goodness and justice of the universe that God has created. It is also the belief that God is intimately engaged in the personal existence of the individual as well as in the world. King says, "The confidence that God is mindful of the individual is of tremendous value in dealing with the disease of fear, for it gives us a sense of worth, of belonging, and of at-homeness in the universe."[52]

Only when fear is overcome at the individual level is the person able to respond to the external barriers that work against a harmonious social order. In a revealing testimony, King shares how he overcame fear in the early days of the Montgomery bus boycott. As the frequency of threatening letters and telephone calls began to accelerate, fear for his life and family began to grow. At the end of a particularly stressful day, King received yet another threatening phone call. With it came the realization that he had reached his "saturation point." Exhausted and almost ready to give up, King reflected:

> I determined to take my problem to God. My head in my hands, I bowed over the kitchen table and prayed aloud... 'I am at the end of my powers. I have nothing left. I've come to the point where I can't face it alone.'

> At that moment I experienced the presence of the Divine as I had never before experienced him. It seemed as though I could hear the quiet assurance of an inner voice, saying, 'Stand up for right-eousness, stand up for truth. God will be at your side forever.' Almost at once my fears began to pass from me. My uncertainty disappeared. I was ready to face anything.

Three nights later the Kings' home was bombed, but King was able to receive word of the bombing calmly. "My experience with God had given me a new strength and trust," he said. "I knew now that God is able to give us the interior resources to face the storms and problems of life."[53]

The other internal barrier to community is hate. Hate, King reasoned, is a destructive force which "scars the soul and destroys [the] personality" of its victim and of the one who hates.[54] It has its genesis in irrational fears and ignorance. Racism is an expression of the irrational pathology of hate. White racists who are normally amiable and congenial in their day to day relationships respond from an irrational and distorted sense of values when they are asked to accept black Americans as equals. The great tragedy of race hate, he contends, is that it

> destroys a man's sense of values and his objectivity. It causes him to describe the beautiful as ugly and the ugly as beautiful, and to confuse the true with the false and the false with the true.[55]

Hate also has a spiralling effect which issues forth in violence. The systemic violence inherent in economic injustice, war, and racism is a product of hate, ignorance, and fear.[56] The chain reaction of hate can only be halted and overcome through the redemptive suffering of the hated. Love for the enemy is the true test of *agape*, and the only hope for the future of humankind that stands over the abyss of violent annihilation.

> Upheaval after upheaval has reminded us that modern man is travelling along a road called hate, in a journey that will bring us

destruction and damnation. Far from being the pious injunction of a Utopian dreamer, the command to love one's enemy is an absolute necessity for our survival.[57]

In summary, the personal dimensions of sin reflected in the internal barriers to community are ignorance, fear, and hate—obstacles which the moral agent must overcome in his or her pursuit of the beloved community. The barriers are interrelated and must be consciously dealt with at a personal level as the individual struggles against systemic evil in the world. Inner spiritual and intellectual transformation are essential for external transformation of the social order. Love expressed in redemptive suffering for the other is the key which overcomes these barriers. Such love, it should be remembered, proceeds from an experience of spiritual regeneration and commitment to God. When persons commit their lives to the power of God, they are enabled to overcome the internal barriers which obstruct personal wholeness and the systemic oppression in society reflected in poverty, racism, and war.

Overcoming the Barriers

Traditional Means of Overcoming Evil

King argued that human persons have traditionally relied upon two methods for overcoming evil in the world. One is through reason. Through modern science and technology human beings have been able to reach great heights of discovery and victory over evils that have tormented humanity. Nevertheless, the power of reason is ultimately inadequate to overcome the barriers of race, class, and poverty that work against community. The exalted optimism which arose from the birth of modern science has failed because it has forgotten the human capacity for sin.[58]

> When scientific power outruns moral power, we end up with guided missiles and misguided men. When we foolishly minimize the internal of our lives and maximize the external, we sign the warrant for our own day of doom.[59]

The second traditional method has been the belief that God alone will remove evil from the world. King suggests that this position is ultimately untenable because it is a fatalistic doctrine which relegates the human person to the status of a helpless invalid. Such a belief is born of pessimism and a misconception about the nature of persons and God. Neither God nor persons by themselves will rid the world of evil; rather, the overcoming of barriers which prevent community is a cooperative effort between God and persons.[60] The barriers of evil and sin which have locked people in oppression can only be overcome through the human willingness to receive the gift of God in Christ which issues forth in regeneration and courage to struggle against the external forces that work against community.[61] King argued that the triplets of oppression (militarism, racism, and poverty) are the great social evils which must be overcome if the world is to survive. He recommended a revolution of values and priorities as the only way that these barriers could be overcome. Such a revolution of values is rooted in love, the supreme unifying principle of life.[62]

Community as the Norm and Goal of the Moral Life

The ideal of community, King asserts, serves as the goal toward which all life strives and the norm for ethical reflection. Specifically, the beloved community is the Christian social ideal which is rooted in the interrelatedness of all life and in the unity of human existence under the guidance of a personal God of love and power who works for universal wholeness. The religious and the ethical are positively related in King. Faith serves as the point of departure for ethical reflection and informs his understanding of love as the means of actualization of community, the nature and role of the moral agent, and the church in society.[63]

From the beginning to the end of his rich and controversial career, King upheld the vision of the beloved community as the ultimate norm and goal for his struggle in the arenas of civil rights, economic justice, and world peace. The interrelatedness of all life and the fundamental unity and interdependence of human existence are basic presuppositions in all of his thinking regarding the moral life. In one of his earliest articles, he indicated that the purpose of the Montgomery bus boycott "is reconciliation; the end is redemption; the end is the creation of the beloved community."[64] Later, near the end of his life, he spoke from a global perspective that utilized the same norm and goal as his basis for speaking on world peace.[65]

Love as the Means of Actualization

Love is the ethical principle which creates and maintains community. Community and love are inseparable in the thought of King. Love is the *summum bonum* of life, found in the person and nature of God who is revealed in the redemptive suffering of Jesus Christ. "This principle," he says, "is at the center of the cosmos. It is the great unifying force of life. God is love. He who loves has discovered the clue to the ultimate meaning of reality."[66]

King defined love as *agape*. He often compared his understanding of agapaic love to the kindred Greek notions of *eros* and *philia*. Eros refers to aesthetic or romantic love. *Philia* refers to the intimate, reciprocal affection

137

between friends. But *agape* goes beyond *eros* and *philia* in that it is creative understanding and redemptive goodwill for all persons. *Agape* is the love of God operative in human hearts which seeks to preserve and create community.[67] Unlike *eros* and *philia*, it is overflowing and seeks nothing in return. It simply loves because it is of God. "At this level," says King, "we love men not because we like them, nor because their ways appeal to us, nor even because they possess some divine spark; we love every man because God loves him."[68]

King's conception of agapaic love is expressed as altruism, forgiveness, and reconciliation. In his sermon on "Being a Good Neighbor," he delineates three ways in which love is altruistic.[69] First, love is demonstrated as *universal altruism*. Universal altruism goes beyond the boundaries of race, class, and other provincial loyalties. Such love is rooted in an understanding that all persons are created in the image of God and therefore are lovable because they bear in their individual personalities a common humanity which goes beyond external accidents of race, class, and nationality. The great tragedy of narrow provincialism, as in segregation, is that it fails to recognize the sacredness and universality of human personality. He contended that such a "spiritual myopia limits our vision to external accidents,"[70] and consequently, people outside of our limited ethical fields are treated as things, and not as persons with inherent value and worth. The moral implications of such narrow visions of humanity are far reaching and can be discerned in misdirected ideals of nationalism, economic injustice, and social isolation. Universal altruism, however, enables us to see all persons as inherently equal with dignity and eternal worth.[71]

Love is also expressed as *dangerous altruism*. Love involves risk and requires sacrifice. Here love is other-directed and goes beyond the natural desire for personal security. The key question that this love asks in ethical situations requiring neighborly concern for others is not, "What will happen to me if I act lovingly in this situation?" Rather it asks, "What will happen to my neighbor, if I fail to act on his/her behalf?" On the eve of his assassination, King said this was the question that motivated him to go to Memphis on behalf of the garbage collectors.[72] "The true neighbor," according to King, "will risk his position, his prestige, and even his life for the welfare of others."[73]

Love is also expressed as *excessive altruism*. Excessive altruism is concretely expressed in acts of sympathy.[74] As such it is to be distinguished from pity arising from an abstract understanding of humanity. Unlike pity, sympathy is concerned with particularity. "Sympathy is fellow feeling for the person in need—his pain, agony, and burdens."[75] Examples of pity are the paternalistic endeavors of missionaries and philanthropic handouts that are devoid of true love and compassion. True love, as

138

sympathetic concern for others, does not do something *for* others, but seeks creatively to do something *with* others. It is only in this respect, suggests King, that the dignity and self-worth of others are preserved.

Excessive altruism also goes beyond deontological decrees. It seeks not only to fulfill what is perceived as one's duty or that which is in compliance with law, it goes "the second mile." Love is a "purely spontaneous, unmotivated, groundless, and creative" act which arises out of genuine concern for the neighbor.[76] Therefore, it cannot be enforced by external decrees, but must be motivated by unenforceable, self-imposed sanctions. He makes a distinction between *enforceable* and *unenforceable* obligations. Enforceable obligations refer to moral demands (rules, laws, statutes) which are imposed from without, while unenforceable obligations refer to the inner sanctions of persons which are self-imposed.[77] Unenforceable laws "concern inner attitudes, genuine person-to-person relations, and expressions of compassion which law books cannot regulate and jails cannot rectify."[78] Enforceable obligations are human laws which insure justice; unenforceable obligations belong to higher law, rooted in the moral order of the cosmos, and they produce love.[79] Although behavior can be regulated by external decrees, morality cannot be legislated. This is the logic of his argument against the limits of desegregation as an enforceable demand and integration as an unenforceable demand.

> Desegregation will break down the legal barriers and bring men together physically, but something must touch the hearts and souls of men so that they will come together spiritually because it is natural and right.[80]

The ultimate solution to the problem of community lies in the human willingness to be bound by the unenforceable obligation of the moral law that is within. This is the nature and scope of love as universal, dangerous, and excessive altruism. There are, however, two other very important, interrelated expressions of love which serve as means of actualization of community: forgiveness and reconciliation.

Forgiveness and reconciliation are salient expressions in King's understanding of love. Forgiveness is the loving act on the part of the wronged individual(s) which removes the barriers that inhibit authentic relationship between her/himself and the other who have been separated by ignorance, fear, hate, and violence.[81] Reconciliation is the result of forgiveness; it is the coming together of disparate parties that have been separated by internal and external barriers that work against wholeness and harmony in relationships between God, persons, and the world.[82]

Forgiveness is the product of moral predisposition; it is not an occasional act, but is part of personal character. The charge of Jesus to Peter to forgive his enemies seventy times seven is not simply a matter of quantity, but of quality. King says, "A man cannot forgive up to four hundred and ninety times without forgiveness becoming part of the habit structure of his being. Forgiveness is not an occasional act; it is a permanent attitude."[83] Forgiveness goes beyond the injunction of *lex talionis*, which actually perpetuates the vicious cycle of ignorance, fear, hate, and violence, and lifts the person to a higher law, the law of love.[84] Love never seeks to humiliate its opponent, but always seeks to find a way of transforming enemy into friend.[85] This is the basis for reconciliation. In fact, King says, "Forgiveness means reconciliation, a coming together again."[86] Both grow out of the command to love the enemy. The degree to which we are able to forgive determines the degree to which we are able to love our enemies.[87]

In King's many statements regarding the need for black Americans to love white segregationists, the themes of forgiveness and reconciliation are fundamental. It is his insistence that the oppressed must develop the capacity to forgive if the beloved community is to become a reality. While the oppressor has responsibility to request forgiveness from the one(s) he or she has violated, the willingness to forgive is always the responsibility of the wronged person(s).[88] King asserts that "The Negro must love the white man, because the white man needs his love to remove his tensions, insecurities, and fears."[89] He suggests that this was the greatness of Jesus's redemptive suffering on the cross, his willingness to forgive his enemies. For King, the highest expression of love was when Jesus uttered the words from the cross, "Father, forgive them, for they know not what they do."[90] A testament to the power of forgiveness and reconciliation exemplified in the suffering of Christ is the historical chronicle of failed kingdoms and empires that were built on force, contrasted with the kingdom of love that Jesus established.[91]

Love is not a sentimental, passive emotion, but the creative synthesis of a strong, rational principle wedded with sentience. King characterizes this combination of reason and sentience in the person as a "tough mind and a tender heart." Tough-mindedness represents "incisive thinking, realistic appraisal, and decisive judgment."[92] This rational principle, which is part of love, allows the individual to be discriminating and astute in making moral judgments. Tough-mindedness without tender-heartedness, however, can carry over into a moral disposition which begets insensitivity, bitterness, and violence, and thus, destroys community. Hardcore rationality creates a false dichotomy between fact and value, science and religion, external and internal dimensions of life, and is ultimately responsible for the negation of human personality.[93] The moral life, contends King, must continually uphold the creative synthesis between a disciplined mind and a tender heart.[94]

Closely related to his understanding of the rational/sentient nature of love is King's correlation of love, justice, and power. Love is power to achieve justice.[95] Like Paul Tillich, King did not see a necessary conflict between love, justice, and power; rather, the three, properly understood, form a creative union which issues forth in wholeness and community. As noted earlier, King rejected Nietzsche's conception of Christian love as a glorification of weakness. He argued that Nietzsche failed to understand the true nature of Christian love as *agape* because he restricted love to the emotional level or "soft-mindedness." Consequently, Nietzsche identified love with the resignation of power. For King, the rational nature of persons, which incorporates freedom and self-transcendence, is the basis for their power over nature, time, and space, and the crippling human circumstances that work against community.[96] Power, properly understood, King argued, "is the ability to achieve purpose." Love and justice are regulating ideals for power. Justice, however, does not have ontological status; rather, it is fulfilled in love as the *summum bonum* of life. For King, "Love that does not satisfy justice is no love at all. It is merely sentimental affection, a little more than what one would have for a pet. Love at its best is justice concretized. Love is unconditional."[97] Justice is the politico-social ideal which "at its best is love correcting everything that stands in the way of love." Power, therefore, without love is "reckless and abusive and...love without power is sentimental and anemic. Power at its best is love implementing the demands of justice."[98]

This was a critical argument for King because it enabled him to move beyond the Niebuhrian analysis of love as an impossible possibility in social and political affairs. Unlike Niebuhr's contention that justice is an approximation of love which can only be achieved in individual relationships, King actually grants to justice the potentiality of becoming one with love in an ontological union wedded with power. Walter G. Muelder, one of the personalists whom King credits as influencing his intellectual development, succinctly captures this crucial point in the following:

> Since love is freely given, writers often contrast it with justice, which measures to each what is due and which supposedly can be coercively commanded. Justice and mercy are to be held in conflict, the one may be enforced and the other not. This supposed conflict arises when justice is first abstracted from love, with which it is in fact indivisible, and then treated as an absolute principle. But the limits of the idea of justice point to the larger context of love of which it is an indispensable aspect. When one thinks through any serious problem of justice, i.e., how to give persons their due, he is confronted by deep dimensions of integral responsibility. In the Bible the righteousness of God and his mercy

are an indivisible whole. The components are distinguishable but not separable in him. His righteousness is a justice of mercy which offers salvation and reconciliation.[99]

Theologically, King resolves "the crisis of powerless morality and immoral power"[100] by understanding justice within the context of the redemptive suffering of Christ. Along with Muelder, King believed that the cross is the ultimate expression of the fact that "self-sacrificing and forgiving compassion are the ultimate fulfillment of person-in-community and the ultimate revelation of the character of God."[101] King maintained that "Jesus eloquently affirmed from the cross a higher law," the law of love, which transcended "the old eye-for-an-eye philosophy," which is the demand of justice as expressed in *lex talionis*.[102] The cross is the symbol of the length that God will go to restore broken community.[103] As co-workers with God, persons are called to create a just and loving society through redemptive suffering. King writes

> My personal trials have taught me the value of unmerited suffering... I have lived these past few years with the conviction that unearned suffering is redemptive. There are some who still find the cross a stumbling block, others consider it foolishness, but I am more convinced than ever before that it is the power of God unto social and individual salvation. So like the Apostle Paul I can now humbly say, 'I bear in my body the marks of the Lord Jesus.'[104]

Nonviolence: Love in Action

Love as redemptive suffering is the central theme which informs King's understanding of nonviolent resistance. He maintained that it was through Gandhi's emphasis on love and nonviolence that he discovered the method of social reform which was both morally and practically sound for oppressed people in their struggle for freedom.[105] Nonviolent resistance was more than a method of action; it was a moral imperative, born of his Christian conviction, which defined his way of life.[106] It is love in action, creating and preserving community.[107]

For King, *agape* is most concretely expressed in the philosophy of nonviolent direct action. In his famous recapitulation of his intellectual odyssey, "Pilgrimage to Nonviolence," he delineates six basic characteristics of his understanding of nonviolent resistance:

1) Nonviolent resistance is not a method for cowards, but it is ultimately the way of the strong person, i.e., it is not "passive" in the sense that it succumbs to evil, rather it *actively* seeks to confront the opponent with the error of his/her ways. "It is not passive nonresistance to evil, it is active nonviolent resistance to evil." [108]

142

2) Nonviolence does not seek to humiliate or defeat the opponent, but to win the opponent's friendship. As such, its ultimate goal is redemption and reconciliation. "The aftermath of nonviolence is the creation of the beloved community..."[109]

3) Nonviolence makes a distinction between evil and the evil-doer. Here King's understanding of the inherent goodness of all persons as bearing the image of God is operative. Therefore, nonviolent resistance is not directed at the persons themselves, but against the forces of evil by which they are victimized.[110]

4) Nonviolent resistance emphasizes redemptive suffering. It is a willingness on the part of the votary to accept suffering without retaliation. King believed that redemptive suffering has tremendous educational and transformative power. Redemptive suffering is the highest expression of love as symbolized in the cross of Christ.[111]

5) Nonviolent resistance not only avoids physical injury, but psychological violence as well. "The nonviolent resister not only refuses to shoot his opponent, but he also refuses to hate him."[112] Related to this belief is the idea that nonviolence recognizes the interrelatedness of all life. King maintained that to do harm to another is to harm oneself because human existence, as with all of life, is interdependent. Therefore, when whites uphold unjust statutes of segregation, they ultimately hurt themselves.

6) Nonviolent resistance is based on the conviction that the universe is ultimately on the side of justice. The person who accepts nonviolence as a way of life must also accept the belief in a creative force which works for universal wholeness. At the root of nonviolence is a deep faith in the future based on a belief in the moral order of the universe. Implied in King's belief in a moral order is the belief in the ultimate actualization of community.[113]

Nonviolence: The Only Road to Freedom

Nonviolence represented love in action for King. For him, it was the only method for achieving the beloved community.[114] A fundamental presupposition in King's thinking is the principle that "means and ends must cohere because the end is preexistent in the means."[115] If the end of a peaceful and just society is to be achieved, it must be accomplished by a method that is peaceful and just. Violence, whether physical or psychological, cannot achieve constructive and creative ends because it carries within itself the seeds of its own destruction. This affirmation was the basis of his criticism of some advocates of Black Power. The philosophy of violent revolution was not only impractical, but foremost it was immoral. King argued that as a practical method of revolution, violence is counterproductive for black Americans because of their relative size in relation to the larger population and their lack of resources and technology to sustain a revolution.[116] King also maintained that Black Power's advocacy of violence failed to recognize the relationship between power and morality. "Power and morality," he explained, "must go together, implementing, fulfilling, and ennobling each other."[117] Violence is immoral because ultimately it works against community.[118] Nonviolence is the only practical and moral method capable of bringing about genuine community because the ends it seeks are in coherence with the method itself.

King also rejected the argument for self-defense. Although he acknowledged that defense of property and person are constitutional rights, he maintained that there is a very thin line between self-defense and retaliatory violence. Self-defense fails to address the real issues that cause segregation, disenfranchisement, economic deprivation and other social ills, and, instead, actually furthers the vicious cycle of violence. In this sense, self-defense creates more problems than it solves. King argued that

> Only a refusal to hate or kill can put an end to the chain of violence in the world and lead us toward a community where men live together without fear. Our goal is to create a beloved community and this will require a qualitative change in our souls as well as quantitative change in our lives.[119]

King's political posture also informed his method for creating community. Politically, King was a reformist.[120] Although some have labelled his latter years as a radical stage in his development, his basic political outlook remained reformist. Coupled with his reformist political posture, he believed that it was the divinely appointed mission of black and other oppressed peoples to save the soul of America through redemptive suffering.[121] They could only accomplish this mission by working for creative and constructive change within American society, not through violent revolution. Nonviolence as a strategy was the most complementary method to achieve this end.[122] Therefore, liberation, for King, was not based on defeat or humiliation of the white man, but through the willingness of the black American to suffer redemptively for his sake and to call the nation to a higher destiny.[123] Liberation, in King's thinking, is inextricably bound to integration.[124] Integration and liberation are analytically distinct, but practically they are inseparable. To be truly liberated within American society requires that there be an interpersonal venture of cooperation and responsibility. Unlike other nations where the oppressor is occupying a foreign land and is forced to leave after revolution occurs, black and white Americans are both at home, and the situation can only be changed by the responsible sharing of power which is expressed in authentic, interpersonal living. Liberation, therefore, can only be achieved within the context of an integrated society. This places America in a unique position in world history and has implications for its destiny as a moral force in international affairs among other nations.[125]

Nonviolence and Civil Disobedience

King's understanding of nonviolence as strategy for social change also included his belief that noncooperation with an evil system is a moral imperative. This belief informed his conception of nonviolent civil disobedience. Along with Thoreau, King felt that it was a moral obligation to disobey unjust laws. Unlike Thoreau, he believed that civil disobedience must be nonviolent.[126]

An adequate understanding of King's view of civil disobedience demands an analysis of his conception of law. King made a distinction between just and unjust laws. King agreed with Aquinas that "an unjust law is no law at all." "A just law," he argued, "is a man made code that squares with the moral law or the law of God. An unjust law is a code that is out of harmony with the moral law." He further argued that "any law that uplifts human personality is just" and that "any law that degrades human personality is unjust."[127] He stated this distinction more concretely by demonstrating the difference between just and unjust laws. He argued that an unjust law is a code that the majority inflicts upon the minority that is not binding on itself. This is *difference* made legal. An unjust law is also a code the majority imposes upon the minority which the minority had no part in enacting or creating, i.e., segregated statutes came into being without the Negro's exercise of the ballot. A just law, King maintained, is the opposite. It is *sameness* made legal. It is a code which the majority, who happen to believe in that code, compel the minority (who had opportunity through the ballot to express dissent) to follow because they believe in the law themselves and consequently are willing to be governed by it.[128]

King believed that one has not only a legal but a moral obligation to obey just laws. Conversely, one has a moral responsibility to disobey unjust laws. When one disobeys an unjust law for the sake of calling attention to circumstances that cripple and demean human personality, then that individual is showing the highest respect for law. The nonviolent resister, then, must not only disobey unjust laws but must be willing to accept the penalty for civil disobedience. Such an attitude of respect for the principle of law counters the charge of anarchy and uplifts the value of redemptive suffering for higher ends.[129]

The techniques King used in his campaign of nonviolent civil disobedience included marches, demonstrations, wade-ins, boycotts, and prayer pilgrimages. Underlying these tactical maneuvers was the basic presupposition that power and morality must be wedded to bring about creative social change. First, he maintained that the primary purpose of nonviolent

145

civil disobedience is to dramatize an evil by mobilizing the forces of goodwill and generating pressure and power for change.[130] This underlying principle of strategy reflects his understanding of the nature and role of conflict in the realization of human community and it underscores his thesis that the nonviolent campaign is ultimately directed at the evil system, not the individual.[131]

Second, at work in his understanding of civil disobedience is the notion that was fundamental to the efficacy of redemptive suffering, i.e., that a time interval of sufficient duration is essential to bring about the projected change that issues forth in wholeness and reconciliation. While violence tends to be quick and efficient, nonviolence requires a type of "revolutionary patience."[132] Although King strongly opposed the kind of tolerance that breeds greater injustice,[133] by implication his doctrinaire stance on liberation through integration and peaceful, nonviolent change, confirms the argument that social change requires patience rooted in steadfastness.[134]

Third, the forces of goodwill must be *organized*. King believed that the "children of darkness" tend to be wiser and better organized than the "children of light." King was both a theoretician and practitioner of this principle.[135] He fervently believed and practiced his words: "To produce change people must be organized to work together in units of power."[136] Critics of his nonviolent stance who cite his strategy as lacking "realism" in effecting creative and constructive social change often fail to recognize that he was well aware of the nature and depth of recalcitrant, systemic evil and the need to be "realistic" in regard to power relationships.[137] His dialectical method of resolving conflict,[138] however, would not allow him to maintain the "real" without the ideal, rather both are held in creative tension and resolved at the higher level of redemptive suffering in love. For King, the theological resolution of the conflict between "power" and "morality" is symbolized in God in Christ, who is revealed in redemptive suffering on the cross. Jesus Christ, the ideal human personality, willingly suffers and dies in love as a symbol of God's willingness to share power and to create community. The moral resolution of the conflict is demonstrated in the individual's willingness to become a co-sufferer with Christ for the realization of the beloved community. This is not to suggest that King's love ethic is born of a superficial sentimentalism, for as it has been demonstrated, he understood well the relationship between morality and power. King's emphatic position regarding the organization of power to achieve a just and loving society is a clear indication of his belief that oppressors do not relinquish power without struggle and conflict. His call for massive civil disobedience in The Poor People's March on Washington is an illustration of his understanding of the need to confront immoral power with the power of love through nonviolent direct action. During the latter months of his life, King said:

Nonviolent protest must now mature to a new level to correspond to heightened black impatience and stiffened white resistance. This higher level is massive civil disobedience. There must be a force which interrupts its functioning at some key point. That interruption must not, however, be clandestine or surreptitious. It is not necessary to invest it with guerilla romanticism. It must be open, and above all, conducted by large masses without violence.[139]

Smith and Zepp suggest that King's matured understanding of nonviolence and massive civil disobedience reflects a critical change in strategy from "liberalism" to "radicalism." The former refers to social change through moral suasion, legislation, and education, which is basically reformist.[140] The latter refers to King's matured vision of radically transforming the priorities and structures of American society.

Liberalism stresses persuasion; radicalism emphasizes power and coercion. For the liberal, cooperation and consensus are the important social processes; for the radical, conflict and confrontation are important. As King became more and more radical in his thinking, he placed more and more stress upon power, coercion, conflict and confrontation.[141]

Even with changed emphases in strategy, King's major concern remained that power be used to achieve the goals of the beloved community which is defined within the context of integration. To the end of his life, nonviolence remained the only practical and moral method to achieve human community. But the overall strategy and political position is essentially reformist. When King speaks of a "revolution of values and priorities" and of overcoming the triplets of oppression (poverty, racism, and war), he speaks within the framework of American democratic society with the willingness to suffer the penalties imposed by law for his civil disobedience.[142] Nowhere in his writings, sermons, or speeches does he speak of overthrowing the system. His political, economic, and social vision is one of transformation through nonviolent protest, not violent revolution.

In summary, King's understanding of love as redemptive suffering finds its most practical application in the method of nonviolent resistance. Nonviolent resistance, for King, is *agape* in action; it is both a method of bringing about constructive social change and a way of life. Love, law, and civil disobedience are not mutually exclusive ideas; rather, they are seen as harmonious elements in one singular quest to create the beloved community. Power and morality are treated in a creative dialectic which is resolved theologically and morally in redemptive suffering for others.

His reformist political posture also informed his understanding of nonviolence as the only method for bringing into realization the beloved community. Since liberation is defined within the context of an integrated society, nonviolent resistance is the only viable method to create the kind of society and world in which love and justice reign. Such a vision of community requires a type of patience wedded with steadfast endeavor for social change. King was well aware of the cost of such a lofty vision. Near the end of his life he wrote:

> There is no easy way to create a world where men and women can live together, where each has his own job and a house and where all children receive as much education as their minds can absorb. But if it is created in our lifetime, it will be done in the United States by Negroes and white people of good will. It will be done by people who have the courage to put an end to suffering by willingly suffering themselves rather than inflict suffering upon others. It will be done by rejecting the racism, materialism and violence that has characterized Western civilization and especially by working toward a world of brotherhood, cooperation and peace.[143]

King's recommendations for overcoming the barriers to community have been discussed. The beloved community ideal ("community ordered by love") serves as norm and goal of the moral life. The barriers to community, according to King, can only be overcome by the power of *agape*, the ethical principle which creates community. *Agape* is expressed as altruism (universal, excessive, dangerous), forgiveness, and reconciliation. The true test of *agape* is the love of the enemy. In King's thinking, there is a correlation between love, power, and justice. Love is the power to achieve justice. Justice does not have ontological status, rather it is fulfilled in love. More specifically, justice is love concretized. Love is ultimately revealed through redemptive suffering for others. The redemptive suffering of Jesus Christ is the highest expression of *agape* and is the symbol of the length that God will go to create and preserve community. The moral agent, therefore, is under mandate to suffer redemptively for the sake of the other. The crisis of power and morality ("loveless power" and "powerless love") is resolved through redemptive suffering.

Nonviolent resistance, for King, is love in action. Redemptive suffering is the key element informing his philosophy of nonviolent resistance. King felt that nonviolence was the only moral and practical method for achieving community in American society and the world. The way of nonviolence is moral because the means it employs informs the end that it seeks. A peaceful and just society or world, King says, cannot be created through violent struggle because the method of violence only perpetuates the climate of violence which works against community.

Community, Religion, and Social Action

Persons and Social Action

The discussion turns now to King's understanding of the nature and role of the moral agent (or persons) and the church in social action. As stated, the nature of persons in the thinking of King includes the sacredness of human personality, human freedom and responsibility, the moral law, the rational nature of persons, the dialectical nature of persons, and the communitarian nature of personality. These respective themes in his conception of persons inform his understanding of the moral agent and his or her responsibility to become a co-worker with God in the creation of the beloved community.

King's understanding of the moral nature of personality is religious; faith precedes morality. While it is true that all persons are created in the image of God, yet there is "a tension at the heart of human nature" between good and evil which tends to drag persons down to lower levels of existence.[144] Because of the dialectical nature of the self, there is an endless struggle between freedom and finitude which prevents the moral perfection of the individual. King affirmed with the Apostle Paul, "The good that I would, I do not; and the evil that I would not, I do."[145] In other words, persons are powerless to realize the ideal of *agape* by their own will and power.[146] For King, the power of human reason alone is insufficient to attain the moral ideal of love. The arrogant abuse of reason and freedom accounts for the moral irresponsibility that works against harmonious human relations, and ultimately, against community.[147] The humanist hope of redeeming the world through reason and science, King postulates, is a product of "exalted Renaissance optimism," which attempted to free the mind of humankind, but forgot about the human capacity for sin.[148] The only remedy for the question of human sin is grace.[149] The grace of God, which is freely given, must be freely received by the penitent sinner. In commentary on the Parable of the Lost Son, King speaks symbolically of the son who returns home (to his original nature, the *imago dei*) to his father who freely forgives him for his waywardness. He suggests the glory of the Christian religious experience is, "that when a man decides to rise up from his mistakes, from his sin, from his evil, there is a loving God saying, 'Come home, I still love you.'"[150]

King firmly believed that an experience of inner transformation was primary to involvement in social transformation. Salvation, however, is not equated with moral perfectionism, rather it is understood as an inner quality of life which issues forth in deeds of goodwill and love for the

149

neighbor. "In the final analysis," says King, "what God requires is that your heart is right. Salvation isn't reaching the destination of absolute morality, but it's being in the process and on the right road."[151] Those who open their lives to God in Christ experience a new birth and a reorientation of values which enable them to struggle for social transformation. "Only through an inner spiritual transformation do we gain the strength to fight vigorously the evils of the world in an humble and loving spirit."[152] The regenerated individual is a "transformed nonconformist" in society, and following the way of Christ, is willing to suffer redemptively for others.[153] The "transformed nonconformist" refuses to cooperate with evil systems which exploit and destroy human personality, and willingly suffers the penalty of law for his or her nonconformity. The life of the person who suffers redemptively for the sake of others becomes a living sacrament of the Presence of God in the world, working for universal wholeness.[154]

The Nature and Role of the Church

For King, the nature of the church is Christocentric, i.e., the church as the Body of Christ is the symbol of the beloved community in the world.[155] The Christian church is the place in which *agape* is realized in common sharing and nurturing, and is a sign of faith, hope, and love for the world.[156] While Christ is the central figure of the Christian fellowship, the all-embracing, unifying principle of love is the key which binds other religious faiths in unity.[157]

According to King, the church exists both in time and eternity; it is in the world, but not of the world. Its highest loyalty is to God, who is revealed in Christ.

> Living in the colony of time, we are ultimately responsible to the empire of eternity. As Christians we must never surrender our supreme loyalty to any time-bound custom or earth-bound idea, for at the heart of our universe is a higher reality—God and his kingdom of love—to which we must be conformed.[158]

Second, the church is also the center of worship for the gathered community. King understood worship to be primarily a social experience which transcends all forms of sectarianism, class, and race.[159] Early in his pastoral ministry, he proclaimed that "worship at its best is a social experience with people of all levels of life coming together to realize their oneness and unity under God."[160]

Third, King believed that the church is the moral custodian of society. It is entrusted with the responsibility both to proclaim to the world and to demonstrate in its fellowship the dynamics of human community. The church's role as moral custodian is first a call to demonstrate *agape* within its own fellowship. The great tragedy of the Christian church has been its conformity to unjust mores and customs of society within its own fellowship which work against human community. The racism reflected in the creation of Negro and white churches is a tragic expression of the disunity within the Christian church which scars the soul of the Body of Christ.[161] The church's cooperation with classism and exclusiveness within its fellowship destroys its witness in the world.[162] As moral custodian of society, the church is called to a prophetic role as a creative minority which refuses to conform to unjust statutes of the state, but boldly and courageously confronts the systemic evil which prevents the realization of the beloved community. As the prophetic witness of Christ

> The church must be reminded that it is not the master or the servant of the state, but rather the conscience of the state. It must be the guide and the critic of the state, and never its tool. If the church does not recapture its prophetic zeal, it will become an irrelevant social club without moral or spiritual authority.[163]

King believed that the church must be involved as an institution in the struggle for social justice. He maintained that the institutional church is entrusted with the "ideals of a higher and more noble order."[164] It is the *ekklesia* which gives moral guidance and direction to society, and willingly suffers the penalty for nonconformity and noncooperation with social evils which destroy human personality and ultimately impede the actualization of human community.[165] The moral failure of the church is that as the very institution which should be in the forefront of the call for justice and peace in society, it has actually participated in and perpetuated social evils.[166] Its conformity to patterns of racism, exclusiveness, sectarianism, economic injustice, and violence has made it a thermometer which records and registers majority opinion, rather than a thermostat which regulates and transforms the temperature of society.[167]

While King was often critical of the black church for what he perceived as two extremes, classism and emotionalism,[168] he also maintained that the role the black church played in the Civil Rights Movement was a glorious example in the history of Christendom. From Montgomery to Memphis, the black church was the central motivating force behind the movement which King led. He felt that the witness of the black church in the Civil Rights Movement was reminiscent of the early Christians:

> For never in Christian history, within a Christian country, have Christian churches been on the receiving end of such naked brutality and violence as we are witnessing here in America

today. Not since the days of the Christians in catacombs has God's house, as a symbol, weathered such attack as the Negro churches.[169]

In summary, King believed that the nature and role of the church is to serve as the moral custodian of society. It is called to proclaim and to demonstrate in its fellowship the power of *agape* to create community. The moral failure of the church is that it has conformed to the mores and customs of society which work against community. He called upon the church to recapture the zeal of the early Christians and to see themselves as citizens of two worlds, of time, and of eternity. The church must participate as an institution in the struggle for social justice. It must be the true *ekklesia* of Christ in the world. The black church symbolized the authentic mission of the church in society through its redemptive suffering for justice in the Civil Rights Movement. While the moral agent derives his/her strength from the gathered community in worship, King's understanding of the church is decidedly social in its formation and intentionality. The social gospel influence of Rauschenbusch, the personal theism of DeWolf, and most importantly, "the black Christian tradition" contributed to this radically social understanding of the nature and purpose of the church.[170]

In the discussion above, King's understanding of the barriers to community and his recommendations for overcoming them have been examined. Part III of this study will explicate the continuities and discontinuities in Thurman's and King's thinking regarding the ideal of community (Chapter 7) and will offer findings and conclusions (Chapter 8).

152

Part III

They Looked for a City:
A Comparison of the Ideal of Community
in Howard Thurman and Martin Luther King, Jr.

The secret things belong to the Lord our God; but the things that are revealed belong to us and to our children forever.

—Deuteronomy 29:29

Chapter 7

Keep A Inchin' Along

The tough minded person always examines the facts before he reaches conclusions.

—*Martin Luther King, Jr.*

Life must make sense. Whatever seems to deny a fundamental structure of orderliness upon which rationality seems to depend cannot be countenanced.

—*Howard Thurman*

Keep a inchin' along,
  Massa Jesus comin' by an' by,
Keep a inchin' along like a po' inch worm,
  Massa Jesus comin' by an' by.

—*Negro Spiritual*

Introduction

In this study, the ideal of community in Howard Thurman and Martin Luther King, Jr. has been analyzed. It has been demonstrated that the ideal of community is the defining motif of their lives and thoughts. The discussion began by raising fundamental questions which served as the basis for an analytical construct or method to examine each thinker's view of community. First, *the experiential and intellectual sources of community* in their lives and thoughts were examined. The question raised was, What were the personal, social, and intellectual sources which informed and shaped their understandings of community? Second, *the nature of community* was examined, i.e., How is community conceived? What is its character? What are the dynamic elements involved in their respective views and how are they related? And third, the question of *the actualization of community* was raised: What barriers did they identify that must be overcome in the actualization of community? What were the recommendations of each thinker for overcoming the barriers and creating community? or How is community actualized? In each section, particularly under the experiential and intellectual sources of community, this study has shown how the black American experience of oppression was related to and helped to mold their respective responses to the questions outlined above. The comparison of the ideal of community and the conclusions that follow are products of this analysis.

This chapter is divided into two sections. The first treats the continuities between the two thinkers and the latter, the discontinuities. The final chapter will be concerned with findings and conclusions.

Continuities

The Experiential and Intellectual Sources

The Black Family, Church, and Community

The analyses of the experiential and intellectual sources of the ideal of community in Thurman and King demonstrate that their respective understandings of community arose initially from their common experience of oppression and segregation as black Americans in the Deep South.[1] It has also been shown that out of the particularity of their experiences of community and non-community in the segregated South, there emerged a universal vision of human community which transcended race, class, religion, and other forms of sectarianism. Their early childhood experiences in the contexts of family, the black church, and black communities of Daytona, Florida, and Atlanta, Georgia, provided them with a sense of personal worth and an awareness of the interrelatedness of life which became central elements in their respective views of community.

These early experiences also gave them a sense of mission and purpose in their personal and intellectual quests to find a method to overcome the barriers which they perceived as antithetical to community. While each subject represents distinct social origins and class orientations within the black community itself, the common experience of being black and victimized by segregated statutes and policies of the Deep South, combined with the distinctive insights of the black American religious experience, led both to raise fundamental questions about the relation of Christianity to racism and formed the backdrop for their respective methods of creating community. For both Thurman and King, the central, axiomatic questions underlying their visions of community are: *How does Christianity address the problem of American racism?* and *What is the most moral and practical method for overcoming racism in American society?* This is not to suggest that the issue of class and other forms of exclusiveness[2] were not important barriers which each sought to overcome, but the question of racism within the context of American society was their point of departure.

156

Their respective intellectual searches for community must be understood within the social contexts of these early experiences. For black Americans, education has been traditionally perceived as a path to liberation from the bondage of white racism. Thurman says that his grandmother thought there was something "magic" about reading.[3] Frederick Douglass wrote that education was "a direct pathway from slavery to freedom."[4] Angela Davis suggests that knowledge is precursive to liberation. In her "Lectures on Liberation,"[5] she explores the notion of freedom in light of the philosophical concepts of identity, self-knowledge, and the philosophy of history. Education, she argues, is a form of resistance for the slave in which the slave discovers the extent of his or her alienation from self and consequently from freedom. The recognition of this condition of alienation through self-knowledge is at the same time the rejection of that condition. "Consciousness of alienation entails the absolute refusal to accept that alienation." For the slave, Davis says, "enlightenment does not bring happiness, nor does it bring *real* freedom—it brings desolation, misery…" Real freedom is a product of resistance and struggle against the condition of alienation created by enslavement. Davis's astute analysis of the role of knowledge in the liberation of the slave is certainly *apropos* to the early intellectual development of Thurman and King in their searches to answer their primary concern of the relation of faith to the prevalence of American racism. Education for both was promoted by their families, their churches, and the black communities from which they came. Thurman was encouraged by his grandmother, the church, and members of the Daytona community such as Mary McLeod Bethune, and later by Mordecai Johnson and Benjamin Mays. Mays and Johnson, as our biographical treatments indicate, were pivotal influences for both subjects. King was born into a middle-class black family where the mother and father were educated and the surrounding black Atlanta community encouraged him to pursue higher education. Thurman and King were both graduates of Morehouse College, an historically black institution which has always understood its mission as a training center for future black leaders. Morehouse College reinforced in each a sense of mission and purpose begun early in their families, churches, and communities. Their later intellectual pursuits (which were informed by the questions mentioned above) at prestigious white institutions and with noted professors find their basis in the early development of these men within the environment of the black community.

While the black experience of community is fundamental in understanding the development of the ideal of community in Thurman and King, it is equally important to see how their common experiences of struggle to achieve universal community out of the particularity of the black religious experience found creative affinity with the intellectual tradition of liberal Protestant theology. Such a perspective also helps in understanding the parallel themes found in both and answers in part the question of Thurman's influence upon King.[6] The continuities between liberal Protestant theology and the black religious experience and their impact on the thinking of King and Thurman can be seen in their common themes of *the interrelatedness of all life, the primacy of religious experience, the moral order of the universe, the love and power of God, the dignity and worth of human personality,* and *the social nature of human existence.*

In each thinker there is an apparent evolution in his understanding of community. Both acknowledge that early in their development, their conceptions of community were primarily relegated to the black community. Thurman says that when he was growing up in Florida, white people did not even fit into an ethical field, rather, relationships with whites were considered amoral.[7] Similarly, King indicates that it was not until his experience on the Atlanta Intercollegiate Council that he was able to conquer his "anti-white feeling."[8] As their biographical profiles demonstrate, through knowledge and exposure, both grew beyond these narrow understandings of community into a vision which was inclusive of, yet transcended racial, cultural, religious, and national loyalties. For both, the growth of the ideal was rooted not only in their intellectual quests, but in practical engagement with their initial problematic: the relationship between race and American Christianity and the search for the most moral and practical method to overcome this barrier. A major theme which emerges for each is that *out of the particularity of their oppressed status as black men in American society, their respective understandings of faith provided the source and the method to seek universal fellowship.*

The Nature of Community in Thurman and King

Conception of Community

There are striking continuities which exist in the conceptions and characteristics of community in Thurman and King. For both thinkers, the nature of community is rooted in the interrelatedness of all life, which is teleological.

For Thurman, community or "common ground" refers to wholeness, integration, and harmony. All life is interrelated and involved in goal-seeking. In each particular manifestation of life, there is the potential for it to realize its proper form, or to come to itself. The actualization of any form of life is synonymous with community. Community as "actualized potential" is true at all levels of life. There is, for him, a fundamental structure of interrelatedness and interdependability inherent in all living things, at microscopic levels of existence and in human society. The theological dimension of Thurman's understanding of community is the affirmation that the mind of God realizes itself in time. The origin and goal of community, therefore, is in the Mind of God, which is coming to Itself in time. This theological dimension of community is fundamental for all his philosophical and ethical claims. The nature of the problem of "community" is rooted in the relationship of the individual to social existence. While the primacy of the individual is a major concern for him, his ultimate vision is one of the harmonious human society. Life, in this sense, is a dynamic, ongoing project. God is at work in creation in a manner akin to an artist shaping and re-shaping his or her masterpiece. God is not finished with creation, and consequently, God is not finished with the human story, which is ever-unfolding and coming to itself in history. Similarly, personality is an unfinished project involving the individual in relation to God in a concerted endeavor of free and responsible acts that issue forth in commitment and maturity.

Like Thurman, community is the single, organizing principle of King's life and thought. The conception of community in King, which he referred to as "the beloved community," is rooted in the interrelatedness of all life and in the unity of human existence under the guidance of a personal God of love and reason who works for universal wholeness. The theological dimension of the "beloved community" is primary for King, and, therefore, the idea of a personal God who is a creative force working for universal wholeness informs his philosophical and ethical claims. "Community" refers primarily to the Christian social eschatological ideal, and is synonymous with the Kingdom of God. Concretely expressed, it is the mutually cooperative venture of persons in which they realize the solidarity of the human family by assuming responsibility for one another as children of God.

The Triadic Character of Community

For Thurman and King there is a triadic relationship between God, persons (individuals), and the world. These three principals are integrally related and form the basis for the dynamic character of community. Also for each thinker, community is a cooperative affair involving the three elements. Religious experience is the fundamental category for their thinking regarding the moral life.

In their anthropologies, both stress the sacredness of personality, the rational nature of human beings, freedom and responsibility, the communitarian nature of self, and the autonomous nature of the self in moral judgment. Human persons and individuals have their ground and being in the personal God of love and power who wills human community. God is the creator, ground, and sustainer of community. God is transcendent and immanent; the divine signature is on all creation. God's love is the basis for redemption and reconciliation. God's love and power, for both, are manifested in the divine ability to overcome the forces of evil in human history and in individuals (persons). God's will for community can be discerned in the world, the vast totality of the cosmos, nature, human history, society, and the state. God's activity in the world is characterized by loving, reasoned, and totally self-determined activity. Human persons and individuals are called to participate freely and responsibly with God in the creation of human community.

Of primary importance for both Thurman and King is the role of the state in the creation of community, particularly in America. A just and equitable society for both is based upon the democratic model expressed in the Constitution of the United States and the Declaration of Independence, which uphold the freedom and dignity of the individual. Thurman and King saw in the founding principles of American democracy the potentiality for the creation of world community. For each, America has a unique destiny and responsibility as a nation to demonstrate the truths of democratic idealism in the world. Black Americans and other oppressed ethnic groups have a redemptive role to play in "saving the soul" of America by calling the nation back to its founding principles and moral responsibility in the world.[9]

The Actualization of Community

Common themes in Thurman's and King's treatments of the actualization of community include: evil and sin as barriers to community, community as the norm and goal of the moral life, love as the means of actualization for community, and the nature and role of the moral agent in the creation of community. While their views of evil differed, both recognized that sin is both a personal and social phenomenon which erects internal and external barriers that must be overcome in the creation of community. For each, the internal barriers of sin find greater manifestation in social evils such as racism, classism, and religious exclusiveness.

Thurman and King believed community is the goal toward which all life strives and the norm for ethical reflection. The religious and the ethical are positively related in both. Faith serves as the point of departure for moral decision making and informs their views of love, the nature and role of the moral agent, and the church in the actualization of community.

Love, the two men contend, is the method for creating and maintaining human community. While Thurman's treatment of love also emphasizes its relationship with truth, both agree that all love is of God, and that love is the profoundest act of religion and life. Love has a strong rational core and is wedded to sentience. Love transcends justice and is expressed most completely in forgiveness and reconciliation. Love is ontologically related to justice and power. While this is more explicit in King, as it is

expressed in social relations, Thurman ŀ
correlation of justice, power, and love in in
of the enemy is the true test of love. Redem
nonviolent resistance, for Thurman and
practical means of creating community. Bot
making, *means and ends must cohere*, i.e., th
(community) cannot be achieved through
(hate, violence, war, etc.). For each, revolution
or legitimate option for the person who seeks
human relations. Love, as it is demonstrated
imperative for the actualization of human con

A clearly articulated theme in both subjects is that the person who works for community in the world must also seek community within. While this is the dominant strand in the thinking of Thurman, we have demonstrated that King also had a clear understanding of internal barriers that must be overcome in the actualization of community. For both, therefore, spirituality is inextricably bound to the struggle for social justice and liberation. Spirituality, as personal encounter and commitment to the God of love, provides the *ground* (the love of God), the *means* (the power of love) and the *goal* of social action (a just human society, i.e., human community ordered by love).

Discontinuities

The Nature of Community in Thurman and King

Conceptions of Community

Thurman's treatment of community is more clearly developed and systematic than King's. This is due primarily to their respective lifestyles, careers, and lengths of life. By virtue of longevity, academic positions, pastoral offices, and chaplaincies, Thurman had time and opportunity to develop a more systematic articulation of his ideas. King, on the other hand, was catapulted into the midst of the civil rights struggle at an early age and had less time to devote to a systematic presentation of his understanding of community. This fact, however, has no bearing on the profundity nor the fruitfulness of his intellectual contributions. The comparison of their conception of community is most revealing in respect to their treatments of the individual and society and their understandings of God. These two pivotal concerns are intricately related in Thurman and King and have significant implications for their recommendations for the actualization of community.

...ent differences in the two thinkers' conceptions of ...d in the elements which comprise community. Their respec-...tions of community proceed from different points of departure ...ect, to some extent, their personal pilgrimages toward community. ...individual serves as the point of departure for Thurman's under-...tanding of community. King's conception begins with the social existence of persons. This is not to suggest that Thurman does not see the individual in relation to the social order or that King does not value the significance of the individual in the interrelatedness of social existence. Their respective *emphases*, however, have implications for their particular constructions of community.

Thurman's ministry can be seen, in part, as a priestly/pastoral endeavor of enriching the spiritual life of individuals and empowering them for the work of community in society. Mozella Mitchell[10] referred to Thurman as a "modern day sophisticated shaman" and "a technician of the sacred,"[11] suggesting that he stands somewhere between the priest and the shaman while maintaining a distinctive posture as a social prophet. King embraced a prophetic model of ministry and was visibly and concretely engaged in the quest for social justice. The shaman, unlike the prophet who speaks to the community, "Thus says the Lord," leads the community to God by "giving others access to the spiritual world and effects a care for their ailing condition." According to Mitchell,

> Thurman, in his shamanistic function, does not simply bring the message of truth from God to the religious community, but he leads individuals and the community to have an experience with the divine from which they may gain a sense of wholeness themselves.[12]

Thurman's conception of community or "common ground" arises out of the individual's identification with the natural processes of the created order. The theme of the "aliveness of life" is rooted in his early affinity with nature and his own propensity toward solitariness. Life, as such, serves as a hermeneutical principle. By observing the extreme orderliness and exquisite harmony of living things, Thurman discovered an inherent vitality at work which issues forth in harmony and directiveness. This principle of vitality operative in the natural order finds correspondence in the inner workings of the mind of the individual. In each manifestation of life, there is the inherent potential for it to realize its proper form, or to come to itself. The quest for personal identity is also part of the mind's inherent logic, which seeks wholeness and integration. An individual's identity stands in direct relationship to the mind's actualization of its inherent potential. Therefore, *a healthy sense of self or personal identity is the clue and ground for community with others.*

King's conception of community begins with the social existence of persons. For him, the universe of shared values is decidedly social. The person can only exist in relationship with other persons, of whom God is the Supreme Person. This is a direct inheritance from personalism:

> The implication is that the nature of human beings is such that they need fellowship and thus they naturally seek community. Individuals are constantly interacting with each other in society, and such interaction affects their experience, consciousness, and history. An individual reaches the level of personhood only in social relations, a person grows and develops through social relations with other persons.[13]

In Thurman and King, the character of community is triadic, i.e., there are three basic elements in their conceptions of community: the individual or persons, God, and the world. However, for Thurman, the emphasis is on the individual and God; the world, as such, is secondary. The "creative encounter" between God and the individual is the basis for religious experience and is the place where the individual begins the quest for community. Community begins within, through the individual's commitment to the God of life. In the presence of God, the committed individual is both enabled and required to work for community in the world. The individual begins with his or her "own working paper," with the internality of religious experience, which serves as the point of departure for what he called "the outwardness of religion."[14] Hence, the methodology involves a movement from "the inwardness of religion" to "the outwardness of religion."[15]

In King, the three principals (persons, God, and the world) are equally related in a positive, creative relationship that constitutes "the dimensions of a complete life." For him, ideal human society is the product of the creative interaction of all three elements; one cannot be divorced from the other. The personal and social dimensions of religious experience are treated in a dialectical framework which endeavors to maintain a balanced treatment of the two modes of existence. The autonomy and the sociability of the person are guarded in a creative interplay between the inner and outer dimensions of religious experience. The ethic that emerges, therefore, is able to incorporate a more positive vision of the nature and role of persons as *social actors* within society. This crucial distinction has implications for King's and Thurman's views of freedom and responsibility.

Thurman's emphasis on the cultivation of the inner life as the basis for the development of a genuine sense of self, and consequently for authentic existence in the world, rests on his distinction between the *inner* and *outer* modes of self-existence. The inner mode of existence is primary to the outer, i.e., the internality of experience informs the externality of existence. Freedom and responsibility are treated in similar fashion. As noted, "freedom" for Thurman refers to a quality of being and spirit; freedom is located within; its locus is the human will. "Liberty," on the other hand, refers to external prerogatives, privileges, and grants that are conferred upon the individual from a social arrangement or context. The freedom of the individual, as it is interpreted by Thurman, places ultimate responsibility upon the *individual* to work for justice within society. Although Thurman treats responsibility as a shared experience in which the individual interacts responsibly with others, the accent is on the individual and the inner struggle to become whole. The need for social transformation arises from the individual's entrapment in the economic and political forces of oppression which hinder self-actualization.[16] The normative character of community, therefore, is not an external imposition upon the individual, but it is essentially within and is a disclosure of what life is about as it seeks to realize itself in myriad time-space manifestations. Martin Luther King, Jr., like the faithful pilgrim, Abraham, according to Thurman, "looked for a city where the builder and maker is God."[17] However, the clue to the search for the ideal city was first and foremost within him. This is the lesson, says Thurman, that every crusader for social justice must ultimately learn, that which one seeks for "without" is found "within," for the beyond is within.[18]

King's dialectical method and his emphasis on the sociality of persons inform his treatment of freedom and responsibility. Like Thurman, an inclusive human community in which people are able to develop and realize their potential is the goal of life. Political and economic systems should reflect the social nature of persons and their interdependency; and social institutions are responsible for the development of human personality. However, he does not make the distinction between "freedom" and "liberty" as it is articulated by Thurman; rather, freedom and liberty are conjoined in the context of social destiny. Here the emphasis is placed on society and its responsibility to persons. King, like Thurman, makes a distinction between the internal and external modes of existence. However, he attempts to maintain a dialectical tension between the two realms which is resolved in the quest for a "responsible society." The definition of a "responsible society" as offered by the First Assembly of the World Council of Churches in Amsterdam in 1948 is the model which best captures King's emphasis:

> Man is created and called to be a free being, responsible to God and his neighbor. Any tendencies in State and society depriving man of the possibility of acting responsibly are a denial of God's intention for man and his work of salvation. A responsible society

is one where freedom is the freedom of men who acknowledge responsibility to justice and public order, and where those who hold political authority or economic power are responsible for its exercise to God and the people whose welfare is affected.[19]

Also like Thurman, personality, as understood by King, is only meaningful within the context of other persons and society.[20] Freedom, however, is always within destiny; it is not limitless nor can it be relegated to a function of the will. Thurman's understanding of freedom is rooted in the nature and function of the will.[21] This conception of freedom arises from Thurman's methodological grid for spirituality and social transformation. The sanctity of the will is the citadel where freedom is either preserved or forfeited. It is also the place for the creative adventure with the Divine Presence which calls the individual forth into engagement with the world. While Thurman submits that freedom is a birthright, an inalienable quality of the individual which cannot be granted by external prerogatives, King's understanding of freedom suggests that outside of social existence with others, freedom is a misnomer. He emphasizes the purpose and responsibility of society in insuring what Thurman refers to as the "liberty" of persons. This is the nucleus of King's argument against segregation as a social system which impedes the person's capacity to deliberate, decide and respond; in essence, to be free.[22] Again, it is important to state that Thurman's view of freedom is not ultimately opposed to King's. The difference is one of accent, not of substance. Thurman was an astute observer and keen interpreter of the American democratic process, especially its implications for the eradication of white supremacy.[23]

Perspectives of God

The discontinuities in their respective emphases on the conception of community are most revealing in respect to their treatments of God. An important distinction between King's and Thurman's understandings of God is that the latter's vision of ultimate reality is theocentric while the former's is Christocentric. Both perspectives are firmly rooted in the black theological and ethical traditions.[24] This distinction may also reflect Kenneth Cauthen's distinction between "evangelical liberalism" and "modernistic liberalism" as the two types of American Protestant liberalism. As indicated, both thinkers were influenced by proponents of evangelical liberalism. Thurman, however, falls more appropriately into the designation of modernistic liberalism. Cauthen claims that the main distinguishing feature of the two schools of thought are their respective treatments of Jesus Christ.

The loose connection of the modernistic liberals within the traditional faith can be seen clearly in their estimate of Jesus. The thinking of these men was not Christocentric. Jesus was important—and even unique—because he illustrated truths and values which were universally relevant. However, these truths and values can be validated and even discovered apart from Jesus. He is not so much the *source* as he is the *exemplar* of the religious norm. Jesus might be psychologically helpful, but he was not usually thought to be logically necessary for the highest experience of God in human life.[25]

For King, Christ is the *source* of the norm of the beloved community. he redemptive love of God, revealed in the cross of Christ, is King's nswer to the possibility of achieving community within history. The :surrection of Jesus Christ is the symbol of the power of God and of the ltimate defeat of the forces which block the realization of community. hurman, on the other hand, sees Jesus as an *exemplar* of the possibilities f the committed individual in the quest for community. Jesus is not the orm of community, but an expression of the inherent potentiality of uman nature to achieve the highest goal of the moral life, love.

It should be noted that while there are clear distinctions between the wo thinkers' conceptions of community, this does not suggest that their ositions are mutually exclusive. Their perspectives of Jesus Christ should ot be interpreted apart from the socio-historical patterns of black Ameri- an oppression, rather the existential reality of black oppression is the rimary context in which the question of Christology is appropriately aised for Thurman and King. The fundamental question for the black :hristian tradition cannot be relegated to an abstract, sanitized concern for roper theoretical formulations. The critical issue is always, "Who is Jesus :hrist for us today?" James Cone contends, "If our existence were not at take, if we did not experience the pain and the contradictions of life, then he Christological question would be no more than an intellectual exercise or professional theologians."[26] The pivotal questions for Thurman and <ing which *form* and *in-form* their interpretations of Jesus were raised luring their early years within a cruel social environment where lynch- ngs and other barbarous acts of brutality against black people in the Deep :outh were daily occurrences.[27]

These two major differences in Thurman's and King's conceptions of :ommunity (the individual and society and their perspectives of God) nform their particular recommendations for the actualization of commu- iity.

The Actualization of Community

The Barriers of Sin and Evil

For Thurman and King, evil and sin are barriers to community. Their treatments of evil differ, however, and are related to their respective conceptions of the nature of God, their anthropologies, and their emphases on the individual and the social dynamics of community. For Thurman, evil is the positive and destructive principle that works against harmony, wholeness, and integration. It is not an intruder, rather, it is a constituent part of life. Life is good in the sense that includes both good and evil. Evil serves a purpose in the evolution of life as an upender which upsets the balances and insures a dynamic, creative quality in all living things. Since evil is a part of life, it must be interpreted within the divine context. Therefore, God is able to use evil as an instrument for the divine and ultimate purposes in the world. The creative resolution of the conflict between good and evil in the universe is guaranteed by the very logic of life, which works against all dualisms. For Thurman, the contradictions of life are not final. Life is ultimately one. This is the basis of hope and the ground for the ultimate achievement of community within history.

Thurman makes a distinction between natural, punitive, and moral evil. He claims that most of the suffering and pain in the world can be attributed to moral evil. Moral evil is a consequence of human disobedience to God. It is rooted in egoism and is an abuse of human freedom and responsibility. The locus of sin is the human will and freedom. Although Thurman recognizes the personal and social dynamics of evil and sin, his primary concern is how the individual deals with evil at the personal and private levels of his/her existence. The emphasis in Thurman is on the internal barriers of evil and sin that work against community within the self (fear, deception, and hate). The individual's personal response to the internal barriers imposed by sin has implications for the eradication of the social manifestation of evil in the world. Because of Thurman's positive conception of human nature, he maintained that the individual, through spiritual discipline, could ultimately overcome the internal barriers separating him or her from the vision of God. He maintained that when a solitary individual chooses not to cooperate with evil at the personal level, but instead places his or her life on the side of goodness, that individual anticipates community at the level of his or her functioning. What the person experiences within as impediments to harmonious self-existence, she or he also discovers in society. The struggle to overcome the barriers within propels the individual into the world as an agent of reconciliation.

Unlike Thurman, King sees evil as an intruder in God's creation. Evil is positive and destructive and works against God's purposes for community. The question of evil as being part of the will of God is dismissed by

King as contrary to divine benevolence. Evil exists, according to King, because of God's self-imposed limitation to assure human freedom and cooperation in the realization of the divine purposes for creation. Although there is a tension at the heart of the universe between good and evil, King believed that ultimately goodness will triumph over evil. King's belief is rooted in the Christian affirmation of the efficacy of the cross and resurrection.[28] Unlike Thurman, King sees the resolution of evil as a fact accomplished in the death and resurrection of Christ and in the proleptic realization of the Kingdom of God.[29] Evil is overcome not because of the individual's struggle to overcome it, but because of God's power to defeat it. For King, this is most dramatically illustrated in the cross of Christ.[30]

King's understanding of sin differs from Thurman's in that the latter identified sin as egoism or pride. King refused to equate sin with egoism or pride alone. His treatment of sin is rooted in the existential struggle between freedom and finitude. King suggested that sin is a product of the "civil war of the soul" or the "tragic schizophrenic personality"[31] which wills righteousness but is unable to attain it.[32]

While King, like Thurman, upheld the sacredness of human personality, he also had a profound understanding of sin both as a personal and a social phenomenon. King's understanding of the radical nature of sin within human personality and its heightened dynamic in social groups led him to a position which rejected any suggestion that human agency alone could overcome the forces that work against community.[33] King was acutely aware of the pervasive nature of human sin. In particular, his astute understanding of power and its relationship to social evil demanded a doctrine of grace which made available extraordinary resources to overcome the barriers erected by evil and sin in personal and social existence.

King firmly believed that as persons choose to become co-workers with God through faith, they are empowered to overcome the barriers erected by evil and sin. Unlike Thurman, who stressed the significance of internal barriers in the realization of community within oneself, King's emphasis is on the social manifestations of evil and sin which impede the actualization of community in the world. He identified them as poverty, racism, and war. King does not neglect internal barriers that prevent the realization of authentic self- existence. His emphasis, however, is on the social dimensions of evil and sin and the need for cooperation between persons and God in the struggle to overcome these barriers.

Overcoming the Barriers to Community

Their respective treatments of the individual and society and their ultimate construals of reality have direct implications for their recommendations for overcoming the barriers to community. For Thurman, the religious grounding of the moral life proceeds from a theocentric vision of reality. He maintained that the historical Jesus is a religious subject rather than a religious object; he is not God, but "the for instance of the mind of God." "Jesus is the revelation of how personality perfects itself and creates community."[34] When Jesus is elevated to the status of God the universality and inclusiveness of religious faith are jeopardized by a principle of exclusiveness. A theocentric understanding of God, on the other hand, frees the individual for a direct, immediate encounter with the living God and creates the grounds for authentic community in the world.[35] The fruit of this creative encounter is love, which is the means of actualizing community.

For King, Jesus Christ is the ground and goal of the moral life. His Christocentric treatment of the moral life combines both the historical Jesus and the cosmic Christ as the normative character for community.[36] Jesus is not only the *exemplar* of community, but is the *source* of the norm for community, which is love. The cosmic Christ is not interpreted by King in a christomonistic fashion, but rather in broad and universal categories which openly accept and embrace the truth claims of other religious orientations.[37]

These distinctions between theocentric and Christocentric understandings of the moral life and the roles of the individual and society are important as they relate to concrete, historical application of ethical principles and the creation of community. For both thinkers, love is the ethical principle which brings about the realization of human community. For Thurman, there is no mediator involved in the divine encounter. The creative encounter with the God of love is immediate and personal. This understanding of the moral life and the potentiality of human response to the divine initiative in such an encounter is rooted in a profoundly positive anthropology and a doctrine of sin which is psychological rather than racial. Hence, his understanding of the fall and sin, and consequently redemption, arise primarily from an affair between God and the individual. While the world (human society) is important, it is related in a secondary sense.

As stated, a key concept in Thurman's anthropology and ethical theory is the distinction he makes between "innocence" and "goodness."[38] Innocence, for Thurman, is given; community is "achieved goodness." In Thurman's treatment of creation myths, the fall is treated as "a fall from innocence." In each account, human beings' original experience of community is both potential and actualized potential within the framework of innocence. In the state of innocence, the things which work against community are dormant or unactualized, but once they are actualized by the agency of free-will, disharmony results and innocence is lost. After the fall from innocence, the divine-human project of "goodness" or "community" becomes the goal toward which human endeavor must be directed.

"Community" or "goodness" must be achieved through free and responsible actions. Goodness as achieved community is brought about through the radical freedom of the individual who makes a conscious, deliberate choice to strive for wholeness within the self and the world. Innocence is given without knowledge; goodness, however, comes through knowledge and responsibility. In the individual's struggle to achieve goodness, there is no savior figure; rather, the locus of the individual's moral initiative is the human will. For Thurman, sin is understood primarily as willful disobedience to God. Individuals are not sinners by virtue of a fallen existence, but through conscious, deliberate decisions that are antithetical to community. Redemption, therefore, is not a cosmic remedy offered outside the will and freedom of the individual. Rather, redemption is a divine-human possibility for the individual who already has the power within to choose wholeness and harmony with God.[39]

King's understanding of sin and the need for redemption through the efficacy of Christ had a profound impact on his view of nonviolence as the means of actualizing community.[40] Like Thurman, King recognized an individual fall, not a racial one. He stressed, however, the cumulative, structural, and social nature of human sin and its destructive consequences for human personality. Although he distinguishes individual responsibility from collective responsibility, the emphasis is on overcoming the social barriers of sin through the power of nonviolent love. Such an endeavor, says King, requires a doctrine of extraordinary grace which is effected in the cross of Christ. The soteriology present in King's understanding of the crucifixion of Christ emphasizes social redemption and the creation of a new situation.[41]

The Nature and Role of the Church in Society

The two thinkers' conceptions of God and the related treatments of the individual and society inform their views of the nature and role of the church in social change. For Thurman, the church is the social institution which is entrusted with "the Jesus idea." Jesus is not the central object of worship for the church, rather the ideal of community and the ethic of love which he taught as the means of actualizing community form the basis of the idea with which the church is entrusted. The church is the inclusive religious fellowship in which the committed individual seeks communion with those who share the common encounter with the Divine Presence.[42] The central theme underlying Thurman's ecclesiology is his belief that experiences of unity and fellowship are more compelling than the fears, dogma, and prejudices which divide and separate people. He believed that if these spiritual experiences of unity could be multiplied over a time interval of sufficient duration, they should be able to undermine any barrier that separates one person from the other. These barriers include racism, classism, denominationalism, and religious beliefs which hinder authentic fellowship between individuals as children of God.

The primary emphasis of Thurman in respect to the church is the spiritual cultivation of the individual through the worship/teaching ministry of the church. The church is called upon to actualize the vision of community within its own fellowship and the world. Thurman does not counsel the church as an *institution* to confront unjust social arrangements, rather he sees the church as a spiritual enabler and interpreter in the quest for social justice.

For King, the nature and goal of the church is Christocentric. It is the Body of Christ and the symbol of the beloved community in the world. As in Thurman, the church is called upon to demonstrate community within its own fellowship and the world. Both thinkers are critical of racial, classist, and denominational exclusiveness within its institutional structures. Thurman, however, identifies exclusiveness beyond race, class, and denominationalism, and raises the issue of exclusiveness among other religions. For Thurman, the principle of exclusiveness among religions is centered around Jesus as a religious object. While King embraces love as the universal bond between all religions, he does not clearly articulate how this claim is actualized in religious fellowship.

King understood worship to be primarily a social experience in which persons from all levels of life realize the oneness and unity of God and the human family. Thurman's emphasis lies with the immediacy of religious experience between God and the individual which has implications for the gathered community and its relationship to society. King begins with the social nature of the church, and worship as such is an expression of the social mission of the church in the world. This difference is most dramatically illustrated in the two men's ministries and their understanding of *the church's role as an institution* involved in the creation of community. Thurman's pastorates and chaplaincies, and eventually his work with the Howard Thurman Educational Trust Fund, served primarily as spiritual resources for those engaged in the quest for social justice. King, on the other hand, was able to mobilize churches as participants in the struggle for social change. From Montgomery to Memphis, the black church served as the primary source and the means through which he struggled for community.[43] Whereas Thurman identified the church's mission basically as an enabler and interpreter for individuals engaged in the work of community, King's social vision of the church allowed him to see that institution as the moral custodian of society. For King, this means that the church as an institution, the *ekklesia* of Christ, has a prophetic role as a creative minority within society. Its mission is to give moral direction to society and to willingly suffer as an institution the penalty for nonconformity and noncooperation with social evils which destroy human personality and ultimately impede the actualization of human community.

171

The treatments of community in Howard Thurman and Martin Luther King, Jr., represent two responses to the same questions which guided their personal and intellectual quests for community: How does Christianity address the problem of American racism? and What is the most moral and practical methodology for overcoming racism in American society? Thurman's personal pilgrimage, which he called "the search for common ground," culminated in a theocentric vision of reality which emphasized the nature and role of the committed individual in the actualization of community. King's personal odyssey toward the beloved community resulted in a Christocentric conception of community which stressed the nature and role of society in the actualization of community.

While both thinkers maintained different points of departure in respect to the nature and actualization of their central concern, there are striking parallels in their thoughts and recommendations for the creation of human community. Both were products of the black American experience of oppression and segregation. The resolution of this initial problematic became the labor and goal of their lives; and it was out of the particularity of this experience that their universal visions of community arose. Although Thurman and King differed in respect to their conceptions of evil and sin, they both recommended the same means of actualization: love as redemptive suffering. King's treatment of power and its correlation with justice and love enabled him to raise the ethical vision of community to a level of social consciousness which is not as pronounced in Thurman. Also, their respective conceptions of God and the relationship of individual and society informed their approaches to the role of religion and the church in social change. The discussion now turns to findings and conclusions of this comparative analysis in the final chapter.

Chapter 8

To See What the End Will Be

Upheaval after upheaval has reminded us that man is travelling along a road called hate, in a journey that will bring us to destruction and damnation. Far from being the pious injuction of a Utopian dreamer, the command to love one's enemy is an absolute necessity for our survival.

—Martin Luther King, Jr.

For this is why we were born: Men, all men belong to each other, and he who shuts himself away diminishes himself, and he who shuts another away from him destroys himself.

—Howard Thurman

Done made my vow to the Lord,
And I never will turn back.
I will go, I shall go,
To see what the end will be.

My strength, Good Lord, is almost gone,
I will go, I will go,
To see what the end will be.
But you have told me to press on,
I will go, I shall go,
To see what the end will be.

—Negro Spiritual

The discontinuities that exist between Thurman and King are perhaps as important as the continuities. They reveal different dimensions of the common problems addressed by their conceptualizations and recommendations for the actualization of community, and consequently, they provide new insights and direction toward a constructive Christian social ethic. This final chapter is concerned with the findings of this comparative analysis and their significance for the conception, character, and actualization of community.

The two thinkers' approaches to community (their emphases on the nature and role of the individual and society and their construals of ultimate reality) can serve as helpful resources in the explication and application of the principal elements involved in the conception, character, and actualization of community. These elements, or formative principles, include their common themes of *spirituality as a basis for social transformation, the relationship between love, justice and power, the nature and role of the church in the work of community, the nature and role of the state, and specifically, the distinctive role of black Americans and other historically rejected groups in the realization of community within the context of American society and the world.* In both, their respective points of departure and emphases combine to form constructive outlines for the achievement of human community.

Spirituality and Social Transformation

Both Thurman and King agreed that spirituality is the basis for social transformation, but the theme is more pronounced in Thurman's treatment of the individual and social responsibility. Thurman maintains that the movement from the inner experience of community within the self is the basis for social transformation. His understanding of the movement from the "inner" to the "outer" dimensions of religious experience has profound implications for spirituality and social change, and serves as a corrective to the tendency of one-dimensional theological discourse that exalts the social dynamics of community at the expense of the individual relationship between God and the self. Mozella Gordon Mitchell suggests that Thurman's contribution to black theology rests on his provision of an intellectual framework for a proper *sense of self* and *urge toward community*.[1] Thurman's shamanistic endeavor to lead the individual to the inner resources of being, which he described as "the hunger of the heart"[2] is a cogent reminder that the work for harmony and wholeness in the world cannot be accomplished without the cultivation of the inner life.

As Thurman's conception of community serves as a corrective to overemphasis on the social dimension of community building, King's view of community warns against the temptation to quietism and detachment, which is a chief criticism of Thurman's position.[3] By stressing the importance of maintaining a sense of self in the midst of a hostile society where privileges and prerogatives are granted on the basis of race and social status, Thurman's accentuation of the freedom of the individual is essential. Its shortcoming, however, lies in the absence of a viable social ethical foundation for calling society into accountability.[4]

Thurman's strong insistence on the immediacy of religious experience as an encounter between God and the individual could be interpreted as placing inordinate responsibility on the individual for the work of community in the world. Meanwhile, his relegation of the world to a secondary status in relation to the individual and God and his relative depreciation of institutions and social structures in his theocentric construal of reality, result in an ethical framework which comes perilously close, at points, to atomizing individuals within society. As illustrated later, this is not his intention. Thurman was an outspoken advocate of racial and social change within American society. The problem rests, however, in his theoretical formulation.

King's vision of community gives a more prominent place to the role of social institutions and structures in shaping the destiny of persons and social groups. This is a direct product of King's conception of community as a totality in which God, persons, and the world are integrally related as it is articulated in his sermon, "The Dimensions of a Complete Life." Also, King's understanding of the Kingdom of God allowed him to interpret theologically and ethically the nature of the responsible society and enabled him to fashion a more balanced view of the individual's relationship to society and society's relationship to the individual. Utilizing the Kingdom as a paradigmatic instrument in interpreting the relationship between individual and collective responsibility in the creation of a loving and just society, King wrote: "The Kingdom of God is neither the thesis of individual enterprise nor the antithesis of collective enterprise, but a synthesis which reconciles the truths of both."[5] The redemptive love of God, revealed in Jesus Christ, is King's answer to the possibility of achieving community or realizing the Kingdom within history. While he did not believe that human efforts alone could bring the Kingdom of God into realization, he strongly believed that the power of God, demonstrated in the cross and the resurrection of Christ, was the assurance that God would accomplish the divine and eternal purposes.[6]

Despite this difference in emphasis and ethical formulation, it is instructive to note how the two thinkers' complement each other in understanding the totality of interaction between the individual/persons, God, and the world. Thurman's point of departure is the individual and his/her relationship with God as *preparation* for the work of community in the world. The movement as such is from the inner to the outer mode of existence (or, in his words, from the "inner consciousness" to "world-mindedness"). Here the committed individual is highlighted as the key to social transformation. His conception of the committed individual has striking parallels with King's conception of the "transformed nonconformist."[7] Vincent Harding, a keen interpreter of the black American struggle and an equally astute student of both Thurman and King, offers this insightful commentary on the role of spirituality and social transformation in the quest for human community:

> Largely as a result of such grapplings with history, self, and community, I have felt a renewed urgency to emphasize the role of religion and spirituality in our freedom struggle. I have also

become increasingly dissatisfied with any analysis of the external forces opposing our liberation which sees only racism and capitalism at work in the world. Like others before me and around me, I have long sensed that these were necessary but insufficient definitions of the malaise that has grasped the white mainstream of America. Beneath such distortions of human community lies a deeper illness, a lack of attunement, a loss of sense of self, an unspoken fear. I have yet no satisfactory name for this ailment of the spirit, but I am now more certain than ever that it has been at work throughout the history of our black and white—and red—encounters in this land, and that there will be no hope for a truly just society on these shores until we address the issue of the human spirit and its role in our struggles for political transformation. (When Martin King first came among us speaking of the need to carry on a struggle for justice and truth that would 'redeem the soul of America,' many of us tended to smile patronizingly or to turn away in annoyed disbelief at such naivete. It appears to me now that we rather than he may well have been the innocents.)[8]

To King, there is a direct correlation between persons, God, and the world. The ideal city of humanity or community is the product of the cooperative venture between persons and God in relation to the world. The point of departure is social. Social transformation takes place in a cooperative network between God and persons. While the individual's commitment and development are important, the accent is on society's role and responsibility in the creation of community.

Both thinkers, however, ultimately stress an organic pluralism as the goal of community, but with different points of entry.[9] The language of both men suggests this distinction. Thurman's primary concern is always with the "creative individual," which is reflected in his appropriation of Cross's and Schreiner's thought and his personal inclination toward solitariness.[10] King, however, emphasizes the redemptive possibilities of the "creative minority."[11] Ultimately, Thurman's insistence on the individual's spiritual development as a prelude to creative social engagement is not in conflict with King's accentuation of the social nature of persons involved in the creation of community. Thurman's individualism is a product of his mystical orientation. He explains that while the basic ethical significance of mysticism is individualistic, the ascetic impulse of the mystic ultimately brings him or her to face with the society in which she or he functions as a person. The mystic, Thurman maintains

discovers that he is a person, and a personality in a profound sense can only be achieved in a milieu of human relations. *Personality is*

176

something more than mere individuality—it is a fulfillment of the logic of individuality in community.[12]

King's treatment of community follows the pattern of personalism. Muelder writes:

What personalism offers as a social philosophy is the hypothesis that community conceived normatively as rational love and as organic pluralism is consistent and coherent with the metaphysical actualization of the person.[13]

The discontinuities which exist between Thurman and King in respect to the individual and society, therefore, find "common ground" in their agreement that spirituality is the basis for social transformation and that the ultimate model of community is a type of organic pluralism which seeks unity in diversity and guards individuality in society. For both, the political framework that best represents this model is democratic idealism as represented in the Constitution of the United States and the Declaration of Independence. The discussion will return to this important observation in the latter part of the chapter.

Love, Justice, and Power

Thurman and King recommended love as the means for overcoming the barriers to community. Thurman concentrated on the power of love as a means of overcoming the internal barriers of deception, fear, and hate. King emphasized love in respect to social justice and the organization of power in the creation of a responsible society. King identified the major crisis of our times as the collision between immoral power and powerless morality. His resolution of the dialectic created by this crisis is rooted in his understanding of *agape*. This interpretation of *agape* is decidedly Christocentric. Muelder succinctly states that the central question for King in his quest for a method to eliminate social evil is "How was love as redemption related to just power? Is there a loving way to change unjust expressions of power and powerful embodiments of injustice?"[14] While this question was also a serious concern of Thurman's, King's struggle with "social evil" created a deeper need to understand the relationship of power, justice and love in social situations. Although Thurman recognizes the necessity of the just or equitable distribution of power in social relationships, his primary concern is with the individual's response to unjust political and economic arrangements, which is equally important in the quest for social justice.[15] King, on the other hand, concentrates on the political and economic nature of social existence and its relationship to love, justice, and power. Personal morality for King is weighed in the scales of one's commitment to social justice; the interior religious experience has meaning only in the external context of social relations which are based on *power*. James P. Hanigan makes a significant observation about King's social ethic:

> Faith for him had its realization or its truth in some new situation outside the subjective experience and attitudes of the individual believer. Whatever interior changes of attitude and affections this might require, faith demanded more than a new heart or a new attitude. It demanded a new situation, a new relationship that could be seen and evaluated. Truth was to be found in doing, and the only test of faith was the quality of the activity and of the actor.[16]

Again, it is important to note that King's and Thurman's respective treatments of love, justice, and power combine to create the basis for their common concern of overcoming barriers that militate against community. Thurman's insight into the problem of identity and the need to maintain a balance between one's self-fact (one's inherent worth and dignity as a child of God) and self-image (which is given by the social environment) are rooted in his belief that in the encounter with the Divine, one discovers the love of God as an experience which goes beyond good and evil. Therefore, in the Presence of God, one experiences wholeness, integration, and a profound sense of being ultimately secure despite the ravages and pronouncements of the surrounding culture. This fundamental conception, he argues, forms the background for a healthy sense of self and is the quintessence of social transformation and revolution. Referring to the Black Awareness movement of the late '60s and early '70s, Thurman says:

> I didn't have to wait for the revolution. I have never been in search for identity—and I think that (all) I've ever felt and worked on and believed in was founded in a kind of private, almost unconscious autonomy that did not seek vindication in my environment because it was in *me*.[17]

Thurman claims that once the individual understands that she or he is loved by God, that person is both empowered and required to become an agent of reconciliation in the world. Therefore, while King's accentuation of the social correlation of love, justice, and power is important, it is equally enlightening to reflect on the correlation of love, justice, and power in confronting the internal struggles to overcome the psychological forces which conspire against personal wholeness and communion. This is Thurman's invaluable contribution.

The Nature and the Role of the Church in Society

As with other important points of difference, Thurman's understanding of the church's role in society, ultimately, is not in conflict with King's. His emphasis, however, is on the need for the interior life of the individual to receive nourishment and direction through the spiritual resources of the church. He viewed the church as the place where "the individuals who were in the thick of the struggle for social change would be able to find renewal and fresh courage."[18] His experiments in worship in university settings, and most notably with the Fellowship Church, are examples of his emphasis. Also, his long-standing role as counselor to activists engaged in the struggle for creative social change is confirmation of this belief. On at least one occasion, even King was a beneficiary of this ministry.[19]

It can be argued that the experiences of community created by Thurman in his respective ministries in particular situations were accomplished by King at a greater social level through organization and mobilization of churches as institutions within American society. This is probably due, in part, to King's more traditional understanding of the Christocentric nature of the church, as opposed to Thurman's broader interpretation of the church as a fellowship which transcended different religious beliefs. Although the movement which King led was supported by other religions, it is doubtful whether he would have been able to organize the masses of black people, and many whites, if he had begun initially with the paradigm of inclusiveness utilized by Thurman. King's success as a leader was rooted in his unique embodiment of black folk culture and his supreme ability to articulate the religious idiom of the black church experience.[20] Thurman's appeal tended to be more universal and less adaptable to the particularity of black folk culture and religious life. This is not a criticism of Thurman, but a crucial observation.

Again, their understandings of the church need not be viewed as mutually exclusive, but represent two related dimensions of the church's mission in the actualization of human community: *the church as both a spiritual resource where experiences of unity occur* and *the church as moral custodian of society*. A creative synthesis of both views could provide the basis for an ecclesiastical model in which the pastoral and prophetic offices of the church are fulfilled in a balanced construct which holds in tension the care and nurture of the individual committed to social change and the role of the church as an institution involved in the moral issues of society. This is a major concern for thinkers such as Archie Smith, Jr., Edward and Anne Wimberly, and Cheryl Townsend Gilkes.[21]

The American Dream and Black Americans

It is no small wonder that out of the particularity of their oppressed status as black Americans, Thurman and King sought a universal vision of humanity which transcended the barriers of race, class, denominationalism, and other forms of sectarianism. This study has shown that for Thurman and King, the central, axiomatic questions underlying their visions of community were, *How does Christianity address the problem of American racism?* and *What is the most moral and practical method for overcoming racism in American society?* The other issues they raised, such as classism, war, and religious exclusiveness, have their origin in this initial problematic. To miss this fundamental concern in Thurman and King is to obscure the essential matter of their life-long projects. Certainly, the ideal of community was an evolutionary conception with which each wrestled in his respective empirical settings, but its origin and development cannot be divorced from these basic questions. Their early experiences of community and non-community in the Deep South, their later academic and intellectual quests, and the work of community to which they devoted themselves attest to their relentless searches for community within the American system dominated by racism and segregation.

Thurman and King provide the contemporary church with important answers to the two questions which informed their personal and intellectual quests for community. First, both thinkers called upon the American church not merely to redress its racist practices, but to repent. In fact, both claimed that the transformation of American society is inextricably bound to the transformation of American Christianity. The absence of community within the church, for Thurman and King, was a tell-tale commentary on the church's spiritual condition and its lack of moral authority in society. They claimed that the moral failure of the church is directly related to the demise of American democracy.[22]

Second, both agreed that the only moral and practical method to overcome the racism within American society is through nonviolent direct action. Thurman and King recommended that black Americans, because they are victims of the violence of racism in American society and because of their distinctive appropriation of Christian faith from their masters who had bastardized and disgraced the religion, stood in candidacy as redemptive sufferers for the soul of America. Both agreed that somehow experience and history had uniquely prepared black Americans for this sacred task.[23]

It is also important to note that King and Thurman were political reformists. For each, liberation and integration are inseparable and integrally related to the realization of the American dream. It should be underscored, however, that their respective loyalties to the principles inherent in American democracy did not prevent them from openly and critically denouncing the rampant hypocrisy and racist practices of their country. Indeed, these principles (integration and liberation), combined with the ethical insights of the Judeo- Christian tradition and the black American religious experience, formed the basis of their critique of American society. The recurring universal themes of the dignity and worth of human personality, the equality of human persons, and the concomitant freedom and responsibility in the former two are dominant themes in their writings, sermons, and addresses. Both thinkers believed that America not only had a responsibility to its citizens of color, but that America had a moral responsibility to the world. They felt that because of its vast national resources, its multi-ethnic, multi-cultural composition, God had called America to set an example for world community. Thurman and King, in this respect, are luminous exemplars of a long tradition in the black church experience which Peter Paris calls "the prophetic principle."[24]

It has been suggested that in some respects Thurman's and King's visions of America can be identified with themes in Robert N. Bellah's classic "transcendent universal religion of the nation," which interprets the American experience as being subject to blessing or judgment in light of ultimate and universal reality. In his celebrated article, "Civil Religion in America," Bellah stated:

> There actually exists alongside of and rather clearly differentiated from the churches an elaborate and well-institutionalized civil religion in America...(which) has its own seriousness and integrity and requires the same care and understanding that any other religion does.[25]

For Bellah, the sources of American Civil Religion are the writings and official documents of the founders of the republic. Among these are the Declaration of Independence and the Constitution. However, his understanding of the historical and mythic motifs of these sources goes beyond formal statements and national polity. His favorite and most often cited source is a sermon preached by John Winthrop, the first leader of the Massachusetts Bay Colony, on board ship in 1630 before landing in the New World. The sermon is entitled, "A Modell of Christian Charity."[26] Bellah argues that this sermon is an illustration of the "covenant" that was presented to the new settlers. This covenant between the Divine and the Puritans is a formula for divine blessing or judgment, dependent on the type of ethic the new society chose to embrace. The keeping of the covenant was predicated on the obedience of the settlers to *virtue* as opposed to *interest*, i.e., *caritas* versus *cupiditas*.[27] According to Bellah, this covenant was broken almost as soon as it was instituted.[28] Nevertheless, it was from such sources that the covenant idea sprang, an idea which serves as the *mythos* that informs American civil religion.[29]

Bellah speaks of three periods of trial in the American civil religion: the American Revolution, the Civil War, and the contemporary situation brought on by the turbulence of the sixties and early seventies. The Revolution was the period comparable to the biblical imagery of the Exodus, with Washington symbolizing the Moses of the nation. At this point, the Constitution and the Declaration of Independence became sacred scriptures. In the second period, the Civil War, Lincoln emerged as the savior of the nation during internal strife over slavery and political secession. The third and present crisis, for Bellah, presents a new challenge for American civil religion. In the other times of trial, new symbols, peculiar to the American people, were precipitated. Now the present situation entails the possibility of new international symbols and a new world civil religion which transcends nationhood and calls upon America to relinquish greed and power in the rest of the world. The actualization of this possibility, he contends, would actually strengthen America both morally and politically.

> Fortunately, since the American civil religion is not the worship of the American nation but an understanding of the American experience in the light of ultimate and universal reality, the reorganization entailed in such a new situation need not disrupt the American civil religion's continuity. A world civil religion would be accepted as a fulfillment and not a denial of American civil religion. Indeed such an outcome has been the eschatological hope of American civil religion from the beginning. To deny such an outcome would be to deny the meaning of America itself.[30]

While it would be highly inappropriate to characterize King and Thurman as "American civil religionists," at various places, they strike remarkably similar notes to Bellah's thesis. King, in particular, falls easily into the covenantal motif articulated by Bellah, but gives it an important twist in relation to the problem of race within the American ethos.[31] As stated earlier, in his early development as a civil rights leader, the American dream for King was centered on enfranchisement of the American Negro, desegregation and integration through legislation, and the economic empowerment of black people.[32] During his latter years after he had received the Nobel Peace Prize, there was an increased realization of the international implications of the American dream.[33] King's constant references to the Declaration of Independence, the Constitution, and the Emancipation Proclamation and the moral failure of America as a nation and world power are pervasive in his writings and sermons. "King did not support and affirm the bland American dream of comfortable living and material prosperity," writes Cornel West. "Rather, he put forward his own dream – grounded and refined in the black church experience, supplemented by liberal Christianity, and implemented by Ghandian methods of nonviolent resistance – rooted in the American ideals of democracy, freedom, and equity."[34]

There are also definite indicators in Thurman's perspective which parallel the interpretation of covenant enunciated in Bellah. Thurman perceived America as an experiment in the Mind of God to create the climate and opportunity for the actualization of human community. He maintained that the sovereign purposes of God are manifested in the coming together of various races and ethnic groups in one place at a particular time in history to create a new nation. How the various groups arrived in America (i.e., by slavery, conquest, or other means), while significant, is not the most important question for Thurman. In fact, through the human atrocities and errors committed in the enslavement and oppression of black people, the occasion is created for the redemptive possibilities of love.[35] However, Thurman, like King, is concerned primarily with the problem of racism as an obstacle to the realization of the American dream.[36]

For Thurman, the Declaration of Independence, the Constitution, and the Emancipation Proclamation are also the pivotal documents of the American experience which insure freedom for the individual under God and remind America of its role as steward of the great ideal of democracy.[37] In an eloquent and revealing statement, Thurman outlines his vision of the United States of America as a metaphysical and religious manifestation of the sovereign purposes of the Divine Spirit actualizing itself in human history and pointing the way to human community:

> It is my conviction that our nation is involved in the far-flung purpose of God to establish a world community of friendly men living beneath a friendly sky. Think of our startling history at this point just for a moment! It is not chauvinistic to affirm that our total life as a nation has been a schooling in the meaning of human freedom against a time when the only thing that serves the collective life of man is a dynamic faith in the worth of the individual and the freedom which it inspires. Our national life was launched in a revolution against tyranny with its corresponding assertion of human dignity. Our emergence as a nation is a judgment against all dictatorships. From the beginning we have been made up of the widest variety of peoples from the ends of the earth. Our roots go deep in the various cultures, faiths and

heritages of the peoples of this planet. For a long time interval we were isolated by two oceans, and in this isolation we were tutored by a political, social, and religious ideal which placed the premium supreme upon the inherent worth and dignity of persons. Our response as a nation to this tutoring was to inscribe these ideals in the formal arrangements by which we pledged ourselves under God to undertake our social adventure. We were blessed with the kind of climate and the abundance of natural resources which contributed deeply to our individual and our collective emotional security—all this social development against a time when the human race would be faced with a mass crisis created by the almost sudden emergence of vast power over nature that both time and space are canceled out, and for the first time in human history, men, wherever they are on the planet, are, as if they were next door neighbors. The world is a neighborhood, but there is no confidence in the integrity of the neighborliness. For more than a century, we, as token representatives of the many peoples of the earth, have been in school, learning the meaning of human dignity and the responsibility of the freedom which it inspires. Our fatal responsibility before God is to provide the inspiration for the confidence in the possibilities of a way of life on this planet in which no man need to (be) afraid and in which 'the bruised reed will not be crushed or the smoking flax quenched!' No strength of arms, no might of material wealth can qualify our nation for such a role. This possibility of a life of freedom under God is the crown that He holds steadily over our heads with the hope that as a nation we may grow tall enough to wear it.[38]

This lengthy quotation captures the essence of Thurman's understanding of the nature and role of America in world history and what he perceives as a divinely sanctioned mission. During his latter years, Thurman again articulated this view of America in a speech entitled, "America in Search of a Soul."[39] Here he refers to Lincoln's famous Gettysburg Address as a source which outlines the conception of the "new nation" entrusted with the moral responsibility of realizing the democratic ideal in the world with other nations. He also underscores the significance of the inherent worth and dignity of the individual and the freedom and responsibility which a democratic political arrangement insures. In this speech, however, Thurman suggests that perhaps "school is out" for America, referring to the bombings of Hiroshima and Nagasaki and the potential for nuclear devastation wrought by the creation of the atomic bomb. There is a strikingly similar theme in King where he reminds America of its moral responsibility to the poor and other nations of the world, and finally warns the nation that this particular moment in history may be the last chance for humanity to choose between chaos and community.[40] Bellah sounds a similar alarm and calls for a national year of mourning and repentance for the American bicentennial.[41]

Despite their apparent disenchantment with the failure of America as a moral leader among other nations, nonetheless, in Thurman and King, there is an eschatological hope of community which informs their vision of America and its mission to the world. During the latter years of King's life and ministry, he analyzed the difficulties and tensions within and outside of the Civil Rights Movement and identified "the temptation to despair" as being bound to the realization of the deep entrenchment and interrelatedness of the three evils of racism, poverty, and militarism. He also argued that the national policy of discrimination against ethnic minorities and the poor was related to the nation's foreign policy as illustrated in the Vietnam War.[42] Nevertheless, King believed that the international liberation movements arising from the oppressed were a sign of hope for the future of America and humankind. In his last speech, King, while recognizing the pessimistic state of the nation and the world, raised the element of hope for this particular period of history and America's role in it:

> But I know, somehow, that only when it is dark enough, can you see the stars. And I see God working in this period in the twentieth century in a way that men, in some strange way, are responding— something is happening in our world. The masses of people are rising up. And wherever they are assembling today, whether in Johannesburg, South Africa; Nairobi, Kenya; Accra, Ghana; New York City; Atlanta, Georgia; Jackson, Mississippi; or Memphis, Tennessee—the cry is the same—'We want to be free.'[43]

In Thurman's last formal treatise on community within American society, he concludes on a positive note regarding the realization of the American dream. Referring to the crisis within American society, Thurman felt that "the present solution is a stopgap, a halt in the line of march toward full community or, at most, a time of bivouac on a promontory overlooking the entire landscape of American society."[44] In a voice of prophecy, Thurman envisions another creative moment for America when one in the likeness of Martin Luther King, Jr. will come forth bearing the dream of community.[45] For both, therefore, the eschatological hope for America and the world is bound to the struggle of oppressed peoples.

This eschatological hope for America is also a prominent theme in Bellah. As stated, Bellah sees the possibility of the emergence of a world civil religion out of the third time of crisis in America.[46] The denial of such an outcome, however, is the argument of John T. Watts.[47] Watts contends that Bellah's imaginative theory of eschatological hope is idealistic and that it forces an interpretation on American history that is foreign. John Cartwright's criticism of Bellah's transcendent universal religion of the nation is similar. He writes, "Seeking to be normative, it moves so far away from the distinctive American experience that it becomes rather abstract."[48]

Watts argues that the historical personages whom Bellah acknowledges as significant authorities in the development of American civil religion, such as John Winthrop, Benjamin Franklin, Thomas Jefferson, George Washington, and Abraham Lincoln, adhered tenaciously to an exclusivistic "we-they" syndrome which was fundamentally opposed to alien symbols from the beginning. Charles H. Long raises this issue as a methodological concern.[49] Long's criticism is that at the core of American civil religion is a language that is oppressive to non-Europeans, notably black and native Americans, because it ignores their reality, and hence renders them invisible. This language, according to Long, is also repressive in that it hides from social consciousness the European mentality of conquest and exploitation, which too is an integral and vital component of civil religion.

> All interpretations of American religion, whether from the point of view of the revealed tradition or the civil tradition, have been involved with a subjective concealment of the inner dynamics of their own religious-cultural psychic reality and correlative repression and concealment of the reality of the other. This procedure has been undertaken to give American reality a normative and centered mode of interpretation.[50]

Long calls for a new hermeneutic, a reinterpretation of American history, which includes the presence of non-Europeans, and ultimately for a transformation of American consciousness and society. Bellah makes similar recommendations.[51]

Thurman and King make several important contributions which merit further research and closer examination in the American civil religion debate and in understanding the role of religion in the transformation of American society. Thurman's and King's analyses and recommendations for "saving the soul of America" can be helpful in laying the foundations for the "new hermeneutic" called for by Long, and may well be the direction needed for the inculcation of a new moral tone within American culture.

First, Thurman's and King's diagnoses of the malady afflicting the American psyche (and consequently, American civil religion) overcome the tendency towards abstraction, which is a chief criticism of Bellah and other Euro- Western interpreters of American religion and culture. Both not only point to the xenophobic tendency inherent in the American consciousness, but also offer concrete analyses of the dilemma created by the tragic struggle between American democratic idealism and its antithetical twin, racism.[52]

Second, Thurman's and King's respective proposals warrant further discussion in relation to what Bellah et al have termed the recovery of the biblical and republican strands of American culture.[53] Thurman's insistence on the internal cultivation of spirituality as a prelude to social transformation and King's accentuation of the social responsibility of the nation could provide the outline of a creative model for the role of religion as a source of "civic virtue" in the reconstruction of American society.[54] Such a model is needed to address what the writers of *Habits of the Heart* call "the most important unresolved problem in American history," the tension which exists between "self-reliant competitive enterprise and a sense of public solidarity expressed by civic republicans." According to the authors:

> Americans have sought in the ideal of community a shared trust to anchor and complete the desire for a free and fulfilled self. This quest finds its public analogue in the desire to integrate economic pursuits and interrelationships in an encompassing fabric of national institutional life. American culture has long been marked by acute ambivalence about the meshing of self-reliance and community, and the nation's history shows a similar ambivalence over the questions of how to combine individual autonomy and the interrelationships of a complex modern economy.[55]

Both Thurman and King argue that within the religious and cultural lives of rejected groups in American society lies the basis for social transformation and the creation of world community. King's vision of America and the relation of black Americans to its realization have already been discussed. It is sufficient to add that until the end of his short career, King maintained the belief that authentic community would come to America through the redemptive struggles of black Americans and others who dared to follow their glorious example.[56] The 1984 and 1988 presidential campaigns of Jesse Jackson are a part of this legacy. Thurman maintained that the dichotomous scenario of "outsiders" living in the midst of "insiders" is perhaps the greatest threat to American democratic values. A reinterpretation of "the role of minorities in the modern state is crucial not only for the state as a community among world states, but also for the experience of community on the part of minorities themselves."[57] Thurman thought it not unreasonable to infer from the biblical narrative and the republican strand of the democratic ideal that the oppressed and rejected should lead the way to redemption. This, for him, is particularly applicable in regards to the American destiny.[58]

By virtue of their conceptions and recommendations, Thurman and King represent two distinct yet related approaches to the problem of community. Their proposals for human community should not be viewed as ultimately conflicting, but as complementary. Although their respective approaches differed at important places, the urgent need and mandate for human community was the common goal and labor of their lives. Both insisted that the goal of human community was not merely a utopian ideal, but the very destiny of the human family. They argued that because of the advances in scientific technology, once distant cultures and nations have now become an international neighborhood with fundamental structures of interdependability and interrelatedness. Therefore, human community and international cooperation are no longer options, but vital necessities for continued existence on the planet. Thurman reflected on this common sense of mission between himself and King:

> Perhaps the ultimate demand laid upon the human spirit is the responsibility to select *where* one bears witness to the Truth of his spirit. The final expression of the committed spirit is to affirm: I choose! and to abide. I felt myself a fellow pilgrim with him and with all the host of those who dreamed his dream and shared his vision.[59]

This study has been a comparative analysis of the ideal of community in the lives and thoughts of Howard Thurman and Martin Luther King, Jr. The purpose of this study was to demonstrate how these two thinkers contributed to the religious and moral formulations of human community. In both, there are major continuities and discontinuities which have significant implications for the conception, character, and actualization of community.

It has been suggested that the two thinkers' approaches to community, i.e., their respective emphases on the nature and role of the individual and society and their construals of ultimate reality, can serve as resources for the explication of the principal elements involved in the creation of community. These formative principles include their common themes of spirituality as a basis for social transformation; the relationship between love, justice, and power; the nature and role of the church and religion in the work of community; the nature and role of the state, and specifically, the unique role of black Americans and other historically rejected groups in the realization of community within the context of American society and the world. Thurman and King, in many ways, represent the best in the American dream. Their views of integration and liberation within American society and the method they upheld as the only moral and practical one available to the men and women of conscience are, at once, a critique of American society and a distant goal to which the nation is called.

Finally, and of particular importance for this examination, has been the fact that these two pastors and social prophets were black Americans whose understandings of community were rooted in their personal searches to find the most moral and practical method to overcome the barrier of racism in American society. It is of no small consequence that out of their own oppression they searched for a universal human fellowship which transcended the artificial barriers of race, class, and religious exclusiveness. This study makes clear that these two faithful pilgrims were looking for a city which has foundations, whose builder and maker is God.

Epilogue

It was my good fortune to have known Dr. Martin Luther King, Jr. and Dr. Howard Thurman rather well. Therefore I have followed with special interest the research Professor Fluker has been doing on the thought of the two men in relation to the concept of community. I consider it an honor to have been invited to do this epilogue.

Martin Luther King, Jr.

One approaches the task of lifting up special insights from the thought of these two great men with a degree of reluctance. However, let me offer some suggestions. Here are lessons that to me stand out in Dr. King's life.

He had the ability and courage to deliver the gospel of truth and justice with such clarity and passion that the ordinary person could understand it. He was a gifted communicator of the Word at a critical time in the history of our nation. Crowds heard him gladly.

He described injustice and social inequities as being in radical conflict with the heart of the Christian faith which he defined as "the courage to love." And he designated the contradictions and disorders in society which result in maimed, broken, and defeated lives as sin. Once again, he gave us the opportunity in our day to see the epitome of the Christian community in the form of the crowds that followed him in Montgomery, Selma, Chicago, Memphis, etc., and who sat at his feet in Washington, D.C. They were people of all colors and religious affiliations, the physically weak and strong, different cultures and backgrounds, great and small, differing in ages, economic standings and educational achievement, all concerned to some degree about a common pursuit, the cause of justice. When the Christian community arrives as an historic reality, this is the mix of which it will be made. This is a part of the King bequest to our world.

When I was twelve years old I became a member of Ebenezer Baptist Church here in Atlanta and as a boy I was active in the life of the church until I was graduated from Morehouse College. During this time my father was a deacon and clerk of the church. For most of my years in the church Reverend A. D. Williams was pastor of Ebenezer. The Reverend M.L. King, Sr. was a college classmate of mine, and M.L. Jr. (as he was fondly called) was born January 15, 1929 in my junior year in college. He was born into a very favorable family setting consisting of both parents, loving grandparents, and a wide circle of uncles, aunts, and cousins on both sides. Moreover, the families maintained close relationships. It is clear that M. L. Jr.'s growing up and maturing were strongly influenced and directed by participating in the life of a large immediate family as well as the attention and love of members of the church family. It occurs to me also that in this setting one finds the seed bed for the cultivation of much of M. L.'s early thought life.

Mrs. Alberta King, Dr. King's mother, received a college education and lived with her parents, the Reverend and Mrs. A. D. Williams, who managed a lower middle class style of living. She had not suffered for want of any of life's necessities. She had experienced loving concern within the family, and when M. L. Jr. appeared, he inherited the same love and concern. Throughout his adult and married life he did not lack attention. It seems to me, therefore, there was ingrained in his approach to life a species of optimism. It is not that he did not later experience some of life's brutal and unjust treatment. In his writings he recognized unmistakably the negative components of existence. In spite of this, he paid a heavy tribute to the human spirit's capability to deliver in daily life situations that toughness of mind, and that forgiving attitude prompted by love of Jesus Christ which in the end would produce the Beloved Community here on earth.

Mrs. Jennie C. Williams, wife of the Reverend A. D. Williams, frequently invited me home to have Sunday dinner with the family. She was a first–class cook and I enjoyed the meals and also the family table conversation. During his college years, the Reverend M. L. King, Sr. was called to be the pastor of a local church. The Williams' daughter, Alberta, found herself being greatly attracted by Reverend King's preaching, and occasionally I would be asked to accompany her to his church or to another local church where he was to be guest preacher. As time passed such visits became more significant until they led to the marriage of these two, a marriage, though unknown at the time, laden with great joy, peril, and pathos.

Let me record here that Alberta's father, the Reverend Williams, was a genuine friend of young ministers and in numerous ways helped many of them during his long ministry. It was in my first year of study in the Oberlin Graduate School of Theology that I received a long letter from him telling me of happenings at Ebenezer, congratulating me, and wishing me good success in the ministry. This readiness to be helpful to young men in the ministry was passed on as a heritage to the Reverend M. L. King, Sr., and his two sons in the ministry. It was my good fortune to have had the opportunity to maintain a similar relationship with young Martin during his doctoral studies at Boston University.

One event occurred in the relationship between Dr. King, Jr. and my family which will be for me a lasting memory. It was an instance in which the minister's compassionate spirit was demonstrated. After long years of membership and service in Ebenezer Baptist Church, my father died on July 1, 1967. At the time, Dr. King, Jr. was the co-pastor of the church. On the day the funeral service for my father was set, Dr. King had an appointment to be out of the city and had an airplane reservation, but he was gracious enough to alter his travel plans in order that he could be in the church to deliver the eulogy at the funeral service for my father. It was a tribute paid both to my father and my family.

Howard Thurman

This statement about Dr. Thurman is made in full recognition of the fact that no single statement can gather up adequately the several streams of influences that have flowed from his life and work and impacted in some way the life of our times. Thurman was an uncommon thinker, a man who thoroughly enjoyed playing with ideas, a man who thrived on allowing his mind to roam in places seldom travelled. His writings give ample evidence of his skill in fashioning the apt phrase with which to clothe the ideas his mind had discovered. He was a creative spirit; he meditated both day and night, and like a tree planted by the rivers of the water, he brought forth bountiful fruit in his season.

Howard Thurman was also a superb counselor, whose informal counseling was done from the perspective of a God-centered life. In his counseling sessions one could see aspects of the man's life which were not obvious from the pulpit or speaker's platform. A host of persons of a diversity of callings and endeavors has been enriched by patient and wise words that have fallen from the lips of this man.

Howard Thurman was one of the truly great preachers of our times. He never achieved the popularity which has come to a number of ministers today. But in Thurman there always was a genuine effort to know the truth before proclaiming it. One was aware that in him the medium and the message were united. His interpretation of the Gospel was in the tradition of the great Hebrew prophets, Jesus, and other great Teachers of the spirit. "If one is moved from within one's own spirit to do the deed of ministering to the need of another, and if the need of another is the point at which the spirit is most highly sensitized to communication, then it follows that the good deed is a meeting place for the mingling of one life with another," so Thurman wrote. And this is the point at which his vision of community emerges.

Dr. Thurman's long and fruitful life began much earlier and lasted longer than Dr. M. L. King, Jr.'s brief years. This means that he was able to draw upon an ever widening body of experience in the process of developing and examining his own thought and structure. Growing up as he did in the Waycross neighborhood of Daytona Beach, Florida, Dr. Thurman lived in a friendly extended family, but he was not favored as Dr. King was to grow up with the strong support of a large immediate family. For

193

him life showed its tough side early. At a relatively tender age, he was introduced to life's woes. The achievement of a high school and college education resulted in a full initiation into a life of struggle.

By the time Howard Thurman entered college, he had already begun to sharpen his intellectual appetite and to confront life with profound questions. After he had completed his course of study at Rochester Theological Seminary in Rochester, New York, a two–year pastoral experience in Oberlin, Ohio, and a year of study with Professor Rufus Jones at Haverford, Dr. Thurman was invited to serve on the faculties of Morehouse and Spelman Colleges. It was during my senior year at Morehouse that I enrolled in a course taught by him in the second semester of that year. It was a course of study based principally on the Gospel of John, with some attention given to the Johannine tradition. Oh, how I wish I had today the notes taken in that class! His interpretations were penetrating and he had such a dramatic way of giving expression to them. But it was during his ministry at the Fellowship Church For All Peoples, in San Francisco, and Boston University that his reputation as a writer was clearly established.

In Fellowship Church, where in my judgment his career reached its peak, Dr. Thurman sought to test and refine his approaches to be used in his effort to get men and women as individuals to internalize the church, to add new dimensions to their spirituality. This spirituality takes concrete form in its performance of deeds in history. As a pastor, Dr. Thurman was aware often, no doubt, of the role of the church as an agent of social change and approved it. Yes, and he just as surely recognized the need of individuals who out of the enriched spirituality of their personal lives were creative spirits prompting and enabling the church and other social institutions to affirm their faith in people expressing a concern about people and a just society in which people can live in peace and harmony. The steady and deep enrichment of personal spirituality was a profound concern of Dr. Thurman's ministry and life to the end.

During my two and a half years in the Bay area, I spent the week days in Berkeley working toward the doctorate degree and my Sundays in San Francisco at Fellowship Church and in the home of the Thurmans. I was operating on a short budget, so Dr. and Mrs. Sue Bailey Thurman made a room available to me at all times and provided food aplenty without charge. Both were excellent culinary artists; but Dr. Thurman was the boaster. They were indeed my family away from home, and this I cannot forget. Believe it or not, there was frequent bantering in the home involving the parents and two daughters which I could rarely escape. There were times when Dr. Thurman allowed me to be his companion on short trips when he was a guest speaker somewhere to a small or large group. Through him I came to know and to make some fine friendships in and out of Fellowship Church. At times there was outside traffic in the home, but

Mrs. Thurman directed it with a gentle touch. Generally, the Thurman home was a nest, a quiet place where a person could settle down and be at peace with nature, people and God.

At the theological level, there is much kinship between Dr. King and Dr. Thurman. Both were Christian ministers; they believed in God. Both accepted the Christian estimate of Jesus as the key to a full and necessary understanding of God and of his love for the world and all humankind. Both saw the kingdom of God as a communal expression of the love which was fully revealed in the life and mission of Jesus. A point of difference here rests in the fact that Dr. Thurman reached forward eagerly to this God–like love in prophetic spirits other than Jesus and in forms of religious worship and expression other than the strictly Christian forms. In all of these, however, he saw the hand of God seeking to pull humankind in all of its rich variety, dreams and failures, hopes and fears, into a vital and peaceful harmony. It is obvious, I think, that Dr. Thurman reaches beyond the traditional view of Christology. And yet, it seems to me, we can be grateful that in his thinking he was led by the Spirit to provide a broader base upon which the Good Society can come into existence. It should be added that in his writing, Howard Thurman goes to great lengths to explicate the nature and quality of that love which is to be the substance uniting all humankind into a community of brothers and sisters, shining through all relationships.

Dr. Melvin H. Watson
Professor Emeritus,
Morehouse College
Atlanta, Georgia
1988

Notes

Introduction

1. Thurman writes, "...a strange necessity has been laid upon me to devote my life to the central concern that transcends the walls that divide and would achieve in literal fact what is experienced as literal truth: human life is one and all men are members of one another. And this insight is spiritual and it is at the hard core of religious experience." Howard Thurman, *The Luminous Darkness: A Personal Interpretation of the Anatomy of Segregation and the Ground of Hope* (New York: Harper and Row, 1965), p. x. King comments, "In a real sense, all life is interrelated. All men are caught in an inescapable network of mutuality, tied in a single garment of destiny. Whatever affects one directly affects all indirectly. I can never be what I ought to be until you are what you ought to be. This is the interrelated structure of reality." Martin Luther King, Jr., *Strength to Love* (Philadelphia: Fortress Press, 1981), p. 70.

2. See Luther E. Smith, *The Mystic as Prophet* (Washington, D.C.: University Press of America, 1981), pp. 118-19; Ricardo A. Millett, ed., "Simmering on the Calm Presence and Profound Wisdom of Howard Thurman" *Debate and Understanding*, Special Edition (Spring 1982): 71-90; Henry J. Young, ed., *God and Human Freedom: A Festschrift in Honor of Howard Thurman* (Richmond, IN: Friends United Press, 1983), pp. xiii-xix.

    Several writers have made reference to the influence of Howard Thurman on his younger fellow visionary, but no scholarly treatment has demonstrated a *formal* tie between the two. The writer has also conducted a search for a formal connection between the two without success. This research consisted of interviews with both of their widows, a review of the King and Thurman collections at the Mugar Library, Boston University, the Thurman materials at the Howard Thurman Educational Trust Fund in San Francisco, and the archives at the Martin Luther King, Jr. Center for Nonviolent Social Change, Atlanta, GA. See also John Ansbro, *The Making of a Mind* (Maryknoll: Orbis Books, 1982), pp. 27-29, 272; Lerone Bennett, *What Manner of Man*, 2nd rev. ed. (Chicago: Johnson Publishing Co., 1976), pp. 74-75; "Dr. King Mentor Remembered," *Boston Globe*, 15 January 1982, pp. 13-14. The influence of Thurman on King's conception of community is suggested by Lewis V. Baldwin in an article entitled, "Understanding Martin Luther King, Jr. within the Context of Southern Black Religious History," *Journal of Religious Studies* 13:2, (Fall,

1987): 19; see also Lewis V. Baldwin, "Martin Luther King,the Black Church and the Black Messianic Vision," *The Journal of the Interdenominational Theological Center* 12:1-2 (Fall 1984/Spring 1985):1; and Larry Murphy, "Howard Thurman and Social Activism," in *God and Human Freedom*, pp. 154-55.

The influence of Thurman on King seems to be that of a counselor concerned primarily with the younger man's spiritual life and emotional well-being. Perhaps Thurman's own accounting of the nature of their relationship is sufficient. Thurman relates only two specific instances of meeting with King: one, in the informal setting of his Boston home, while King was a Ph.D. candidate, and the other, after the tragic stabbing of King in Harlem. Neither meeting seems to indicate any substantive exchange on philosophies of thought and action. See Howard Thurman, *With Head and Heart: The Autobiography of Howard Thurman* (New York: Harcourt, Brace, Jovanovich, 1979), pp. 254-55; At another place, Thurman comments, "I am one of a few and maybe the only person who was a member of the faculty of the Graduate School of Theology at Boston University when Dr. King took his doctorate degree who did not have him in the classroom. I think that's a mark of distinction. We had contacts, but our most primary contact was sitting around my television watching the World Series...I've known him and his family, his mother and his father for many years. And Mrs. Thurman's and my relationship to those two young people [Martin and Coretta King] was a personal and primary one. It was not involved in the light and the drama. My concern was about the state of his spiritual life all the time. And I felt it was my relationship with him that gave me this right to do it, while Mrs. Thurman's interest was always in the little things involving the children and the wife of a man who had to live so much of his private life in public. And this is a great agony. I understand from one of his biographers that a book that I wrote in 1949 was very influential on his thinking: *Jesus and the Disinherited*. But I did not hear this from him and I do not make a claim to it; but lest someone may know that it is in this biographical statement you will think that I am trying to be falsely modest by not mentioning it; so I've done it and now I can go on with my work." Thurman, "Litany and Words in Memoriam for Martin Luther King, Jr.," Fellowship Church, San Francisco, 7 April 1968. Such modesty, however, was characteristic of Thurman's style and temperment. It is difficult to believe that in their encounters, there was not a level of discourse which carried over into recommendations regarding specific items relative to the black struggle for liberation. For one example, see their correspondence in which

Thurman offers his counsel after the incident of the Harlem stabbing, "Howard Thurman to Martin Luther King, Jr.," 20 October 1958, and "Martin Luther King, Jr. to Howard Thurman," 8 November 1958. King Papers, Special Collections, Mugar Memorial Library, Boston University.

3.   Few studies to date have given significant attention to the impact of the black experience on either of these thinkers. For Thurman, Smith's work, *The Mystic as Prophet*, comes closest to treating this dimension. See also Irving S. Moxley, "An Examination of the Mysticism of Howard Thurman and Its Relevance to Black Liberation" (Ph.D. dissertation, Louisville Presbyterian Theological Seminary, 1974). Neither Ansbro nor Smith and Zepp, in their treatments of the intellectual sources of King's thought, give any serious attention to the role of the black church and its impact upon King. See Kenneth L. Smith and Ira G. Zepp, Jr., *Search for the Beloved Community: The Thinking of Martin Luther King, Jr.* (Valley Forge: Judson Press, 1974); see James H. Cone, "Martin Luther King, Jr., Black Theology—Black Church," *Theology Today* (January 1984): 409-20; Paul R. Garber, "King Was a Black Theologian," *Journal of Religious Thought* 31 (Fall-Winter): 16-32; William D. Watley's treatment of the relationship between the black religious experience, evangelical liberalism, and personalism and their impact upon the thinking of King is the most serious treatment to date on this important aspect of his intellectual development. See William D. Watley, *Roots of Resistance: The Nonviolent Ethic of Martin Luther King, Jr.* (Valley Forge: Judson Press, 1985), pp. 17-45. Katie G. Cannon is the only scholar who has offered a comparative analysis of the two thinkers' conceptions of community. While Cannon's brief and enlightening correlation of their views of community with the thought of Zora Neale Hurston has as its basic concern the construction of a black womanist ethic, it is an excellent resource for the purposes of this study. *Black Womanist Ethics* (American Academy of Religion Series No. 6 Atlanta: Scholars Press, 1988), pp. 168-174.

4.   Raymond Plant, *Community and Ideology: An Essay in Applied Philosophy* (London, Boston: Routledge and Kegan Paul, 1974), p. 8.

5.   In order to speak meaningfully about "community," given the varieties of experiences to which it refers, it is helpful to understand that it is both a *descriptive* and *prescriptive* term. It is both *empirical* and *normative*. It has to do with *fact* and *value*. David W. Minar and Scott Greer offer this definition:"Community is both empirically descriptive of a social structure and normatively toned. It refers both to the unit of a society as it is and to the aspects of the unit that are valued

if they exist, desired in their absence." Comp., *The Concept of Community: Readings With Interpretation* (Chicago: Aldine, 1969), p. ix. While such a sociological definition is instructive, still it is susceptible to ideological bias, i.e., it varies according to the ideological position of the definer and ultimately raises questions regarding perspectival and methodological issues relative to the term. See Plant, p. 12 and Richard P. Hiskes, *Community Without Coercion: Getting Along With the Minimal State* (Newark, NJ: University of Delaware Press, 1982); Steven Lukes, *Individualism* (New York: Harper Torchbooks, Harper and Row, 1973); and Stanley Hauerwas, *A Community of Character: Toward A Constructive Christian Social Ethic* (Notre Dame, IN: University of Notre Dame Press, 1981). Other significant issues related to the normative and descriptive meanings of community include the central question, "What is it that is shared or held in common in communal relation?" (Hiskes, p. 23.) This question entails a variety of complex and conflicting claims which plague contemporary ethical discourse. Looming large in the foreground of this serious debate are the questions of authority, rules, and justice. What is the degree of authority necessary in community? Related to the question of authority are the questions of who makes the rules, who enforces the law, and what is a just law? How are conflicts between the law of the community and individual perspectives of morality resolved? The issues of entitlement, rectification, and desert are other variables which figure prominently in the contemporary socio-political scheme of justice and equity. Robert Nozick, *Anarchy, State, and Utopia* (NY: Basic Books, 1974) and John Rawls, *A Theory of Justice* (Cambridge: The Belknap Press of Harvard University Press, 1971) are examples of these concerns. The latter issue of "desert," however, is camoflaged behind a mirage of presuppositions left over from the failed Enlightment Project discussed in Alasdair MacIntyre's *After Virtue* (South Bend, IN: University of Notre Dame Press, 1984), pp. 244-255.

6.   James E. Blackwell, *The Black Community: Diversity and Unity* (New York: Dodd, Mead, and Co., 1975), p. xi.

7.   Ibid., p. 5. Blackwell's definition should be understood within the broader context of "the lingering memory" of "African tribalism" in "the minds of American slaves." This sense of history and connectedness with the past, according to Sterling Stuckey, "enabled them to go back to a sense of community in the traditional African setting and to include all Africans in their common experience of oppression in North America." See Sterling Stuckey, *Slave Culture: Nationalist Theory and the Foundations of Black America* (New York: Oxford University Press, 1987), p. 3. Here Stuckey suggests that "slave ships

were the first real incubators of slave unity across cultural lines, cruelly revealing irreducible links from one ethnic group to the other, fostering resistance thousands of miles before the shores of the new land appeared on the horizon—before there was mention of natural rights in North America." See also Vincent Harding, *There Is A River: The Black Struggle for Freedom in America* (New York and London: Harcourt Brace Jovanovich, Publishers, 1981), Chap. 1, "From The Shores of Africa," pp. 3-23.

8. H.B. Acton, "Idealism," in *The Encyclopedia of Philosophy*, vol. 3. Edited by Paul Edwards (New York: Macmillan Publishing Co., Inc., and The Free Press, 1967), pp. 111-14.

9. Cornel West, "The Prophetic Tradition in Afro-America," in *Prophetic Fragments* (Grand Rapids, Michigan: Eerdmans Publishing Co. and Trenton, New Jersey: African World Press, 1988), p. 41.

10. See Frank G. Kirkpatrick, *Community: A Trinity of Models* (Washington, D.C.: Georgetown University Press), p. 2.

Chapter 1

1. Millet, ed., *Debate and Understanding*, p. 83.
2. Ibid.
3. Bennett, *What Manner of Man*, pp. 74-75.
4. Muriel Bullard, *The Church For the Fellowship For All People* (San Francisco, CA). Interview, 11 August 1982.
5. Millet, ed., *Debate and Understanding*, p. 5.
6. Introduction, Howard Thurman, *For the Inward Journey: The Writings of Howard Thurman*. Selected by Anne Spencer Thurman (New York: Harcourt, Brace Jovanovich, 1984), p. xiv.
7. Mozella Gordon Mitchell states, "I see Thurman as having subconsciously mythologized his entire life and become the hero of an epic journey of which God is the author. But he himself is the co-author and interpreter of the religious experience he undergoes." *Spiritual Dynamics of Howard Thurman's Theology* (Bristol, Indiana: Wyndham Hall Press, 1985), p. 51.
8. Thurman had two sisters: Henrietta, the eldest, and a younger sister, Madeline. In reference to Thurman's affinity with nature, he says in his autobiography, "When I was young, I found more companionship in nature than I did among people." Thurman, *With Head and Heart*, p. 7. See also Lerone Bennett, Jr., "Howard Thurman: Twentieth Century Holy Man," *Ebony* (February 1978): 76. Bennett describes Thurman as a "loner, a brooder, a sensitive suffering spirit who sought solace in the woods and on deserted beaches and

communicated with forces that are not visible and audible to other mortals."

9. *The Life and Thought of Howard Thurman*, A Documentary Film in Two Parts. The British Broadcasting Company, 1976.

10. In speaking of the assurance and immunity which his friends from nature offered, Thurman said, "I felt rooted in life, in nature, in existence." Thurman, *With Head and Heart*, p. 8.

11. Howard Thurman, "Windbreak Against Existence," *Bostonia* 34:2 (Fall 1960): 8.

12. Thurman, *With Head and Heart*, p. 6.

13. Thurman, "Windbreak Against Existence," pp. 7-8.

14. Thurman, *With Head and Heart*, p. 12.

15. Years later, Thurman remarked that his mother worked so hard to support the family that she actually forgot the correct date of his birth. BBC documentary film.

16. Unpublished manuscript, concluding chapter, *With Head and Heart*, p. 6. Thurman Papers, Mugar Memorial Library Special Collections.

17. Smith, *Mystic as Prophet*, p. 32. See Jacquelyne Jackson, "Black Grandparents in the South" in Robert Staples, ed., *The Black Family: Essays and Studies* (Belmont, CA: Wadsworth Publishing Co., 1978), pp. 207-14; and E. Franklin Frazier, *The Negro Family in the United States* (Chicago, 1939), pp. 114-24.

18. BBC documentary film.

19. "You felt that she contained and honored all of our feelings and all of hers, but they didn't spill over. I got a certain strength from her. That was very fortunate for me..." Mary E. Goodwin, "Racial Roots and Religion," *The Christian Century* (3 May 1973): 533; see also Thurman, *With Head and Heart*, p. 12: "She was always there. She was the receptacle for the little frustrations and hurts I brought to her."

20. Ibid. p. 21; see also Goodwin, p. 534 and BBC documentary film.

21. Ibid.

22. Howard Thurman, *For the Inward Journey: The Writings of Howard Thurman*, pp. 275, 279-80.

23. Thurman, *With Head and Heart*, p. 17

24. Ibid., p. 9.

25. For discussion of the concept of "extended family" in the black community, see Robert B. Hill and Lawrence Shackleford, "The Black Extended Family Revisited," in Robert Staples, ed., *The Black Family: Essays and Studies*, pp. 201-06; Andrew Billingsley, *Black Families in White America* (Englewood Cliffs, NJ: Prentice-Hall, 1968); see Jualynne Dodson, "Conceptualizations of Black Families," and Niara Dudarkasa, "Interpreting the Afro-American Family Organi-

zation," in Hariette Pipes McAdoo, ed., *Black Families*, (Beverly Hills: Sage Publications, 1981), pp. 23-25, 37-53.

26. BBC documentary film.
27. Thurman, *With Head and Heart*, p. 11. Parentheses and italics mine.
28. Ibid., p. 21.
29. Ibid., p. 23. See Rackhman Holt, *Mary McLeod Bethune: A Biography* (Garden City, NY: Doubleday and Co., 1984). See especially p. 114. Thurman also delivered the eulogy for Mrs. Bethune in which he said, "Her life was involved with my own life as long as I can remember my own life." "Eulogy for Mary McLeod Bethune," taped recording, Thurman Collection, Special Collections, Mugar Memorial Library, Boston University.
30. Thurman, *Luminous Darkness*, p. 3.
31. Howard Thurman, *Footprints of a Dream: The Story of the Church for the Fellowship of All Peoples* (New York: Harper and Row, 1959), p. 21; Thurman, *With Head and Heart*, p. 51.
32. See BBC documentary film.
33. Thurman, *With Head and Heart*, p. 28.
34. See Edward O. Jones, *A Candle in the Dark: A History of Morehouse College* (Valley Forge: Judson Press, 1967).
35. Thurman, *With Head and Heart*. p. 35.
36. Jones, *A Candle in the Dark*, pp. 79-121; and Ridgely Torrence, *The Story of John Hope* (New York: The Macmillan Co., 1948).
37. Thurman, *With Head and Heart*, p. 36.
38. Ibid., p. 37.
39. Jones, *A Candle in the Dark*, p. 123-29.
40. Thurman, *With Head and Heart*, p. 39.
41. Unpublished manuscript for Thurman, *With Head and Heart*.
42. Thurman, *With Head and Heart*, p. 45.
43. Ibid., p. 46.
44. Ibid., p. 47.
45. See Intellectual Sources.
46. Jean Burden, "Howard Thurman," *The Atlantic Monthly* (October 1953): 40.
47. Thurman, *With Head and Heart*, p. 55.
48. Ibid., p. 60. Thurman shared this occasion with the writer in a conversation in Evanston, IL, April 1978. The impact of Cross's advice, though not fully realized at that moment, in time became a driving principle for decision making in relation to social action for Thurman. Smith comments on the significance of this occasion and its relation to Thurman's baptism. See Smith, *Mystic as Prophet*, p. 24.
49. Thurman, *With Head and Heart*, p. 60.

50. From that time Thurman collected all of her available works and in 1973 he edited and published an anthology of her writings entitled *A Track to the Water's Edge: The Olive Schreiner Reader* (New York: Harper and Row, 1973). Thurman commented, "It seems that all my life I was being readied for such an encounter. Through the years I have secured all available works of this gifted woman. Her ideas have influenced my thought at a very profound level." Thurman, *A Track to the Water's Edge*, p. xi. "The Hunter" is included in this anthology, pp. 84-95; see discussion on intellectual sources later in this chapter.

51. Thurman, *With Head and Heart*, p. 73.

52. Ibid., pp. 73-74; Thurman, *Footprints*, pp. 21-23.

53. For biography on Jones, see Elizabeth Gray Vining, *Friend of Life: The Biography of Rufus M. Jones* (Philadelphia: J.B. Lippincott Co., 1958); David Hinshaw, *Rufus Jones: Master Quaker* (New York: G.P. Putnam's Sons, 1951); and Harry Emerson Fosdick, ed., *Rufus Jones Speaks to Our Time: An Anthology* (New York: The MacMillan Co., 1952). Thurman studied with Jones from January 1929 through June 1929 on a special grant from the National Council on Religion in Higher Education. This grant was primarily for doctoral students, but an exception was made for Thurman. He had considered Ph.D. work up to this point, but the opportunity to study with Jones put these plans to rest. Thurman, *With Head and Heart*, p. 76. See discussion on intellectual sources.

54. Rufus M. Jones, *Finding the Trail of Life* (New York: The Macmillan Co., 1927).

55. Thurman, *With Head and Heart*, p. 74. Parentheses mine.

56. Ibid., p. 79.

57. Ibid., p. 81; see also Melvin Watson, "Howard Thurman, Teacher-Preacher," in *God and Human Freedom*, pp. 161-65; and Mary Jennes, "A Leader of Students," in *Twelve Negro Americans* (Free Port, NY: Books for Libraries Press, 1936), pp. 145-60.

58. Thurman, *With Head and Heart.*, p. 83.

59. Ibid., p. 87.

60. Ibid., p. 90.

61. Ibid., p. 104; Thurman, *Footprints*, pp. 22-23.

62. Howard Thurman, *Jesus and the Disinherited* (Nashville: Abingdon Press, 1949; pb ed., Richmond, IN: Friends United Press, 1981), pp. 13-15; Thurman, *Footprints*, pp. 23-24; Thurman, *With Head and Heart*, pp. 113-18, 132.

63. He says: "I had to seek a means by which I could get to the essence of the religious experience of Hinduism as I sat or stood or walked

into a Hindu temple where everything was foreign and new; the smells, the altars, the flowers, the chanting—all of it was completely outside my universe of discourse. I had to find a way to the place where I could stand side by side with a Hindu, a Buddhist, a Moslem, and know that the authenticity of his experience was identical with my own." Ibid., p. 120.

64. Ibid., p. 129.
65. Ibid., p. 132.
66. Ibid., p. 135.
67. Ibid., p. 136.
68. Ibid., p. 140.
69. For Thurman's full accounting of the story, see Thurman, *Footprints*; see also Howard Thurman, ed. *The First Footprints: The Dawning of the Idea of The Church for the Fellowship of All Peoples, Letters Between Alfred Fisk and Howard Thurman, 1943–1944.* (San Francisco: Lawton and Alfred Kennedy, 1975).
70. Ibid., p. 31.
71. Thurman, *With Head and Heart,* p. 169, 178.
72. Thurman says, "The time of meditation was the heart of the total experience of worship." Ibid., p. 172.
73. "Great Preachers," editors of *Life,* 6 April 1953, p. 128; see also Jean Burden, "Howard Thurman," *The Atlantic Monthly,* (October 1953): 39-44; "Great Preachers," *Ebony* (July 1954): 29; *New York Times* (22 March 1953): 79; "Offering of the Heart," *Yankee* (December 1953): 19–22.
74. Thurman, *With Head and Heart,* p. 175. Manuscripts of "We Believe" television series are located at Special Collections, Mugar Library, Boston University.
75. Thurman, *With Head and Heart,* p. 181.
76. "Apostles of Growth," salutary remarks made at the occasion of Thurman's retirement by Dean Walter G. Muelder, n.d., Thurman Papers, Special Collections, Mugar Library, Boston University; also published in *NEXUS* 25, 9:1 (November 1965).
77. Thurman, *With Head and Heart,* pp. 193-211. In "Windbreak Against Existence," pp. 7-9, Thurman talks candidly about the relationship of the believer to human suffering and oppression around the world.
78. Thurman, *With Head and Heart,* pp. 193-194.
79. Thurman, *The Luminous Darkness,* p. 113.
80. Thurman, *With Head and Heart,* p. 169.
81. Ibid., p. 35.
82. Ibid., p. 41.

83. See Benjamin May's *Born to Rebel: An Autobiography* (New York: Charles Scriber's Sons, 1971), pp. 265-274.
84. Thurman, *With Head and Heart*, pp. 43-44.
85. Ibid., p. 43.
86. Ibid., p. 44.
87. See Thurman, "The Public and Private Results of Collegiate Education in the Life of Negro Americans—An Interpretation of the Significance of Education in a Segregated Society." Speech delivered at the Centennial Banquet of Morehouse College, 15 February 1967. Thurman Papers, Special Collections, Mugar Memorial Library, Boston University.
88. Benjamin Mays, "Introduction," *God and Human Freedom*, xiv.
89. Thurman, *With Head and Heart*, pp. 40-43.
90. Ibid., p. 41.
91. For a treatment of Robins's influence on Thurman, see Smith, *Mystic as Prophet*, pp. 25-27; and for Thurman's own comments on Moehlman, see Thurman, *With Head and Heart*, p. 54. Cross's three books are: *What Is Christianity? A Study of Rival Interpretations* (Chicago: University of Chicago Press, 1918); *Creative Christianity: A Study of the Genius of Christian Faith* (New York: Macmillan Co., 1922); and *Christian Salvation: A Modern Interpretation* (Chicago: University of Chicago Press, 1925).
92. "The Christian faith is identical with the spirit of loyalty to a historic figure of the past who is at the same time the ideal figure of the future. This figure bears the name Jesus Christ." Cross, *Christian Salvation*, pp. 221.
93. Ibid., p. 216.
94. Smith, *Mystic as Prophet*, p. 23. Smith relies heavily on Kenneth Cauthen, *The Impact of American Religious Liberalism* (New York: Harper and Row, 1962). See pp. 27-29 in Cauthen and David E. Roberts and Henry Van Dusen, eds., *Liberal Theology: An Appraisal* (New York: Charles Scribner's Sons, 1942).
95. Smith, *Mystic as Prophet*, p. 20; see also William Adam Brown, *The Essence of Christianity: A Study of the History of Definition* (New York: Charles Scribner's Sons, 1913).
96. Smith, *Mystic as Prophet*, p. 20.
97. Cross, *Christian Salvation*, pp. 219-20; *What Is Christianity?*, pp. 193–96; *Creative Christianity*, p. 130.
98. Cross, *Christian Salvation*, p. 228.
99. Smith, *Mystic as Prophet*, p. 22; Cross, *Creative Christianity*, pp. 23-53.
100. Cross, *What Is Christianity?* pp. 177; see also pp. 186, 189.
101. Smith, *Mystic as Prophet*, pp. 22.

102. Cross, *What Is Christianity?*, p. 185.
103. For a comparison of Cross's and Thurman's thought, see especially, Cross, *Christian Salvation*, chaps. 7-10, Thurman's treatment of "Reconciliation," in *Disciplines of the Spirit*, chap.5, and Thurman, *Mysticism and the Experience of Love*, Pendle Hill Pamphlet 115 (Wallington, PA: Pendle Hill, 1961); also compare Cross's notion of "Creative Christianity" with Thurman's philosophical exposition of community in *The Search for Common Ground*. See also Cross, *What Is Christianity*, chap. 7, pp. 172-204 and *Creative Christianity*, chaps. 3-4 and compare with Thurman's interpretation of the inner and outer dimensions of religious experience in *The Creative Encounter: An Interpretation of Religion and the Social Witness,* (Richmond, IN: Friends United Press, 1972.)
104. Mozella Gordon Mitchell, "Howard Thurman and Olive Schreiner: Post Modern Marriage Post-Mortem," *Journal of Religious Thought* 39:1 (Spring 1981). See also Mitchell, *Spiritual Dynamics*, pp. 11-14.
105. Smith, *Mystic as Prophet*, p. 35, footnote 1.
106. Thurman's own acknowledgment of Schreiner's contribution to his developing thought is sufficient. He says, "She possessed what comes through to me as an innate, instinctual sense of the unity of all life. It is this emphasis in her writing that was the first external confirmation of what had always been an active ingredient in my own awareness of life... It was not until I read Olive Schreiner that I was able to establish sufficient psychological distance between me and the totality of such experiences to make the experience itself an object of thought. Thus it became possible for me to move from primary experience, to conceptualizing that experience, to a vision inclusive of all life. The resulting creative synthesis was to me *religious* rather than *metaphysical*, as seems to have been true in Olive Schreiner's case. Thurman, *Track to the Water's Edge*, pp. xxvii-xxviii.
107. Mitchell makes a similar observation. "It may be thought remarkable, perhaps even paradoxical, that this oppressed black man in America should be `wedded' to the spirit of a white Englishwoman, native South African, who becomes champion of the causes of both her own oppression and that of the indigenous South Africans. Yet, it should not be surprising, however, that the oppressed who are able to transcend should teach the way to healing and wholeness, as both Schreiner and Thurman do." "Howard Thurman and Olive Schreiner," p. 65.
108. Thurman, *Track to Water's Edge*, p. xii. It is also informative to note Thurman's reaction to Schreiner when he discovered that though she was sensitive to the issues of indigenous South Africans, she still

remained a victim of her times. He was appalled by her use of the term 'nigger' in some of her writings. Ibid., p. xxix; see also the reference to Schreiner's use of derogatory terms to describe black South Africans in Ruth First and Ann Scott's biography, *Olive Schreiner* (New York: Schocken Books, 1980), p. 23.

109. See Schreiner's "The Dawn of Civilization," *The Nation and the Athenaeum*, (26 March 1921); "The Hunter," *A Track to the Water's Edge*, pp. 84-95; and "From Three Dreams in the Desert," Ibid., pp. 53-56. These selections were favorites of Thurman from which he often quoted.

110. James E. Massey, "Bibliographical Essay: Howard Thurman and Rufus M. Jones, Two Mystics," *Journal of Negro History* (April 1972): 191.

111. Thurman, *With Head and Heart*, p. 77.

112. Thurman, *Mysticism and the Experience of Love*, p. 3. A fundamental theme in Thurman's treatment of the individual and the religious experience is the mystical distinction between the "inner" and "outer." His language is remarkably similar to Jones's. Jones writes: "So, too, there is an outer way and an inner way and both are one. There is no inner life that is not also an outer life." Rufus M. Jones, *The Inner Life* (New York: The Macmillan Co., 1916), pp. viii-ix. Compare with Thurman's line of dedication to Eleanor Lloyd Smith in *Meditations of the Heart*, of whom Thurman writes, "in whom the inner and outer are one"; see the chapter headings in *The Creative Encounter*: "The Inwardness of Religion," "The Outwardness of Religion," "The Inner Need for Love," and "The Outer Necessity for Love"; see also Massey, "Bibliographical Essay," pp. 190-93.

113. Smith, *Mystic as Prophet*, pp. 27-30; Cauthen, *Impact of American Religous Liberalism*, p. 36.

114. Smith, *Mystic as Prophet*, p. 28.

115. See Rufus M. Jones, *Social Law in the Spiritual World. Studies in Human and Divine Inter-Relationship* (Philadelphia: J.C. Winston Co., 1904), where this argument is more fully developed. Also in the foreword to his *The Double Search* (Philadelphia: J.C. Winston Co., 1904), Jones writes: "Life as soon as it becomes rich with experience is deeply interfused with mutual and reciprocal correspondence moving both ways from above down and from below up. Our conjunct lives can no more be sundered into separated compartments than the convex and the concave curves of a circle can be divided." p. 6.

116. Jones, *Social Law*, p. 133.

117. Ibid., p. 136. Parentheses added.

118. Massey, "Bibliographical Essay," pp. 190-93.

Chapter 2

1. Thurman says, "The degree to which the potential in any expression of life is actualized marks the extent to which an expression of life experiences wholeness, integration, community. The clue to community can be found in the inner creative activity of living substances." Thurman, *Search*, p. 4. In a lecture entitled "Community and the Will of God," Thurman says: "Community, or the functional and creative wholeness, is a manifest tendency in life itself, that the intent of the Creator of life gives to all forms of life the communal potential, that the degree to which the potential becomes actualized, community results." Mendenhall Lectures, DePauw University (February 1961), Thurman Papers, Boston University.

2. Thurman, "Man and the Experience of Community," Long Beach California State College, n.d. Thurman Collections, Boston University, p. 2.

3. Howard Thurman, *Disciplines of the Spirit*, (Richmond, IN: Friends United Press, 1973) pp. 13-15.

4. Thurman borrows this term from E.S. Russell, "The Directiveness of Organic Activities," an address delivered before the Zoology Section of the British Association, 1934. "Directiveness" is used as a neutral term in distinction from "purposiveness," which has a psychological connotation. See Mendenhall Lectures, p. 2.

5. Thurman, *Search*, p. 3; see also Howard Thurman, "Man Cannot Be Indifferent to Man," *Meditations of the Heart* (Richmond, IN: Friends United Press, 1976), pp. 121-23.

6. *The Search for Common Ground* is a philosophical exposition of the nature of community where each of the above sources is examined. See also his Convocation Address, Pittsburgh Theological Seminary (November 1971) and his Mendenhall Lecture, "Community and the Will of God" (February 1961).

7. Ibid., p. 5.

8. Thurman, *Search*, p. 22.

9. The discussion will return to this theme in chap. 8.

10. "Innocence," says Thurman, "is the state of being which exists without knowledge and responsibility." It is that "which is essentially untried, untested, unchallenged. It is complete and whole within itself because it has known nothing else." Thurman, *Search*, pp. 26-27.

11. Ibid., p. 27.

12. Ibid., p. 24.

13. Ibid., p. 30.

14. "Consciousness" refers to "awareness," "irritability"; consciousness is not separate from, but a vital part of, the functioning of the non-conscious universe. *Ibid.*, p. 32.
15. Ibid., p. 34.
16. See Mendenhall Lectures, III, "Community and the Prophet's Dream," p. 1.
17. Thurman, *Search*, p. 34.
18. Thurman says, "The interesting thing about Utopias is this: they have within their limitations all the elements of community. They do not say anything about whom they are excluding, but theirs is a custom-made projection of dreams of order and harmony which the individual projects and holds at dead center in his soul and mind, seeking thereby to bring to pass in his contemporary experience that which indicates his contemporary experience is under the tutelage of this creative transcendent projection." Convocation Address, Pittsburgh Seminary, Pittsburgh, PA (4 November 1971). Thurman Papers, Boston University, p. 6.
19. Thurman, *Search*, p. 44.
20. See Thurman's Convocation Address, Pittsburgh Seminary; and Thurman, *Search*, p. 57.
21. See discussion of love as ethical principle in the actualization of community in chap. 3.
22. "The body is a man's intimate dwelling place; it is his domain as nothing else can ever be." Thurman, *Search*, p. 78.
23. Ibid., pp. 79-80, 41.
24. Ibid., p. 80.
25. See discussion of "The World" under the next section, "The Triadic Character of Community."
26. Thurman, *The Luminous Darkness*, p. x.
27. Thurman, *Deep Is the Hunger* (New York: Harper and Bros., 1951), p. 64; see also Howard Thurman, "What Can I Believe In?", *Journal of Religion and Health* 12 (November 1972): 111-19.
28. Thurman, *The Creative Encounter*, p. 19; see also Thurman, *Deep Is the Hunger*, p. 62.
29. According to Smith, the emphasis on the centrality of personality places Thurman in the heart of the Protestant Liberal position where "personality centered Christianity is a basic tenet of liberalism." Smith, *Mystic*, p. 49.
30. Thurman, *Deep Is the Hunger*, p. 93.
31. Thurman, "What Can I Believe In?" pp. 111-13.
32. Thurman, *The Creative Encounter*, p. 19; Thurman, *Disciplines*, p. 57; and Thurman, *Search*, p. 21.

33. "The Inner Life and World Consciousness," Thurman Papers, Boston University, n.d., p. 3.
34. Ibid., p. 3.
35. Thurman, *Creative Encounter*, p. 57.
36. Ibid., pp. 57-58.
37. See Thurman, "Man and the Experience of Freedom," California State College, Long Beach, CA (19 March 1969), Thurman Papers, Boston University, p. 1.
38. Ibid., p. 1; see also "America in Search of a Soul," the Robbins Lecture Series, University of Redlands, Redlands, CA (20 January 1976), Thurman Papers, BU, p. 9.
39. Thurman, "America in Search of a Soul," p. 10.
40. Ibid., p. 10.
41. Thurman, "Freedom Under God," Washington University, Second Century Convocation, (February 1955), Thurman Papers, BU, p. 2.
42. See Luther Smith's "Community: Partnership of Freedom and Responsibility," in *God and Human Freedom*, Henry J. Young, ed., pp. 23-31. Here Smith indicates that responsibility in Thurman means both "response-ability" and "accountability."
43. Thurman says, "The moment I transfer responsibility for my own actions, I relinquish my own free initiative. I become an instrument in another's hands. This is the iniquity of all forms of human slavery. The slave is not a responsible person and the result of slavery is the destruction, finally, of any sense of alternatives." Thurman, "Freedom Under God," p. 2.
44. Thurman, "Man and the Experience of Freedom," p. 5.
45. "The Freedom of the Human Spirit," Carmel Valley Manor, 24 January 1971, Thurman Papers, Boston University.
46. Thurman, "Freedom Under God," p. 3. , Thurman Papers, Boston University.
47. Ibid.
48. Ibid.; see also, Thurman, "America in Search of a Soul."
49. Although Thurman begins with the individual, his understanding of community is theocentric. Thurman believes that the individual personality is the medium through which God realizes Godself in the world. Thurman, *Deep Is the Hunger*, p. 94.
50. See Thurman's commentary and exposition of Habbakuk in *The Interpreter's Bible*, esp. pp. 980-982; see also Thurman, "The God of Life Is the God of Religion," in *Meditations of the Heart*, p. 23; Ibid., "Surrounded By the Love of God," pp. 210-11.
51. Thurman, *Creative Encounter*, p. 28; Thurman, *Deep Is the Hunger*, p. 146.

52. Thurman, *Creative Encounter*, p. 29; see Smith, *Mystic as Prophet*, pp. 62-64.
53. Thurman, *Search*, p. 5.
54. There seems to be a discernible, rational order in life, according to Thurman, which discloses the "intent of the Creator." He argues, therefore, that it is reasonable to assume that "wherever life is found, evidence of creative intent must also exist in that which is being experienced, reacted to, observed or studied. One such sign, and the most crucial one, is the way life seeks always to realize itself in wholeness, harmony, and integration within the potential that characterizes the particular experience of life." Thurman, *Search*, p. 7.
55. Thurman, Mendenhall Lectures, p. 2.
56. Thurman, *Deep Is the Hunger*, p. 144; Thurman, *Creative Encounter*, pp. 24, 31.
57. Howard Thurman, *The Inward Journey* (Richmond, IN: Friends United Press, 1971), pp. 130, 133, 139-55; Thurman, *Deep Is the Hunger*, p. 147. Thurman's favorite scripture was Psalm 139, which emphasizes the individual's experience of the presence of God.
58. Thurman, *Creative Encounter*, p. 46.
59. He writes, "Man and God do communicate.... Eckhart insists that there is in the soul of man an apex, a spark which is God, the Godhead. This is the very ground of the soul. It is in and of itself the Godhead." Ibid., p. 43. See also Thurman, "Our Spirits Remember God," *The Inward Journey*, p. 133.
60. Thurman sees Jesus as an historical personage and a fellow-worker in the actualization of human community. Jesus is not God, nor does he deserve worship; worship is reserved for God alone. He does recognize Jesus, however, as the revelation of how the committed individual creates community through the transforming power of love and truth. For an outline of Thurman's interpretation of Jesus, see Smith, *Mystic as Prophet*, pp. 54-62.
61. Thurman, *Deep Is the Hunger*, p. 147.
62. To be loved, according to Thurman, is "to have a sense of being dealt with at a point in one's self that is beyond all good and evil." "We Believe" Television Series, p. 91; Thurman, "The Experience of Love," *The Inward Journey*, p. 35.
63. Howard Thurman, *The Growing Edge* (Richmond, IN: Friends United Press, 1974), p. 68; see also, Thurman, *Creative Encounter*, p. 115.
64. Ibid., p. 124.
65. It will be shown in chap. 3 how Thurman's theocentric vision of reality is the basis for the moral life and the creation of human community.

66. Thurman, *Search*, p. 5-6, 29.
67. Ibid., p. 31.
68. Ibid., p. 34.
69. Ibid., chap. 3, "The Search in Living Structures," pp. 29-41.
70. Mendenhall Lectures, p. 8.
71. Thurman, *Search*, p. 5.
72. Ibid., p. 3; see also, Thurman, *Disciplines*, p. 57.
73. Thurman, *Disciplines*, p. 41ff; see also discussion in *Creative Encounter*, "The Inner Need for Love," where Thurman analogizes "mother-love" with God's love as being the basis of the individual's assurance of being cared for at a personal and intimate level. He writes, "...the need for love is an essential element in the structure of personality. It is responsibility for the establishing of a pattern of response to other human beings that makes possible all forms of community and relatedness between human beings in society" (pp. 105-06).
74. Thurman, *Search*, pp. 81-82; see also Thurman, "What Can I Believe In?" pp. 111-12.
75. Thurman, *Search*, pp. 84-85.
76. See Howard Thurman, "The Fascist Masquerade," *The Church and Organized Movements*, chap. 4, Randolph Crump Miller, ed. "The Interseminary Series" (New York: Harper and Brothers, 1946), pp. 82-100; Howard Thurman, "Religion in a Time of Crisis," *The Garrett Tower* 43:4 (August 1943): 1-3. Thurman's view of the state bears close affinity with American Civil Religion ("transcendent universal religion of the nation") as espoused by Robert Bellah in both its positive and negative potentialities. See Bellah in Russel Richey and Donald G. Jones, eds., *American Civil Religion* (New York: Harper and Row, 1974), pp. 3-18; also, Robert Bellah's *The Broken Covenant* (New York: Seabury Press, 1975); "Evil in the American Ethos," Conference on the Legitimation of Evil, Grace Cathedral, San Francisco, 22 February 1970; and "Reflections on Reality in America," *Radical Religion* I (1974); see also Gail Gehrig, *American Civil Religion: An Assessment*, Society for the Scientific Study of Religion Monograph Series no. 3 (Society for the Scientific Study of Religion, 1981).
77. Thurman, *Search*, p. 87.
78. Ibid., pp. 87-88.
79. Ibid., p. 5.
80. Thurman, "The Inner Life and World-Mindedness," p. 3-4, Thurman Papers, Boston University.
81. See Robert Carroll Williams's very informative discussions of "Self, God, and Existence," in *God and Human Freedom*, pp. 44-56.
82. Thurman, *Creative Encounter*, p. 20.

83. Ibid., p. 39.
84. Ibid., p. 30-31.
85. Ibid., pp. 33.
86. Ibid.
87. Ibid, pp. 37-38.
88. "Residue of God-meaning" refers to the pattern and contents of one's beliefs, value judgments, strengths, weaknesses; in sum, the individual's totality. *Ibid.*, pp. 26-27.
89. Ibid., p. 40.
90. Thurman also treats commitment, growth, and reconciliation as disciplines of the spirit. A detailed discussion is found in Thurman, *Disciplines*. See especially Thurman's discussion of "singleness of mind" at p. 19.
91. Ibid., p. 66. Suffering is rooted in pain, but is distinct from the latter in that it involves consciousness. Apart from the consciousness of pain, says Thurman, there can be no suffering. Thus, the question of theodicy is raised in this dimension.
92. Thurman, *Creative Encounter*, p. 50.
93. Thurman, *Disciplines*, p. 75.
94. Thurman, *Creative Encounter*, p. 53-54.
95. Ibid., p. 124.

Chapter 3

1. The obstacles which prevent the actualization of human community are multifarious, ranging from deep psychological perplexities to complex matrices of political, economic, and social forces. While Thurman does acknowledge the sundry and complex problems associated with the actualization of human community, in the language of James Gustafson, his basic concern is with the practical moral question, "What is God requiring and enabling us to be and do?" The general answer, according to Gustafson, is "We are to relate ourselves and all things in a manner appropriate to their relation to God." *Ethics from a Theocentric Perspective* vol. 1, (Chicago: The University of Chicago Press, 1981), p. 327. Thurman's specific answer is that we are *required* and *enabled* by the love of God to remove all barriers which prevent the actualization of community in the affairs of men and women. See later discussion in this chapter, "Community as Norm and Goal"; see also Thurman, "The Search for God in Religion," *Laymen's Movement Review* 5:6 (November-December 1962).
2. For Thurman, evil is not an illusion, therefore it must be acknowledged and dealt with. He describes evil as being *positive* and *negative*

as opposed to good being *positive* and *creative*. Thurman, "What Can I Believe In?" Typewritten manuscript, Thurman Papers, BU, p. 5. At another place, he writes, "There seems to be present in life a dramatic principle that is ever alert to choke off, to strangle, the constructively creative." Thurman, *Deep Is the Hunger*, p. 51.

3. Thurman, "What Can I Believe In?" p. 5. See earlier discussion of pain and suffering under "The Totality: Disciplines for Preparation"; see Thurman, *Disciplines*, pp. 67, 72.

4. Thurman, *With Head and Heart*, p. 268.

5. He says, "Things do not merely happen, they are part of some kind of rationale. If this rationale can be tracked down and understood, then the living experience, however terrible, makes sense." Thurman, "Exposition to the Book of Habbakuk," *The Interpreter's Bible*, vol. 6, George A. Buttrick et al eds. (Nashville: Abingdon Press, 1956), p. 980.

6. Thurman, "What Can I Believe In?" p. 5; Thurman, *Creative Encounter*, p. 139. Here Thurman refers to the genesis and development of an idea; evil as an idea follows the same pattern in his thinking. Thurman, *Disciplines*, pp. 74- 75; and Thurman, "Habbakuk," pp. 986–87; Thurman, *Deep River*, pp. 92-93.

7. Thurman, *Disciplines*, p. 66; Thurman, "What Can I Believe In?" p. 6.

8. Thurman, "Freedom Under God," p. 3.

9. Thurman, "Habbakuk," p. 983-86.

10. Thurman, *Deep Is the Hunger*, p. 27.

11. Thurman, "What Can I Believe In?", p. 8.

12. Thurman, "Habbakuk," pp. 980-82.

13. Ibid., p. 982.

14. Thurman, *With Head and Heart*, p. 268.

15. Quoted by Thurman in *Disciplines*, p. 80; Thurman, *Inward Journey*, p. 16; see also Thurman, "The Circle of Life," Cassette Recording, No. 65-8. Howard Thurman Educational Trust Fund, San Francisco.

16. This thesis is present in Thurman, "America in Search of a Soul" and "Freedom under God." See earlier discussion of Thurman's understanding of the state under "The Triadic Character of Community: World." Gandhi's request to hear the delegates of the Indian pilgrimage sing the Negro spiritual, "Were You There When They Crucified My Lord?" carries this basic idea. Thurman quotes Gandhi as saying, "I feel that this song gets to the root of the experience of the entire human race under the spread of the healing wings of suffering." See Thurman, *With Head and Heart*, p. 134. Thurman also suggests that the black slave redeemed the religion the slave master profaned. Thurman, *Deep River*, p. 40.

17.   See later discussion of the redemptive suffering of the individual for the collective destiny of the human race under "Nonviolence as Ethical Imperative."
18.   Thurman, *Disciplines*, p. 83.
19.   See later discussion of nature and function of nonviolence. Redemptive suffering and nonviolence are means of creating a climate of love. Redemptive suffering used in the second sense is synonymous with nonviolence. For both, the motivation, the method, and goal is love or reconciliation. See Thurman, *Disciplines*, pp. 104-27.
20.   Thurman, *Search*, p. 26; see p. 4, also.
21.   Thurman, *Disciplines*, p. 83.
22.   Elizabeth Yates, *Howard Thurman: Portrait of a Practical Dreamer* (New York: John Day Co., 1964), p. 233.
23.   Thurman, *With Head and Heart*, p. 268-69; Thurman, "Habbakuk," p. 981.
24.   Thurman, *Deep River*, p. 64.
25.   Responsibility involves accountability not only for one's action, but for one's *re-action* as well. See earlier discussion of freedom and responsibility under "The Triadic Character of Community: The Individual." For the notion of original sin in Thurman, see *Search*, chap. 2, "The Search Into the Beginnings," pp. 8-28. Here he indicates in several places that the problematic nature of the self created by human potential for harmony or disharmony revolves around the will. The occasion for sin is provided by the freedom of the will and temptation to egosim or self-centeredness. See also Thurman, *The Inward Journey*, p. 92: "The murky motive is the common lot! Its dwelling place the human heart."
26.   Pride is defined as "undisciplined, unrestrained, chaotic manifestations of the ego..." Thurman, "Mysticism and Social Change," n.p., n.d., Thurman papers, BU, p. 4; see also, "Mysticism and Social Change," *Eden Seminary Bulletin*, (Spring 1939): 29.
27.   Thurman, *Deep Is the Hunger*, pp. 35-36; Howard Thurman, *The Centering Moment* (Richmond, IN: Friends United Press, 1980), p. 70; Thurman, *Jesus and the Disinherited*, p. 78.
28.   Thurman, *Disciplines*, pp. 112-113; Thurman, *The Growing Edge*, pp. 65-67.
29.   Thurman, "Habbakuk," p. 995; see also Thurman, "We Believe," 2 May 1958, where Thurman discusses the "dimness of the soul."
30.   Thurman, "Mysticism and Social Change," *Eden Seminary Bulletin*, p. 28.
31.   Thurman is not as clear, however, on his economic theory. See Thurman, *Creative Encounter*, p. 130; see also "A Faith To Live By—

Democracy and the Individual," The Fellowship Church, San Francisco, 19 and 26 October 1952, Taped Recording, Nos. 6 and 7, Thurman Papers, BU.

32. See Thurman, "Freedom Under God," p. 1.
33. See Thurman's discussion on the anatomy of segregation in *The Luminous Darkness*, esp. pp. 5-12.
34. Thurman, "The Act of Confession," *The Centering Moment*, p. 98; Thurman, "The Inward Sea," *Meditations*, p. 15; "I Surrender Myself to God," *Meditations*, pp. 174-75.
35. Thurman, *Meditations*, p. 183; Thurman, *Growing Edge*, pp. 67-68; Thurman *Creative Encounter*, chap. 3, pp. 92-124.
36. Thurman, *Creative Encounter*, p. 124.
37. Thurman, *Disciplines*, p. 84; see John Hick, *Evil and the God of Love* (New York: Harper and Row, 1966), p. 3. The traditional formulation of the problem of evil, according to Hicks, is: "Can the presence of evil be reconciled with the existence of God who is unlimited both in goodness and power?"
38. Thurman, "What Can I Believe In?", pp. 5-6.
39. Thurman, *Inward Journey*, p. 105; see "A Faith to Live By—Man," The Fellowship Church, San Francisco, 1952, Taped Recording No. 5, Thurman Papers, Boston University. Here Thurman talks about the perpetual "tragic sense of life."
40. Thurman, *Inward Journey*, p. 105.
41. "The orderly process seems ever to be at the mercy of the disorderly. Weeds do not have to be cultivated, but vegetables must be." Thurman, "Habbakkuk," p. 981.
42. Thurman, *Deep Is the Hunger*, p. 51; Thurman, "Habbakuk," p. 981.
43. Thurman, *Deep Is the Hunger*, p. 52.
44. See later discussion of love and truth as ethical principles under "The Means of Actualization."
45. Thurman, *Disciplines*, pp. 48-55.
46. Thurman, *Search*, p. 90. Italics added.
47. Thurman, "Mysticism and Ethics," *The Journal of Religous Thought* 27:2 (Summer Supplement, 1970): 23.
48. "To say `Yes' to evil, as if it were ultimate, is to be overcome by evil." Thurman, "Habbakuk," p. 987.
49. Thurman, "Judgment and Hope in the Christian Message," n.p., n.d. Thurman papers, Boston University, p. 11. Also in *The Christian Way in Race Relations*, chap. 12, William Stuart Nelson, ed. (New York: Harper and Brothers, 1948), pp. 229-35.
50. Thurman, "Windbreak Against Existence," p. 9.
51. See Introduction.

52. In a very important respect, Thurman's theocentric view of the moral life is related to Gustafson's treatment in *Ethics from a Theocentric Perspective*. Here Gustafson argues that traditional Western theology and ethics have been anthropocentric in their focus rather than theocentric. Consequently, the anthropocentric focus has prevented us from understanding significant things about "the ultimate power and ordering of life, about the majesty and glory of all that sustains us and about the threats to life over which we have no definite control" (p. 99). He contends that the ultimate power is not the guarantor of human benefits as presupposed in our anthropocentric interpretation of God and the cosmos. Gustafson maintains that a theocentric construal of the world provides the moral agent with a relational ethical framework whereby we can "morally discern" the creative activity of God in nature, culture, society, and the self. See also Gustafson's "Moral Discernment in the Christian Life" in *Norm and Context in Christian Ethics*, Gene H. Outka and Paul Ramsey, eds. (New York: Charles Scribner's Sons, 1968), pp. 17-36. Enoch H. Oglesby makes a similar claim for the theocentric character of black religious ethics in *Ethics and Theology from the Other Side: Sounds of Moral Struggle* (Washington, D.C.: University Press of America, 1979), p. 20.

53. Walter Meulder identifies Thurman's philosophical ethical position as theonomous. He writes, "This means that the imperatives are not imposed from external sources, nor completely devised by inner personal mandates, but express at the deepest level a metaphysical divine moral order which is also the rational law of a person's own being. There is a meeting place for communication between God and the person, a place for yielding private, personal will to transcendent purposes that are at the same time common ground. Here revelation and intuition meet, a place rich with the sense of ultimate worth of the individual as a private and social person." "The Structure of Howard Thurman's Religious Social Ethics," *Debate and Understanding*, Special Edition (Spring 1982), p. 9.

54. Gustafson, *Ethics from a Theocentric Perspective*, p. 327; Oglesby, pp. 19-24.

55. See earlier discussion on the nature of the religious experience.

56. Thurman, Convocation Address, Pittsburgh Seminary, p. 7. See also Thurman's "Search for God in Religion,"

57. Thurman, *Creative Encounter*, pp. 67-71, 121.

58. Ibid., p. 81.

59. Ibid., p. 124.

60. See Carlyle F. Stewart, III, "A Comparative Analysis of Theological-Ontology and Ethical Method in the Theologies of James H. Cone and Howard Thurman," (Ph.D. dissertation, Northwestern University, 1982) chap. 1, "The Structure of Ethical Method in the Theology of Howard Thurman," p. 362.

61. Muelder, "Howard Thurman's Religious Social Ethics," pp. 9-10; John H. Cartwright, "The Religious Ethics of Howard Thurman," *The Journal of the Interdenominational Theological Center* 12:1-2 (Fall 1984-Spring 1985): 33-34.

62. Edward LeRoy Long, *A Survey of Christian Ethics* (New York: Oxford Press, 1967), p. 129.

63. See Frederick S. Carney, "Deciding What Is Required," in *Norm and Context in Christian Ethics*, pp. 3–16.

64. See Thurman, *Disciplines of the Spirit*.

65. Thurman, *Meditations of the Heart*, p. 105.

66. Barnett J. W. Greer, "Howard Thurman: An Examination and Analysis of Thurman's Idea of Community and the Viability of the Fellowship Church," (Doctor of Ministry Project, Claremont School of Theology, May 1983), p. 23.

67. Thurman, *Inward Journey*, p. 36.

68. "We Believe," 25 September 1959, p. 91.

69. Ibid.

70. Thurman, *Mysticism and the Experience of Love*, p. 13.

71. The distinctions between love and truth are made for purposes of analysis, but ultimately they are one. The continuing discussion should justify this important distinction.

72. Thurman, "We Believe," 23 October 1959, pp. 97-98.

73. Ibid., 11 December 1959.

74. Thurman, *The Growing Edge*, p. 79.

75. Ibid., pp. 81-84.

76. Thurman uses the word "mercy," but in this context the meaning is synonomous with love.

77. Thurman, "Freedom Under God," p. 3.

78. Ibid.

79. Thurman, *The Growing Edge*, pp. 27-28.

80. Thurman, *Inward Journey*, p. 121; Thurman, *Mysticism and the Experience of Love*, p. 21.

81. Thurman, *Inward Journey*, p. 29.

82. See Smith, *Mystic as Prophet*, p. 46; see also in Smith, Thurman's treatment of "reconciliation," chap. 5, pp. 104-27.

83. Thurman, *Disciplines*, p. 120.

84. Ibid., p. 122.

85. Thurman, *With Head and Heart*, p. 269.
86. Thurman, *Search*, p. 5.
87. "Wade in the Water/Wade in the water, children/Wade in the water/God is going to trouble the waters."
88. Thurman, *Deep River*, pp. 92-93. Muelder comments on Thurman's strong insistence on the rationality inherent in life: "This intention of rationality corresponds to the rationality of the universe and points to the scientific method." Muelder, "Howard Thurman's Religious Social Ethics," p. 10.
89. Thurman, *Creative Encounter*, p. 46. See also his "Mysticism and Social Change: Mysticism—An Interpretation," *Eden Seminary Bulletin*, 1939, pp. 3-10. Here Thurman offers an exposition of the nature of intuition and its difference from discursive reasoning.
90. Ibid., p. 47.
91. In his analysis of Thurman's ethical method, Carlyle Stewart claims that Thurman's use of intuition in moral decision making is founded upon two ethical paradigms: "natural law" and what Henry Sidgwick calls "perceptive intuitionism." Stewart, "The Structure of Ethical Method in the Theology of Howard Thurman," p. 365. Natural law is defined as "…the inherent and universal structures of human existence which can be discerned by the unaided reason and which form the basis for judgments of conscience about the good (that which realizes the natural end and goal of being) and the evil (that which thwarts the natural end and goal of being)." Van Harvey, *A Handbook for Theological Terms* (New York: Macmillan, 1964), p. 157. And for Sidgwick, "conduct is right when conformed to certain precepts or principles of duty intuitively known to be unconditionally binding." *The Method of Ethics* (Chicago: University of Chicago Press, 1962), p. 3. Stewart claims that for Thurman, "Since individuals intrinsically know right and wrong, this 'knowing' is aided by the principles of natural law mediated through intuition." (p. 366).
92. Thurman, "Mysticism and Ethics," *Journal of Religious Thought*, p. 24.
93. Thurman, "The Inner Light," taped lecture given at a Quaker Meeting, n.p., n.d. Thurman Collection, The Howard Thurman Educational Trust Fund, San Francisco, CA; "The Meaning of Commitment: The Strength of Corporate Worship," Fellowship Church, 8 April 1951, Special Collections, Boston University.
94. See Thurman, "The Inward Sanctuary," *Meditations*, pp. 173-74.
95. Thurman, "The Inner Light." Taped lecture; "The Strength of Corporate Worship."
96. Thurman, *Creative Encounter*, pp. 57-65; Thurman, "I Seek Truth and Light," p. 189.

97. Thurman, "Inner Light," *Deep Is the Hunger*, p. 93.
98. Meulder, "Howard Thurman's Religious Social Ethics," p. 9.
99. Thurman, *Jesus and the Disinherited*, p. 71.
100. Ibid., p. 72.
101. Ibid., p. 65.
102. Ibid., p. 73.
103. Thurman, *Deep Is the Hunger*, p. 80.
104. Thurman, *The Growing Edge*, p. 157.
105. Thurman, *Meditations*, p. 51.
106. Thurman, *Disciplines*, p. 124.
107. Thurman discusses fear, deception, and hate in *Jesus and the Disinherited*. Although we have examined sin and evil as barriers to community, here the emphasis is on internal barriers, particularly as they relate to the internalization of love, truth, and nonviolence.
108. Thurman, *Jesus and the Disinherited*, p. 40.
109. Ibid., p. 48.
110. Ibid., p. 57.
111. Thurman, *Luminous Darkness*, p. 3.
112. Thurman, *Jesus and the Disinherited*, p. 79.
113. Thurman writes, "The logic of development of hatred is death to the spirit and disintegration of ethical and moral values." Ibid., p. 88.
114. Thurman, *Disciplines*, pp. 114, 121. A society in which the climate of love is actualized is also a "personality-centered" society. Such a society is democratic in principle, e.g., the United States. See Thurman, *The Creative Encounter*, pp. 129-34; see also Thurman, "America in Search of a Soul" and "Freedom Under God," where the thesis is elaborated.
115. Thurman, *The Growing Edge*, pp. 80-81.
116. Nonviolence is discussed in this context as it relates to the actualization of human community. Thurman is understood by several scholars to be the chief architect of nonviolent resistance for black Americans, predating its practical implementation by Martin Luther King, Jr., in the Civil Rights Movement. Luther Smith gives a summary of the development of the idea among black Americans. Smith, *Mystic as Prophet*, pp. 118-19.
117. Thurman, *Disciplines*, p. 112.
118. Ibid.
119. Ibid.
120. Ibid., p. 118.
121. Thurman, "Man and Social Change—Violence and Non-Violence," California State College, Long Beach, CA, 29 March 1961, Thurman Papers, BU, p. 10.

122. Ibid.
123. Thurman, *Disciplines*, pp. 118-19.
124. Ibid., p. 19.
125. Thurman, *The Luminous Darkness*, p. 113.
126. Smith, *Mystic as Prophet*, pp. 121-24.
127. Ibid., p. 124.
128. Ibid.
129. Ibid., p. 125.
130. Ibid., p. 122; see also Thurman's *Lawrence Lectures on Religion and Society*. "Mysticism and Social Action," 13 October 1978, First Unitarian Church of Berkeley, CA, pp. 22-23.
131. Thurman, *Deep Is the Hunger*, pp. 11-14, 68.
132. Ibid., pp. 14, 27-28.
133. Ibid., p. 28.
134. "One of the tragedies of the modern liberal," says Thurman, "is the illusion that theory and practice, the ideal and the real can be separated from each other." Thurman, *Deep Is the Hunger*, p. 28.
135. Ibid., p. 38.
136. Ibid., p. 94.
137. See discussion of George Cross and Olive Schreiner as intellectual sources for the thought of Thurman.
138. Thurman often quoted from Petrarch's *Letters of Old Age*: "When a word must be spoken to further a good cause, and those whom it behooves to speak remain silent, anybody ought to raise his voice, and break the silence fraught with evil.... Many a time a few simple words have helped further the welfare of the nation, no matter who uttered them; the voice itself displaying the latent powers, sufficed to move the hearts of men." See his "Exposition on Zephaniah," *The Interpreter's Bible*, p. 1002; Thurman, *Deep Is the Hunger*, p. 25.
139. Ibid., p. 49.
140. Thurman would argue that this was true for Jesus and the Buddha; to some extent, Judas Maccabeus (Ibid., pp. 49-50); Albert Schweitzer (Ibid., pp. 57- 58); Mahatma Gandhi and Martin Luther King, Jr. (*Search*, p. 95; *With Head and Heart*, p. 223), among others.
141. Thurman, *Footprints*, p. 21.
142. Thurman, *Deep Is the Hunger*, p. 21.
143. See especially Schreiner's "Three Dreams In the Desert," pp. 53-56.
144. Ibid., p. 56.
145. Dorothee Soelle has already coined this terminology in her collection of poetry entitled *Revolutionary Patience* (Rita and Robert Kimber, trans.; Maryknoll, NY: Orbis Books, 1974; England: 1977); see also

Cornel West, "Subversive Joy and Revolutionary Patience in Black Christianity," in his *Prophetic Fragments*, pp. 161–65

146. See Thurman's treatment of "waiting" as part of the discipline of growth in *Disciplines*, pp. 39–46.
147. Thurman, *Deep Is the Hunger*, p. 54.
148. Ibid., p. 53.
149. Ibid., p. 67.
150. Thurman, *Disciplines*, p. 112.
151. Thurman, "Man and Social Change," complete citation p. 10.
152. Thurman, *Deep Is the Hunger*, p. 53. For Thurman, the redemptive and creative role of the individual in social change also involves a view of time and history which is radically theocentric. See his "Exposition of Zephaniah," *The Interpreter's Bible*, pp. 1015-19.
153. Luther Smith states, "Thurman's primary identity was that of a mystic; a mystic who recognized the necessity of social activism for enabling and responding to religious experience." *Mystic as Prophet*, p. 9. Martin E. Marty places Thurman in the tradition of Meister Eckhart because of his emphasis on the potentiality of the self and his fusion of the idea of love with divine freedom and mystical union. For Eckhart and Thurman, Marty says, "'The unifying of the will with the Will of the highest' issues forth in fresh action.... `Being precedes work'." "Mysticism and the Religious Quest for Freedom," *God and Human Freedom*, p. 7. Muelder places Thurman's ethical theory in the Troeltschian mystical typology, differing, however, with emphasis on the evangelical Jesus as opposed to Troeltsch's "Christ of mysticism." Muelder, "Howard Thurman's Religious Social Ethics," p. 7. Thurman's reluctance to being labeled a mystic is probably attributable to his insistence that religious experience is non-exclusive and accessible to any person who prepares for the encounter. For him, any individual who surrenders her/himself to God is a candidate for a mystical encounter. He defines mysticism in one place simply as "the response of the individual to a personal encounter with God within his own soul." "Mysticism and Social Action," *The Lawrence Lectures*, p. 18.
154. Thurman said, "Long before I was acquainted with the term `mysticism,' and before such a category provided any frame of reference for my mind and thought, the line between the inner and the outer in my own experience was not closely drawn." *The Lawrence Lectures*, p. 17. See earlier discussion in biographical profile regarding his early childhood and the influence of Rufus Jones.
155. Ibid., p. 18; see Rufus M. Jones, *Studies in Mystical Religion* (London: Macmillan and Co., 1923), p. xv.

156. Thurman, *Mysticism and the Experience of Love*, p. 10.
157. See discussion of Jones's distinction between "affirmation mystic" and "negation mystic" in chap. 1.
158. Thurman, "Mysticism and Social Change," n.p., n.d. Thurman Papers, BU, p. 8.
159. Thurman, *Creative Encounter*, p. 124.
160. Ibid., p. 126.
161. Thurman, "Mysticism and Social Change," *Edens Seminary Bulletin*, p. 29.
162. Ibid., p. 28.
163. Smith argues that though Thurman can be rightly identified within the pietistic tradition because of his insistence on self-awareness and inner transformation, yet he had "just as an intense commitment to community, and his mystical experiences were the basis for this commitment." *Mystic as Prophet*, p. 10. Martin E. Marty, speaking of Thurman's contribution in this respect, writes: "He...has shown us how the path of holiness and enlightenment is not merely parallel to but links up with the path of community and action." "Mysticism and the Religious Quest for Freedom," *The Christian Century* 100:8 (16 March 1983): 246.
164. Thurman, *Creative Encounter*, p. 137.
165. Ibid., p. 135.
166. Thurman, *Footprints*, p. 21; Thurman, *Disciplines*, p. 120; see earlier discussions on Olive Schreiner as a source of Thurman's intellectual development and the ethical imperative of nonviolence.
167. Thurman, *Footprints*, pp. 69-70.
168. See Smith's discussion on the place of Jesus in Thurman's theology in Smith, *Mystic as Prophet*, pp. 70-72, 54-62.
169. See Thurman, "We Believe," 12 December 1958; and Thurman, *Creative Encounter*, pp. 135-36.
170. Thurman, "We Believe," 12 December 1958, pp. 54-55.
171. Thurman, "Black Pentecost: Footprints of the Disinherited," Taped messages. 30-31 May 1942, Eliot Congregational Church, Roxbury, MA. Thurman Collection, Boston University.
172. Thurman, "The Fascist Masquerade," pp. 97-98.
173. Thurman, "Freedom Under God," p. 3; see also Thurman, *The Luminous Darkness*, p. 102.
174. In his discussion of "denominationalism," there are striking similarities to H.R. Niebuhr's analysis in Niebuhr's *The Social Sources of Denominationalism* (New York: The New American Library, 1929, 1957, 1975). See esp. chap. 1, "The Ethical Failure of the Divided Church." Niebuhr says, "Denominationalism...represents the moral

failure of Christianity. And unless the ethics of brotherhood can gain the victory over this divisiveness within the body of Christ it is useless to expect it to be victorious in the world." p. 25.

175. Thurman, *Creative Encounter*, p. 140.
176. Smith, *Mystic as Prophet*, p. 72. This appreciation of ecumenicism is also seen in his respective ministries at Mt. Zion Church, Rankin Chapel, Fellowship Church, and Marsh Chapel.
177. Religious experience is the final authority for Thurman's theological construction. The Bible and Jesus are secondary to experience. See Smith, *Mystic as Prophet*, pp. 71-77.
178. He writes, "It must not be thought that life is static, something that is set, fixed, determined. The key word to remember always is potential; that which has not yet come to pass. It is only the potential, the undisclosed that has a future." Thurman, *Search*, p. 4.
179. This was a comment made by Thurman in a classroom setting at the Interdenominational Theological Center, Atlanta, GA, November 1978, which this writer attended.
180. Thurman, *Creative Encounter*, p. 141.
181. Thurman says that "what is true in any religion is to be found there because it is true, it is not true because it is found in that religion. The ethical insight which makes for the most healthy and creative human relations is not the unique possession of any religion, however inspired it may be." Thurman, *The Luminous Darkness*, p. 112.
182. Smith, *Mystic as Prophet*, p. 77; Thurman, *Creative Encounter*, p. 135.
183. Thurman, *Deep Is the Hunger*, pp. 32-33; Thurman, "The Christian Minister and the Desegregation Decision," *The Pulpit Digest* (May 1957): 13-19; Thurman, "The Facist Masquerade," p. 99; Thurman, "Religion in a Time of Crisis," *The Garrett Tower* (Evanston, IL: August 1943), 1-3.
184. See Thurman, *With Head and Heart*, pp. 144-45; Thurman, *Footprints*, pp. 32-33; see also Smith, *Mystic as Prophet*, pp. 129-35. Thurman also was counselor to civil rights leaders, politicians, artists, civic leaders, and other individuals who were committed to organizations and institutions concerned about the welfare of society. Among the many black social activists who were beneficiaries of his ministry were Jesse Jackson, Martin Luther King, Jr., Vernon Jordan, and Whitney Young. See *Debate and Understanding*, pp. 71-88; Thurman, *With Head and Heart*, pp. 254-55; and *The Listening Ear: A Newsletter of the Howard Thurman Educational Trust* 16:2 (Summer 1985).
185. Thurman, *With Head and Heart*, p. 160.
186. Ibid., pp. 119-20.
187. Ibid., pp. 144; Thurman, *Footprints*, p. 21.

188. "Resident members" refers to members who lived in the San Francisco Bay Area and "members-at-large" were those who lived outside this area.
189. Thurman, *Footprints*, pp. 76-78; Thurman, *With Head and Heart*, p. 159.
190. Ibid., p. 161.
191. Ibid.
192. Smith, *Mystic as Prophet*, p. 133.
193. Thurman describes the climate of race relations in San Francisco during 1944 in *Footprints*, pp. 11-14.

Chapter 4

1. Smith and Zepp, *Search for Beloved*, pp. 119-40.
2. See Martin Luther King, Sr., *Daddy King: An Autobiography*, written with the assistance of Clayton Riley (New York: William Morrow and Co., Inc., 1980), pp. 13, 82-91, 100-01; see also David L. Lewis, *King: A Biography*, 2d ed. (Urbana: University of Illinois Press, 1978), pp. 4-5. The writer is also deeply indebted in this section to of Lewis V. Baldwin, "Understanding Martin Luther King, Jr., Within the Context of Southern Black Religious History."
3. King, Sr., *Daddy King*, pp. 23, 30-32, 40-43, 91, 96-101, 104, 106-11, 122–26, 132 and 135.
4. Martin Luther King, Jr., *Stride Toward Freedom:The Montgomery Story*, (New York: Harper and Row, 1964), p. 6. Italics added; see also, King, Sr., *Daddy King*, pp. 107–09 and 130.
5. King, *Stride*, p. 6.
6. Ibid., p. 5.
7. See King, "An Autobiography of Religious Development," n.p., n.d. King Collection, Boston University.
8. He says, "The church has always been a second home for me." Ibid., p. 8. King, "Thou Fool," a serman preached 27 August 1967, at Mt. Pisgah Baptist Church, Chicago, IL, p. 11, King Archives, Atlanta, GA.
9. King, "An Autobiography," p.8.
10. Ibid., p. 9; see Stephen B. Oates, *Let the Trumpet Sound: The Life of Martin Luther King, Jr.* (New York: New American Library, 1982), p. 14.
11. King's wrestling with the emotionalism and fundamentalism of the black church does not mean that he rejected the church nor does it suggest that it was not a major source of his religious development. To the contrary, the black church experience and his religious family

environment were the cornerstones of his developing vision of community. Lewis V. Baldwin argues that King "can only be understood when he is viewed within the context of a cultural heritage which stems back to his slave forbears. This is to say that the black experience and the black Christian tradition were *the most important sources* in the shaping of his thought, his vision, and his efforts to translate the ethical ideal of the `Beloved Community' into practical reality." Baldwin, "Understanding Martin Luther King, Jr., Within the Context of Southern Black Religious History," p. 1. See also Baldwin, "Martin Luther King, Jr., the Black Church, and the Black Messianic Vision," *The Journal of the Interdenominational Theological Center* 12:1-2 (Fall 1984/Spring 1985):93- 108. James H. Cone makes a similar argument in "Martin Luther King, Jr., Black Theology— Black Church," *Theology Today* 40:4 (January 1984):409-420. James M. Washington identifies King as part of a long, dissenting tradition of the black church within the American context. He writes: "Most of us are sadly unaware however that the black church movement, King's primary spiritual and social mooring, nurtured its own dissenting tradition. For those who are aware, it is still ironic that this tradition could so rapidly produce a world historical figure like Martin Luther King, Jr." Washington, ed., *A Testament of Hope: The Essential Writings of Martin Luther King, Jr.* (San Francisco: Harper and Row, 1986) p. xii. David L. Lewis and Stephen Oates suggest that King's struggle with the powerful authoritarian figure of his father as a preacher and his identification with the culturally and intellectually sophisticated standards of Atlanta's black community were key factors in his struggle within the black church. Lewis, *King: A Biography*, pp. 6-11; Oates, *Let the Trumpet Sound*, p. 14. For discussion of Kelsey and Mays, see Intellectual Sources.

12.   King, "Autobiography," p. 15; see also King, Statement to the American Baptist Convention, 7 August 1959, King Papers, Boston University. Here King shares his call to ministry.

13.   King, "Autobiography," p. 5; Lewis, *King: A Biography*, p. 8.

14.   See Lewis, *King: A Biography*, pp. 8-10.

15.   E. Franklin Frazier, "Inferiority Complex and Quest for Status," reprint in Frazier, *On Race Relations: Selected Papers*, edited and with introduction by G. Franklin Edwards (Chicago: The University of Chicago Press, 1968), p. 254.

16.   James H. Cone, "Martin Luther King, Jr. and Malcolm X," Lecture Series at the Partners in Ecumenism Conference of the National Council of Churches, Howard Inn, Washington, D.C., 25–27 September 1984.

17. King, *Stride*, p. 72.
18. Oates, *Let the Trumpet Sound*, pp. 16, 17.
19. King, *Stride*, p. 73.
20. Oates, *Let the Trumpet Sound*, p. 16.
21. Lewis, *King: A Biography*, p. 18.
22. Mays was considered "a notorious modernist in the eyes of the orthodox." He challenged the traditional educational practices as "accommodation under protest" and called for a new dimension in the education of black students in which liberation through knowledge became his paradigm. "Education," he told his students, "allowed the Negro to be intellectually free; it was an instrument of social and personal renewal." Oates, p. 19.
23. Ibid., p. 21; Lewis, *King: A Biography*, p. 24.
24. Oates, *Let the Trumpet Sound*, p. 20; see also, Ansbro, *Making of a Mind*, p. 76.
25. See earlier discussion regarding King's struggle with the black church and the respective contributions of Kelsey and Mays. The idea of "the call" is an important element in the black church tradition. Henry Mitchell remarks that the black preacher must take the call with the utmost seriousness. Mitchell states, "If Jeremiah (Jer 1:5) could be called before birth, so can they. And if Jeremiah's call could sustain him through unbelievable trials and rebuffs, it can for black preachers also. And it has!" *Black Preaching* (San Francisco: Harper and Row, 1979), p. 211.
26. Lewis, *King: A Biography*, p. 25.
27. King says, "I was well aware of the typical white stereotype of the Negro that he is always late, that he's loud and always laughing, that he's dirty and messy, and for a while I was terribly conscious of trying to avoid identification with it. If I were a minute late to class, I was almost morbidly conscious of it and sure that everyone else noticed it. Rather than be thought of as always laughing, I'm afraid I was grimly serious for a time." Quoted in Lewis, *King: A Biography*, p. 28.
28. In a letter to Davis while he was a student at Boston University, King wrote, "I must admit that my theological and philosophical studies with you have been of tremendous help to me in my present studies." Quoted in Ansbro, *Making of a Mind*, p. 15.
29. See discussion on Intellectual Sources later in this chapter.
30. King, *Stride*, p. 82.
31. Ibid., p. 82; see Intellectual Sources.
32. Lewis, *King: A Biography*, p. 41.
33. See Coretta Scott King, *My Life with Martin Luther King, Jr.* (Holt, Rinehart and Winston, 1969), pp. 46-97.

34. Thurman, *With Head and Heart*, p. 254.
35. Lewis V. Baldwin, "The Minister a Preacher, Pastor, and Prophet: The Thinking of Martin Luther King, Jr.," *American Baptist Quarterly* 7 (June 1988): 92.
36. Thurman, *With Head and Heart*, p. 254.
37. King, *Stride*, pp. 7-8.
38. See Benjamin Quarles, *The Negro in the Making of America* (New York: The Macmillan Co., 1964), pp. 239-50. In Montgomery, the State Board of Education voted unanimously to continue segregated facilities through the 1954-55 school year. Oates, *Let the Trumpet Sound*, p. 51.
39. King, "Annual Address to the Montgomery Improvement Association," Holt Street Baptist Church, 3 December 3 1956. King Archives, Atlanta, GA; King, *Stride*, p. 51; Oates, *Let the Trumpet Sound*, p. 73.
40. See King, "Annual Address to the Montgomery Improvement Association."
41. See Lerone Bennett, "When the Man and the Hour Are Met." C. Eric Lincoln, ed., *Martin Luther King, Jr.: A Profile* (New York: Hill and Wang, 1970), p. 25.
42. Ibid., pp. 24-29.
43. King, *Stride*, p. 66
44. Ibid., pp. 66-67; Oates, *Let the Trumpet Sound*, pp. 77-80. See also Adam Fairlough, *To Redeem the Soul of America: The Southern Christian Leadership Conference and Martin Luther King, Jr.* (Athens and London: The University of Georgia Press, 1987), pp. 23-35.
45. King, *Stride*, p. 67.
46. Ibid., p. 200; King, "The Negro and the American Dream," Address at the Public Meeting of Charlotte, NC, NAACP, September 25, 1960, p. 3.
47. King, *Stride*, p. 15.
48. Ibid., p. 170.
49. Ibid., p. 175.
50. King, "The Negro and the American Dream," p. 1.
51. See King, "Facing the Challenge of a New Age," *Phylon* (April 1957): 25-34; also in James Melvin Washington, ed., *A Testament of Hope: The Essential Writings of Martin Luther King, Jr.*, pp. 135-44.
52. Quoted in William Robert Miller, "The Broadening Horizons." C. Eric Lincoln, ed., *Martin Luther King, Jr: A Profile*, p. 45.
53. See King, "Discerning the Signs of History," a sermon preached at Ebenezer Baptist Church, 15 November 1964, King Library and Archives, Atlanta, GA.

54. Oates, *Let the Trumpet Sound*, p. 144; see also King, "Sermon on Gandhi," Dexter Avenue Baptist Church, 22 March 22 1959, King Library and Archives, Atlanta, GA.
55. *This Is SCLC* (Leaflet: Southern Christian Leadership Conference, rev. ed., 1964), in Meier and Broderick, *Negro Protest*, p. 270; see also Garrow, *Bearing the Cross*, pp. 83-126; and Adam Fairclough, *To Redeem the Soul of America: The Southern Christian Leadership Conference and Martin Luther King, Jr.*, pp. 11-35.
56. Typescript, Special Collections, Mugar Memorial Library, Boston University. After the Pilgrimage, the *Amsterdam News* heralded King as "the number one leader of sixteen million Negroes in the United States." Quoted in Oates, *Let the Trumpet Sound*, p. 12.
57. See Miller, "The Broadening Horizons," pp. 50-51; see also King, "Who Speaks for the South?" *Liberation* (March 1958):13-14.
58. The margin of difference was only 112,881 and Kennedy captured almost three-quarters of the Negro vote. See Oates, *Let the Trumpet Sound*, pp. 165- 66.
59. Oates, *Let the Trumpet Sound*, p. 169.
60. Ibid., pp. 169-70; see King, "Equality Now," *The Nation* (4 February 1961).
61. King's involvement in the Freedom Rides, which began in May, 1961 under the leadership of the Congress of Racial Equality (CORE), challenged him to note the developing militancy among the younger ranks of the Civil Rights Movement. While he acknowledged that the young element represented the "revolutionary destiny of a whole people consciously and deliberately" (quoted in Oates, *Let the Trumpet Sound*, p. 177), King argued, "The Freedom Ride[s] grew out of a recognition of the American dilemma and a desire to bring the nation to a realization of its noble dream... One day America will be proud of their achievements." Statement delivered at a rally to support the Freedom Riders, First Baptist Church, Montgomery, AL, 21 May 1961, King Library and Archives, Atlanta, GA. King, however, was castigated by the Freedom Riders for his failure to accompany them on the buses. Lewis, *King: A Biography*, pp. 133- 34.
62. For an astute analysis of the Albany Movement, see Lewis, *King: A Biography*, pp. 140-67. Lewis claims "that the Albany experiment aborted largely because of the plangent discord among its technicians. The wrong things demanded at the wrong time because there was too little coordination, trust, and harmony within the Movement." P. 167.
63. Oates, *Let the Trumpet Sound*, p. 211.
64. King, *Why We Can't Wait* (New York: Signet Books, The New American Library, 1964) p. 77.

65. King, "I Have a Dream," Lincoln Memorial, Washington, D.C., 28 August 1963. Flip Schulke, ed., *Martin Luther King, Jr.: A Documentary...Montgomery to Memphis*, intro. by Coretta Scott King (New York: W.W. Norton and Co., 1976), p. 218.

66. King, Nobel Prize Acceptance Speech, 10 December 1964. *Martin Luther King, Jr.: A Documentary...Montgomery to Memphis*, p. 219. Parentheses added.

67. See Malcolm X, *The Autobiography of Malcolm X*, with the assistance of Alex Haley (New York: Grove Press, 1965); George Breitman, ed., *Malcolm X Speaks: Selected Speeches and Statements* (New York: Grove Press, 1965); and C. Eric Lincoln, *The Black Muslims in America* (Boston: Beacon Press, 1961).

68. See Malcolm X, "Message to the Grassroots," in *Malcolm X Speaks*, pp. 3-17; Ibid., "The Ballot or the Bullet," pp. 23-44; see also "Kenneth B. Clark Interview (1963)," in Washington, *A Testament of Hope*, p. 331.

69. See King, *Where Do We Go From Here? Chaos or Community*, (Boston: Beacon Press, 1967), p. 63. For King's response to Stokely Carmichael et al and other critics, see Ibid., pp. 23-26. See also Lewis, *King: A Biography*, pp. 299, 321-24; and Louis Lomax, "When `Nonviolence' Meets `Black Power,'" in Lincoln, *Martin Luther King, Jr.: A Profile*, pp. 157-80.

70. Lewis, *King: A Biography*, p. 244; Oates, *Let the Trumpet Sound*, p. 300.

71. David Halberstam, "When `Civil Rights' and `Peace' Join Forces," in Lincoln, *Martin Luther King, Jr.: A Profile*, p. 195; Oates, *Let the Trumpet Sound*, pp. 417-19.

72. Louis Lomax, "When `Nonviolence` Meets `Black Power'," pp. 167-71; see also Lewis, *King: A Biography*, pp. 280-83.

73. King, "Nonviolence: The Only Road to Freedom," in Washington, *A Testament of Hope*, pp. 57-58; see also in same work, "A Gift of Love," pp. 62-63, and "Showdown for Nonviolence," pp. 64-74.

74. King, "Facing the Challenge of a New Age" in Washington, *A Testament of Hope*, pp. 135-36. King was also an astute observer of the South African political situation. As early as 1957 there is correspondence between King and Oliver Tambo on the South African crisis. See "Oliver Tambo to Martin Luther King, Jr.," 18 November 1957; see also "Martin Luther King, Jr. to Albert Luthuli," 8 December 1959; and Martin Luther King, Jr., Eleanor Roosevelt and James A. Pike, "Declaration of Conscience: The Apartheid Issue," 10 December 1957. The author is deeply indebted to Lewis V. Baldwin's unpublished manuscript, "Martin Luther King, Jr., and South Africa."

75. Lewis, *King: A Biography*, pp. 294-96.

76. King, Press Conference, 12 April 1967, Biltmore Hotel, Los Angeles, King Archives, Atlanta, GA.

77. King commented on the relationship between conflict and progress in his refutation of the claims that the increasing violence and militancy of black groups were indications of the failure of his program of peaceful protest. King, *Where Do We Go from Here?*, pp. 12-13.

78. Since the St. Albany campaign, King had become an object of surveillance and scorn for J. Edgar Hoover, the powerful director of the Federal Bureau of Investigation. Lewis, *King: A Biography*, pp. 200–01. Hoover's dislike for King fermented into an all-out onslaught against him and the Civil Rights Movement. David J. Garrow outlines three successive phases of the FBI's assault: the charge that King was a communist, his alleged immoral personal conduct, and his being a pronounced political threat to American society. See Garrow, *The FBI and Martin Luther King, Jr.: From "Solo" to Memphis* (New York: W.W. Norton and Co., 1981), pp. 204-19.

79. King, *Where Do We Go From Here?*, pp. 167-202.

80. Ibid., pp. 173-86.

81. King, *The Trumpet of Conscience*, chap. 2, "Conscience and the Vietnam War," in Washington, *A Testament of Hope*, p. 640.

82. King, *Where Do We Go From Here?*, pp. 135-66; "Discerning the Signs of History," sermon preached by King at Ebenezer Baptist Church, 15 November 1964; King, "A Christmas Sermon on Peace (1967)," in Washington, *A Testament of Hope*, pp. 253-58.

83. Oates, *Let the Trumpet Sound*, pp. 449-52.

84. King, *The Trumpet of Conscience*, chap. 2, "Conscience and the Vietnam War," in Washington, *A Testament of Hope*, p. 639.

85. *Ibid.*, p. 652.

86. *Ibid.*, p. 191.

87. The major intellectual sources of Martin Luther King, Jr., have been documented at several places: Smith and Zepp, *Search for Beloved*; Ansbro, *Making of a Mind*; Carter, ed., *Debate and Understanding*, "The Philosophical and Theological Influences in the Thought and Action of Martin Luther King, Jr."; Oates, *Let the Trumpet Sound*; Watley, *Roots of Resistance*, pp. 17-47; and Lewis, *King: A Biography*.

88. Oates, *Let the Trumpet Sound*, p. 19.

89. King, "Autobiography," p. 10; see also, George Kelsey, *Racism and the Christian Understanding of Man* (New York: Charles Scribner's Sons, 1965).

90. See Jones, *Candle in the Dark*, pp. 133-231; and Mays, *Born to Rebel*, pp. 265-74.

91. King, *Stride*, p. 73.
92. Oates, *Let the Trumpet Sound*, p. 19.
93. See Ansbro, *Making of a Mind*, p. 76.
94. Oates, *Let the Trumpet Sound*, p. 18.
95. Smith and Zepp, *Search for Beloved*, p. 21.
96. See Kenneth, *The Impact of American Religious Liberalism*, pp. 27-29 and Sydney E. Ahlstrom, *A Religious History of the American People* (New Haven and London: Yale University Press), pp. 781-784.
97. Smith and Zepp, *Search for Beloved*, pp. 21-31.
98. Ansbro, *Making of a Mind*, pp. 15-16.
99. Ansbro pinpoints Davis's understanding of moral progress in history, which traces the evolution of the human spirit "to higher levels of self-consciousness, freedom, and active participation by the individual in communal activity." The shifts Davis discovered in the historical process are: 1) the transition from external controls to internal sanctions; 2) the transition from the impersonal to the personal; and 3) the transition from rank individualism to the solidarity of the social group, which enhances the realization of the personal. Ansbro, *Making of a Mind*, pp. 63-70.
100. King, *Stride*, p. 73. Actually King's criticism that Rauschenbusch fell victim to "the cult of inevitable progress" is somewhat questionable. It is important to note that although Rauschenbusch makes numerous suggestions and pronouncements regarding "christianizing the social order," he does at points attempt to balance these claims with an articulate realism. Rauschenbusch also recognized that "however evolution may work in the rest of creation, a new element enters when it reaches the ethical nature of man. Ethically man sags downward by nature." Robert T. Handy, *The Social Gospel in America* (New York: Oxford University Press, 1966), p. 281.
101. King, *Stride*, p. 73.
102. See Max Stackhouse's Introduction entitled, "The Continuing Importance of Walter Rauschenbusch," in Rauschenbusch, *The Righteousness of the Kingdom* (New York: Abingdon Press, 1968).
103. Rauschenbusch, *A Theology for the Social Gospel*, p. 141; see also Handy, *The Social Gospel in America*, p. 281; see later treatment of Rauschenbusch in chap. 5 of this work under "The Conception of Community."
104. King, *Stride*, pp. 74-75.
105. Ibid. This analysis is also found in King's sermon, "How Should a Christian View Communism?" in *Strength to Love*, pp. 96-105, which was a later version of a sermon he preached in Atlanta in 1952 entitled, "The Challenge of Communism to Christianity." See also

"Melvin Watson to Martin Luther King," 14 August 1952, Martin Luther King Collection, Boston University. Watson was a professor of religion at the Morehouse School of Religion and a confidant of the King family, especially for young Martin. Watson also represents an important link between the two subjects of this discussion. In the correspondence noted above, his critique of King's presentation of communism reveals that Watson felt that the future civil rights leader was unclear in respect to Marx's position on historical materialism and communist attitudes toward religion and race. See Epilogue.

106. King, *Stride*, p. 75.
107. Ibid., p. 77. It is instructive to note that King's dialectical treatment of communism and capitalism utilizes the paradigm of community which he refers to as the Kingdom of God. He says, "The Kingdom of God is neither the thesis of individual enterprise nor the antithesis of collective enterprise, but a synthesis which reconciles the truths of both." Ibid., p. 77.
108. See Ansbro, *Making of a Mind*, pp. 1-2, and King's reflections on Nietzsche in *Stride*, pp. 77-78.
109. See earlier discussions of Mordecai Johnson's relationship to Thurman.
110. King, *Stride*, p. 78.
111. Smith, *Mystic as Prophet*, pp. 118-119.
112. King, *Stride*, p. 78.
113. Ibid., p. 79; see William Watley, *Roots of Resistance: Martin Luther King, Jr.'s Nonviolent Ethics* for a most illuminating analysis of King's treatment of Gandhi's method and insights from the black religious experience.
114. Ibid.
115. James P. Hanigan, "Martin Luther King, Jr.: The Shaping of a Mind," *Debate and Understanding* 1:3 (Semester 2), Martin Luther King, Jr. Afro-American Center, Boston University, p. 196.
116. King, *Stride*, p. 79.
117. Reinhold Niebuhr, *Moral Men and Immoral Society* (New York: Charles Scribner's Sons, 1932), p. 242.
118. Ibid., p. 240; Reinhold Niebuhr, "Must We Do Nothing?", *The Christian Century*, (30 March 1932): 415; Reinhold Niebuhr, *The Nature and Destiny of Man*, vol. 2 (New York: Charles Scribner's Sons, 1943), p. 252; Reinhold Niebuhr, *An Interpretation of Christian Ethics* (New York: Seabury Press, 1979), p. 24.
119. Niebuhr maintained, "There can be nothing absolute in history, no matter how frequently God may intervene in it. Man cannot live

without a sense of the absolute, but neither can he achieve the absolute. He may resolve the tragic character of that fact by religious faith, by the experience of grace in anticipatory terms, but he can never resolve in purely ethical terms the conflict between what is and what ought to be." Niebuhr, "Must We Do Nothing?" p. 417.

120. King, *Stride*, p. 80.
121. Niebuhr, *Moral Man*, p. 252.
122. King, *Stride*, p. 81; see also Smith and Zepp, *Search for Beloved*, pp. 71–97; and Ansbro, *Making of a Mind*, pp. 151-160.
123. King, *Stride*, p. 83.
124. Ibid., pp. 81-82.
125. See King, "Reinhold Niebuhr's Ethical Dualism," 9 May 1952, Special Collections, Mugar Memorial Library, Boston University.
126. Muelder, "Reinhold Niebuhr's Conception of Man," *The Personalist* 36 (1945): 292. Quoted in Ansbro, *Making of a Mind*, p. 158.
127. Smith and Zepp suggest that there are four significant themes of personalism which shaped King's intellectual quest for the beloved community: 1) the inherent worth of personality; 2) the personal God of love and reason; 3) the moral law of the cosmos; and 4) the social nature of human existence. Smith and Zepp, *Search for Beloved*, p. 118. King stated that personal idealism was his basic philosophical position. He credits personalism with two valuable contributions to his developing religious and ethical convictions: the metaphysical and philosophical grounding for the idea of a personal God and a metaphysical basis for the dignity and worth of all human personality. King, *Stride*, p. 82.
128. Ibid.
129. Brightman had written that rational coherence is a method of verification of truth. He maintained that a proposition was true if it met the following criteria: 1) it is self-consistent; 2) it is consistent with all known facts of experience; 3) it is consistent with all other propositions held as true by the mind that is applying this criterion; 4) it establishes explanatory and interpretative relations between various parts of experience; and 5) these relations include all known aspects of experience and all known problems about experience in its details and as a whole. Brightman, *A Philosophy of Religion*, (New York: Prentice Hall, Inc., 1940) p. 128.
130. King, *Stride*, p. 82.
131. For example, his sermons, "A Tough Mind and a Tender Heart" and "Transformed Nonconformist" in King, *Strength to Love*, pp. 9-16, 17–25. According to Cornel West, black theologians have either consciously or unconsciously employed dialectical methodology as

hermeneutic all along. See West, *Prophesy Deliverance! An Afro-American Revolutionary Christianity* (Philadelphia: Westminster Press, 1982), pp. 108-111.

132. See Ansbro's treatment of DeWolf's influence on King's conception of God, *Making of a Mind*, pp. 38-63.

133. Brightman referred to his position as "theistic finitism." He argued, "A theistic finitist is one who holds that the eternal will of God faces given conditions which that will did not create, whether those conditions are ultimately within the personality of God or external to it... All theistic finitists agree that there is something in the universe not created by God and not a result of voluntary self-limitation, which God finds as either obstacle or instrument to his will." Brightman, *A Philosophy of Religion*, pp. 313-14.

134. DeWolf, *A Theology for the Living Church*, pp. 140-42; see also DeWolf, *The Religious Revolt Against Reason* (New York: Greenwood Press, 1968), pp. 94–96; and Ansbro, *Making of a Mind*, pp. 53-58. DeWolf supervised King in his dissertation, "A Comparison of the Conceptions of God in the Thinking of Paul Tillich and Henry Nelson Wieman" (Ph.D. dissertation in Systematic Theology, Boston University, 1955). See Ansbro's treatment of King's critique of Wieman and Tillich in *Making of a Mind*, pp. 60-63.

135. Oates, *Let the Trumpet Sound*, p. 38; Lewis, *King: A Biography*, p. 41.

136. Lewis, *King: A Biography*, p. 41.

Chapter 5

1. See John H. Cartwright, "Foundations of the Beloved Community," *Debate and Understanding* 1:3 (Semester 2, 1977), p. 171. Boston University, Martin Luther King, Jr. Afro-American Center. Here Cartwright formulates the primary question for King regarding the problem of social eschatology: "From a Christian perspective, what kind of society must human society be when human society truly becomes?" King, *Stride Toward Freedom*, p. 88; King, *Strength to Love*, p. 70; Smith and Zepp, *Search for Beloved*, p. 119.

2. Ansbro contends that "while several thinkers contributed to King's conception of the beloved community, Personalism emerged as the dominant influence in his thoughts about this community which was the goal of all his endeavors." Anbsro, *Making of a Mind*, p. 187. Smith and Zepp, on the other hand, maintain that both liberalism and personalism provided the theological and philosophical foundations of the concept, p. 119. "The black Christian tradition" refers to Peter Paris's argument in *The Social Teaching of the Black Churches*.

Paris claims that "The tradition that has always been normative for the black churches and the black community is not the so-called Western tradition per se, although this tradition is an important source for blacks. More accurately, the normative tradition for blacks is the tradition governed by the principle of nonracism which we call the black Christian tradition. The fundamental principle of the black Christian tradition is depicted most adequately in the biblical doctrine of the parenthood of God and the kinship of all peoples..." (p. 10). See also Cornel West's treatment of "the prophetic black church tradition" as the most important source that "initially and fundamentally shaped King's worldview." West, "Martin Luther King, Jr.: Prophetic Christian as Organic Intellectual," in *Prophetic Fragments*, pp. 3-12.

3. Royce writes, "All morality, namely, is, from this point of view, to be judged by the Beloved Community, of the ideal of the Kingdom of Heaven. Concretely stated, this means that you are to test every course of action not by the question: What can we find in the parables of the Sermon on the Mount which seems to us more or less directly to bear upon this special matter? The central doctrine of the Master was: So act that the kingdom of Heaven may come. This means: So act as to help, however you can, and wherever you can, and whenever you can towards making mankind one loving brotherhood, whose love is not a mere affection for morally detached individuals, but a love of the unity of its own life upon its own divine level, and love of individuals in so far as they can be raised to communion with this spiritual community itself." Josiah Royce, *The Religious Philosophy of Josiah Royce* (Syracuse: Syracuse University Press, 1952), p. 6; quoted in Cartwright, "Foundations of the Beloved Community," p. 172.

4. King, *Stride*, p. 82; Cartwright, "Foundations of the Beloved Community," p. 172.

5. Edgar S. Brightman, *Nature and Values* (Nashville: Abingdon Press, 1945), p. 165; quoted in Smith and Zepp, *Search for Beloved*, p. 139.

6. Cartwright, "Foundations of the Beloved Community," p. 172; see earlier discussion of Rauschenbusch's influence upon King in chap. 4.

7. Smith and Zepp, *Search for Beloved*, pp. 43-45.

8. Walter Rauschenbusch, *A Theology for the Social Gospel* (New York: Macmillan Company, 1918), p. 131.

9. King, "What a Christian Should Think About the Kingdom of God," King Papers, Special Collections, Boston University, p. 2. Quoted in Smith and Zepp, *Search for Beloved*, p. 129; see also Cartwright, "The Social Eschatology of Martin Luther King, Jr." in *Essays in Honor of*

Martin Luther King, Jr. (Evanston: Garrett-Evangelical Theological Seminary, Leiffer Bureau of Social and Religious Research, 1971), p. 3.

10. King, "The Ethical Demands of Integration," in James Melvin Washington, ed., *A Testament of Hope: The Essential Writings of Martin Luther King, Jr.* (San Francisco: Harper and Row, 1986), p. 121.

11. According to King, in order to achieve integration within American society and the world, there must be a conscious, deliberate decision to cooperate with others. Integration is not an enforceable demand, while desegregation is. *Ibid.*, pp. 121-23.

12. *Ibid.*, p. 122.

13. Lewis Baldwin suggests that "King's firm belief in the `Beloved Community' idea, and his optimism regarding its realization, were deeply rooted in the black church tradition." "Understanding Martin Luther King, Jr. Within the Context of Southern Black Religious History," p. 19; see also p. 18. See also Baldwin, "Martin Luther King, Jr., the Black Church, and the Black Messianic Vision," *The Journal of the Interdenominational Theological Center* 12:1-2 (Fall 1984/Spring 1985): 1.

14. Lawrence N. Jones, *The Journal of Religious Thought* 12:2 (1985): 12-18.

15. *Ibid.*, pp. 12, 19.

16. Baldwin, "Understanding Martin Luther King," pp. 20-21.

17. Larry Murphy, "Howard Thurman and Social Activism," in *God and Human Freedom*, pp. 154-55.

18. *Ibid.*, pp. 27-29; Ansbro, *Making of a Mind*, p. 23.

19. The original source of this claim was the historian Lerone Bennett. See Lerone Bennett, *What Manner of Man*, pp. 74-75. See also Thurman's remarks in respect to this influence in Thurman, *With Head and Heart*, p. 255; and Thurman's sermonic tribute to King after his assassination. "Martin Luther King, Jr. Ceremony." Audio-Tape Cassette, Fellowship Church, 8 April 1968. King Papers, Special Collections, Mugar Memorial Library, Boston University. At both places Thurman speaks of his relationship with the younger visionary in rather candid terms. At neither place does he claim to have had direct influence on King's intellectual formation. See also correspondence between Thurman and King: "Howard Thurman to Martin Luther King, Jr.," 20 October 1958, and "Martin Luther King, Jr. to Howard Thurman," 8 November 1958. King Papers, BU. Thurman's major contribution seems to have been that of a counselor and enabler to the young civil rights leader. See Introduction.

20. Baldwin, "Martin Luther King, the Black Church, and the Black Messianic Vision," pp. 103-04.

21. Ansbro, *Making of a Mind*, p. 29.
22. See King sermons, "The Meaning of Hope," Dexter Avenue Baptist Church, 10 October 1967, pp. 16-17 and "Is the Universe Friendly?" Ebenezer Baptist Church, 12 December 1965, pp. 5-6. King Archives, Atlanta, GA. Compare with Thurman, *With Head and Heart*, pp. 20-21. (Thurman's story of the slave preacher can be found in many of his earlier sermons and writings.) See King, "Antidotes for Fear," in *Strength to Love*, p. 36. Only at one place in his writings does he make a bibliographic reference to Thurman. See King, "Knock at Midnight," in *Strength to Love*, pp. 65-66.
23. See Luther Smith, *Mystic as Prophet*, p. 23. See also Kenneth Cauthen, *The Impact of American Religious Liberalism* (New York: Harper and Row, 1962), pp. 27-29, and David E. Roberts and Henry Van Dusen, eds., *Liberal Theology: An Appraisal* (New York: Charles Scribner's Sons, 1942). See also earlier discussions of the intellectual influences on Thurman.
24. For Jones's indebtedness to evangelical liberalism, see Smith, *Mystic as Prophet*, pp. 27-30; Cauthen, *The Impact of American Religious Liberalism*, p. 36. There are important differences, however, in Thurman and his evangelical liberal mentors in respect to their views on sources of authority (the Bible and Jesus) and the ultimate vision of community. See Smith, *Mystic as Prophet*, pp. 73-77.
25. Cauthen, *The Impact of American Religious Liberalism*, pp. 36-37; Smith, *Mystic as Prophet*, p. 75.
26. See Cone, "Martin Luther King, Jr., Black Church—Black Theology," p. 416; see also Timothy L. Smith, "Slavery and Theology: The Emergence of Black Christian Consciousness in Nineteenth-Century America," reprint from *Church History* 41:4 (December 1972).
27. Ibid., p. 2; see also Lawrence N. Jones, "Hope for Mankind: Insights from Black Religious History in the United States," *The Journal of Religious Thought* 34:2 (Fall-Winter 77-78): 59-65.
28. King, *Stride*, p. 73.
29. Smith and Zepp, *Search for Beloved*, p. 29.
30. King, *Stride*, p. 73.
31. Ibid., p. 82.
32. Smith and Zepp, *Search for Beloved*, p. 99.
33. See earlier discussion in chap. 4 concerning the impact of the black community and black church upon King's development.
34. Brightman, *Nature and Values*, p. 113; quoted in Smith and Zepp, *Search for Beloved*, p. 100.
35. See Smith and Zepp's treatment of personalism, idealism, and theism and its impact upon King in *Search for Beloved*, pp. 100-04; see also

Edgar S. Brightman, *A Philosophy of Religion* (New York: Prentice-Hall, 1940), chap. 11, "The Problem of Human Personality," pp. 342–69.

36. Smith and Zepp, *Search for Beloved*, p. 130.
37. King, "Loving Your Enemies," in *Strength to Love*, p. 49.
38. Martin Luther King, Jr., *Where Do We Go from Here: Chaos or Community?* (Boston: Beacon Press, 1967), p. 97.
39. Ibid., pp. 97-101.
40. King, *Stride*, p. 167.
41. King, *Where Do We Go from Here?*, p. 98.
42. Ibid., pp. 97-98.
43. Ibid., p. 99.
44. King, "What Is Man?" in *The Measure of a Man* (Philadelphia: The Christian Education Press, 1959), p. 8.
45. See Ansbro's treatment of Kant's and Brightman's influence, *Making of a Mind*, pp. 71-86; also Smith and Zepp, *Search for Beloved*, pp. 110–13; and William P. DeVeaux, "Immanuel Kant, Social Justice, and Martin Luther King, Jr.," *The Journal for Religious Thought* 27:2 (1970): 5–15.
46. Ansbro, *Making of a Mind*, pp. 76-77; Edgar S. Brightman, *Moral Laws* (New York: Abingdon Press, 1933); see Walter G. Muelder, *Moral Law in Christian Social Ethics* (Richmond, VA: John Knox Press, 1966). Muelder has demonstrated how King's thought appealed to and embodied the personalistic interpretation of the moral laws in a lecture entitled, "Martin Luther King, Jr. and the Moral Laws," delivered at Morehouse College, 24 March 1983.
47. King, "Our God Is Able," *Strength to Love*, p. 110. King writes, "There is a law in the moral world—a silent, invisible imperative, akin to the laws of the physical world—which reminds us that life will only work in a certain way. The Hitlers and the Mussolinis have their day, and for a period they may wield great power, spreading themselves like a green bay tree, but soon they are cut down like grass and wither as the green herb." Ibid., p. 109.
48. Martin Luther King, Jr., *Why We Can't Wait*, p. 82.
49. Martin Luther King, Jr., "What Is Man?" *Measure of a Man*, p. 8.
50. King, *Where Do We Go from Here?*, pp. 171-72.
51. Ibid; King sermon, "Unfulfilled Dreams," Ebenezer Baptist Church, Atlanta, GA, 3 March 1968, King Archives, Atlanta, GA, pp. 3-5; King sermon, "Thou Fool," Mt. Pisgah Baptist Church, Chicago, 27 August 1967, pp. 4-5, King Archives, Atlanta, GA; and King, "What Is Man?," p. 11.
52. King, "Loving Your Enemies," in *Strength to Love*, p. 49.

53. See King, "An Answer to a Perplexing Question," King Archives, Atlanta, GA, p. 11.
54. Quoted in Ansbro, *Making of a Mind*, p. 66.
55. Although King used the terms "person" and "self" interchangeably, his philosophical grounding in personalism certainly would have led him to agree with Brightman's distinction between persons and selves. Brightman wrote, "A *person* is a self that is potentially self-conscious, rational, and ideal. That is to say, when a self is able at times to reflect on itself as a self, to reason, and to acknowledge ideal goals by which it can judge actual achievements, then we call it a person." Brightman, *A Philosophy of Religion*, p. 350. In another place, Brightman writes: "A self is given; a personality is achieved." Ibid., p. 363.
56. King, "The Ethical Demands of Integration," in Washington, *A Testament of Hope*, p. 122.
57. See King's critique of communism as a political-economic system which depersonalizes human being in King, "How Should a Christian View Communism," in *Strength to Love*, pp. 98-99; also, King, *Where Do We Go from Here?*, pp. 188-90.
58. Ibid., p. 180.
59. Ibid., p. 180.
60. Martin Luther King, Jr., "A Comparison of the Conceptions of God in the Thinking of Paul Tillich and Henry Nelson Wieman" (Ph.D. dissertation, Boston University, 1955), pp. 269-70.
61. King, "Loving Your Enemies," in *Strength to Love*, p. 53.
62. King, "Antidotes for Fear," in *Strength to Love*, p. 124.
63. See Smith and Zepp, *Search for Beloved*, pp. 107-10; Ansbro, *Making of a Mind*, pp. 37-62.
64. See Ansbro on King's critique of Wieman and Tillich, *Making of a Mind*, pp. 60-63.
65. King, "Pilgrimage to Nonviolence," in *Strength to Love*, p. 155.
66. King, "A Tough Mind and a Tender Heart," in *Strength to Love*, p. 16; King, *Stride*, p. 88.
67. Ibid., p. 87.
68. See discussion on the influence of Brightman and DeWolf in Chap. 4.
69. King, "Religion's Answer to the Problem of Evil," Special Collections, Boston University, pp. 12-13.
70. King, "Our God Is Able," in *Strength to Love*, p. 108.
71. Ibid., p. 109.
72. Ibid., pp. 111-12; see also King, "Answer to a Perplexing Question," King Archives, Atlanta, GA, pp. 4-6.
73. In King, "A Tough Mind and a Tender Heart," in *Strength to Love*, p. 15.

74. Ibid., pp. 14-16. King, *Why We Can't Wait*, p. 82; see also King, "Transformed Nonconformist," in *Strength to Love*, pp. 17-25.

75. Ervin Smith has shown how King fused the metaphysical, ethical, and experiential aspects of the idea of God onto a harmonious whole. Ervin Smith, *The Ethics of Martin Luther King, Jr.* (New York and Toronto: The Edwin Mellen Press, 1981), pp. 26-27.

76. King sermon, "Thou Fool," pp. 10-11.

77. King, *Strength to Love*, p. 97.

78. This, too, is an inheritance from personal theism. DeWolf wrote, "The relation between the great system of ideas which we know as causal law and the events of the physical universe becomes intelligible only when we conceive of the ideas as occurring long before men discovered them in a cosmic Mind in which idea and will are perpetually and intimately conjoined." Quoted in Ansbro, *Making of a Mind*, p. 40; see Harold DeWolf, *A Theology for the Living Church* (New York: Harper and Row, 1968), pp. 49-50.

79. King, "What Is Man?" King, "Thou Fool," pp. 9-10.

80. King, "Our God Is Able," in *Strength to Love*, p. 108; King sermon, "Thou Fool," pp. 10-11

81. King, "How a Christian Should View Communism," in *Strength to Love*, p. 97; King, "Is the Universe Friendly?" p. 1.

82. King, *Where Do We Go from Here?*, p. 180; King, "Antidotes to Fear," in *Strength to Love*, p. 124; King, "Discerning the Signs of History," pp. 2, 9.

83. King, "A Tough Mind and a Tender Heart," in *Strength to Love*, pp. 11-12.

84. King, "The Answer to a Perplexing Question," in *Strength to Love*, p. 134.

85. Smith and Zepp, *Search for Beloved*, p. 105.

86. H.R. Niebuhr, *Christ and Culture* (New York: Harper and Brothers, 1951), p. 195.

87. King, "An Address Before the National Press Club," *Congressional Record* 108 (July 20, 1962): 14247-49; quoted in Washington, p. 104.

88. King, "The Death of Evil on the Seashore," in *Strength to Love*, pp. 82–83; King, "The Meaning of Hope," p. 8; see also Ansbro, *Making of a Mind*, pp. 187- 96.

89. King, *Why We Can't Wait*, p. 86.

90. Quoted in Smith and Zepp, *Search for Beloved*, p. 113; see Brightman, *Nature and Values*, p. 117.

91. King, "The Ethical Demands of Integration," p. 122.

92. King, *Where Do We Go From Here?*, p. 190; King, "A Christmas Sermon on Peace," in Washington, p. 253.

93. King, "The Ethical Demands of Integration," in Washington, p. 118.
94. King, *Where Do We Go from Here?*, pp. 135-202; see also, Frank L. Morris, "A Dream Unfulfilled: The Economic and Political Policies of Martin Luther King, Jr.," presented at the Annual Celebration Commemorating the Birth of Martin Luther King at Garrett-Evangelical Theological Seminary, Evanston, IL, January 1977.
95. See King, "The American Dream," in Washington, p. 208.
96. David Garrow, *Bearing the Cross: Martin Luther King, Jr., and the Southern Christian Leadership Conference* (New York: William Morrow and Co., Inc., 1986), pp. 536-37, 564, 591-92; Smith and Zepp, *Search for Beloved*, p. 125.
97. King, "Paul's Letter to American Christians," in *Strength to Love*, p. 140.
98. King, *Where Do We Go from Here?*, p. 163.
99. Ibid., p. 165.
100. King, *Strength to Love*, pp. 139-40.
101. King, "The American Dream," in Washington, p. 208.
102. Ibid.
103. See "Excerpts from Address by Dr. Martin Luther King, Jr. at Public Meeting of Charlotte, North Carolina Branch, NAACP," 25 September 1960, King Archives, Atlanta, GA.
104. King, "I Have a Dream," in Washington, p. 217.
105. King, "Excerpts from Address...Charlotte, N.C. NAACP," pp. 3-5.
106. John H. Cartwright suggests that the struggles of the sixties under the leadership of King may have been "American civil religion's finest hour." "An Affirmative Exposition of American Civil Religion," Research Report No. 001 (Evanston: Bureau of Social and Religious Research, Garrett Evangelical Theological Seminary, 1976), pp. 17-18; see also John Dixon Edler, "Martin Luther King and American Civil Religion," *Harvard Divinity School Bulletin* (Spring 1968): 17-18; West, "Martin Luther King, Jr.: Prophetic Christian as Organic Intellectual," p. 11.
107. Robert Bellah et al, *Habits of the Heart: Individualism and Commitment in American Life* (New York: Harper and Row, Perennial Library, 1985), especially pp. 249, 252.
108. King, "Answer to a Perplexing Question," King Archives, Atlanta, GA, p. 12.
109. Ibid., p. 10.
110. Ibid., pp. 10-20.
111. Ibid., p. 20.
112. King, "A Tough Mind and a Tender Heart," in *Strength to Love*, pp. 11-12.

113. King, "The Answer to a Perplexing Question," in *Strength to Love,* p. 134.
114. King sermon, "Is the Universe Friendly?" p. 9.
115. King, "On Being a Good Neighbor," in *Strength to Love,* p. 35.
116. King, "Loving Your Enemies," in *Strength to Love,* p. 35.
117. King, "Love in Action," in *Strength to Love,* p. 45.
118. King, *Stride,* p. 82. In a telephone interview, 3 February 1986, DeWolf shared with the author his understanding of his influence on King's Christological perspective.
119. DeWolf, *A Theology for the Living Church,* p. 246.
120. Ibid., pp. 243-47.
121. Ibid., pp. 248-49. DeWolf also indicates that he is deeply indebted to Donald M. Baillie's treatment of Christology. Donald M. Baillie, *God Was in Christ* (New York: Charles Scribner's Sons, 1948). See DeWolf, *A Theology for the Living Church,* p. 241.
122. King, *Why We Can't Wait,* p. 87.
123. In Cartwright, *Essays in Honor of Martin Luther King, Jr.,* p. 19.
124. See King, "A Tough Mind and a Tender Heart," pp. 13-14; King, "Transformed Nonconformist," pp. 18-19; King, "On Being a Good Neighbor," pp. 35-46; King, "Loving Your Enemies," pp. 47-55; King, "How Should a Christian View Communism," pp. 96-105; "Antidotes to Fear," pp. 115-26; King, "The Answer to a Perplexing Question," pp. 127-37 in *Strength to Love.* See also King's sermons "Is the Universe Friendly," pp. 8-9, "Thou Fool," pp. 2-4; and "Discerning the Signs of History."
125. King argued, "The trouble with Communism is that it has neither a theology nor a Christology: therefore it emerges with a mixed-up anthropology. Confused about God, it is also confused about man." "How Should a Christian View Communism?" in *Strength to Love,* p. 99.
126. King, "Love in Action," in *Strength to Love,* p. 45; see discussion on the influence of Niebuhr and the contribution of Muelder in respect to King's understanding of redemption in history in the next chapter.
127. King, "How Should a Christian View Communism?" in *Strength to Love,* p. 97.
128. Cartwright, "Foundations of the Beloved Community," p. 171. see note 1.
129. King, *The Measure of a Man,* p. 19.
130. Ibid., p. 33.

Chapter 6

1.   King, "The Death of Evil on the Seashore," pp. 76-78, and "Answer to a Perplexing Question," in *Strength to Love*, p. 127.
2.   King, "The Death of Evil on the Seashore," pp. 76-77.
3.   King sermon, "Unfulfilled Dreams," Ebenezer Baptist Church, Atlanta, GA, 3 March 1968, King Archives, Atlanta, GA, p. 3.
4.   King, "Death of Evil on the Seashore," p. 82.
5.   Ibid., p. 77; see also King, "A Knock at Midnight," in *Strength to Love*, p. 65.
6.   King, "The Death of Evil on the Seashore," p. 76.
7.   Ibid., pp. 77-78.
8.   King's treatment of the problem of evil is deeply indebted to L. Harold DeWolf. See Ansbro, *Making of a Mind*, pp. 53-60.
9.   King, "The Death of Evil on the Seashore," p. 83.
10. King, "Shattered Dreams," p. 90.
11. King, "Suffering and Faith," in Washington, *A Testament of Hope*, p. 41.
12. Ibid., p. 41; see also, King, "Shattered Dreams," pp. 87-90.
13. King, "Suffering and Faith," p. 42.
14. King, "The Death of Evil on the Seashore," pp. 84-85. Both Thurman and King use this metaphor. See design on the cover of Thurman's *Disciplines of the Spirit* (Richmond, IN: Friends United Press, 1977.) The drawing is an expression of Thurman's phrase, "The Spear of Frustration is Transformed into a Shaft of Light." The artwork is credited to Esther Nushbaum of Richmond, IN.
15. King, "Answer to a Perplexing Question," p. 134.
16. King, "The Death of Evil on the Seashore," p. 83.
17. King, "Shattered Dreams," p. 91.
18. King, "Love in Action," p. 45.
19. King, "The Negro and the American Dream," NAACP Public Meeting, Charlotte, NC, 25 September 1960. King Archives, Atlanta, GA, p. 3.
20. King, "Address to the Initial Mass Meeting of the Montgomery Improvement Association," Holt Street Baptist Church, Montgomery, AL, 5 December 1955. King Archives, Atlanta, GA.
21. King, "A Testament of Hope," in Washington, *A Testament of Hope*, p. 316; "Loving Your Enemies," *Strength to Love*, pp. 60-61; King, "Playboy Interview: Martin Luther King, Jr.," *A Testament of Hope*, pp. 346-47.
22. King, "Love, Law, and Civil Disobedience," *New South* (December 1961): 6. "Nonviolence is power," writes King, "but it is the right and

good use of power. Constructively it can save the white man as well as the Negro." King, *Where Do We Go from Here?*, p. 59.

23. King, *Where Do We Go from Here?*, pp. 59-61; King, "Loving Your Enemies," pp. 52-53, and "Antidotes for Fear," pp. 121-22, in *Strength to Love*.
24. King, "Loving Your Enemies," *Strength to Love*, p. 49.
25. King sermon, "Unfulfilled Dreams," pp. 3-5.
26. King, "What Is Man?," *The Measure of a Man*, p. 10.
27. DeWolf, *A Theology for the Living Church*, pp. 179-82.
28. King, "The Drum Major Instinct," in Washington, *A Testament of Hope*, p. 260; King, "What Is Man?" p. 12.
29. Ibid.
30. King, "Love in Action," p. 40.
31. Ibid., p. 45.
32. King, "The Drum Major Instinct," p. 260.
33. King, "The Death of Evil on the Seashore," p. 77. This is also Thurman's position relative to a healthy sense of self. See earlier discussion under "The Individual" in chap. 2.
34. King, "The Drum Major Instinct," p. 262.
35. Ibid., p. 265.
36. King, *Stride*, p. 73.
37. Ibid., p. 13.
38. King, *Where Do We Go from Here?*, pp. 173-86. See also section entitled "World House" in chap. 4 for King's treatment of racism, poverty, and militarism.
39. King, "Love in Action," p. 40.
40. Ibid.
41. "Moral suasionists, like philosophical idealists, appeal to ideas in the form of universalistic notions of reason, truth, and meaning; it is the reflection upon the appeal to ideas and values and truth that constitutes the crux of strategies for social change on the part of moral suasionists." Robert C. Williams, "Moral Suasion and Militant Aggression in the Theological Perspective of Black Religion," *Journal of Religious Thought* 30:2 (73-74): 27- 50.
42. King, *Stride*, p. 84.
43. Ibid., p. 45.
44. Ibid.
45. King, "Transformed Nonconformist," *Strength to Love*, pp. 17-18.
46. King, "Antidotes for Fear," p. 117.
47. Ibid., pp. 117-20. Love is inclusive of truth, faith, and courage.
48. Ibid., p. 118.
49. Ibid., p. 119.

50. Ibid., p. 121. Parentheses added.
51. Ibid., p. 120.
52. Ibid., p. 125.
53. King, "Our God Is Able," in *Strength to Love*, pp. 113-14.
54. King, "Loving Your Enemies," p. 51.
55. Ibid.
56. Ibid., pp. 51-52.
57. Ibid., p. 47.
58. King, "Answer to a Perplexing Question," in *Strength to Love*, p. 130.
59. King, *Where Do We Go from Here?*, p. 172.
60. Ibid., pp. 131-33.
61. Ibid., pp. 135-36.
62. Ibid., pp. 190-91.
63. See Ervin Smith, *The Ethics of Martin Luther King, Jr.*, pp. 40-42.
64. King, "Facing the Challenge of a New Age," *Phylon*, vol. 18 (April, 1957), p. 30; see also, *This is SCLC*, in Meier and Broderick, *Negro Protest*, p. 272, where he says, "Our ultimate goal is genuine group and interpersonal living—*integration*. Only through nonviolence can reconciliation and the creation of the beloved community be effected."
65. King, "A Christmas Sermon on Peace," in Washington, *A Testament of Hope*, p. 253.
66. King, "Paul's Letter to American Christians," in *Strength to Love*, p. 145; King, "Love in Action," p. 46.
67. King, *Stride*, pp. 86-87.
68. King, "Loving Your Enemies," p. 50.
69. King, *Strength to Love*, pp. 26-35.
70. King, "On Being a Good Neighbor," in *Strength to Love*, p. 29.
71. Ansbro suggests that King's perception of *agape* in this respect is indebted to George Davis, L. Harold DeWolf, and other personalists who held that human personality, conceived as "imago dei," has the capacity for love which creates human community. Ansbro, *Making of a Mind*, pp. 15-26.
72. King, "I See the Promised Land," in Washington, *A Testament of Hope*, p. 285.
73. King, "On Being a Good Neighbor," p. 31.
74. See Thurman's treatment of "sympathy" as love and imagination in earlier discussion.
75. King, "On Being a Good Neighbor," p. 32.
76. King, *Stride*, p. 86.

77. Here his indebtedness to personalism's treatment of the moral law of autonomy and Kant's categorical imperative are apparent. See earlier discussion of the moral law under the nature of persons in King.
78. King, "On Being a Good Neighbor," p. 33.
79. Ibid.
80. King, "The Ethical Demands for Integration," in Washington, *A Testament of Hope*, p. 124.
81. King, "Loving Your Enemies," p. 48.
82. Although King never makes this distinction systematically, it is apparent throughout his works. See especially the treatment of community ordered by love in "The Totality" where King's sermon, "The Three Dimensions of a Complete Life," is analyzed. Compare with Thurman's treatment of "Reconciliation" in *Disciplines of the Spirit*.
83. King, "Love in Action," pp. 37-38.
84. Ibid., pp. 39, 40-46; King, "Loving Your Enemies," pp. 51-52.
85. Ibid., p. 52; King, *Stride*, p. 86.
86. King, "Loving Your Enemies," p. 49.
87. Ibid.
88. Ibid., p. 48.
89. King, *Stride*, p. 87.
90. King, "Love in Action," p. 38.
91. King, "Loving Your Enemies," p. 55.
92. King, "A Tough Mind and a Tender Heart," in *Strength to Love*, p. 11. Compare with earlier treatment of love and reason in Thurman, chap. 2.
93. Ibid., pp. 9-12; King *Where Do We Go from Here?* pp. 171-73.
94. King, "Love in Action," p. 45.
95. Ansbro shows how King's treatment of love, justice, and power is appropriated from Tillich's analysis in Paul Tillich, *Love, Power, and Justice* (New York: Oxford University Press, Galaxy Book, 1960), pp. 11, 49-50. First published in 1954. See Ansbro, *Making of a Mind*, pp. 7-8.
96. King, "What Is Man," pp. 8-9; see earlier discussion under King's treatment of the nature of persons.
97. King, *Where Do We Go from Here?*, pp. 89-90.
98. Ibid., p. 36.
99. Muelder, *Moral Law*, pp. 169-70.
100. King, *Where Do We Go from Here?*, p. 37.
101. Muelder, *Moral Law*, p. 170.
102. King, "Love in Action," p. 39.
103. King, *Stride*, p. 87.

104. King, "Pilgrimage to Nonviolence," in *Strength to Love*, p. 154.
105. King, *Stride*, p. 78; Ansbro, *Making of a Mind*, pp. 3-7.
106. Smith and Zepp, *Search for Beloved*, pp. 132-38.
107. King, *Stride*, pp. 83-88; King, "An Experiment in Love," in Washington, *A Testament of Hope*, p. 17; see earlier discussion in Chap. 4 under "Montgomery: The Proving Ground."
108. King, *Stride*, p. 84.
109. Ibid.
110. King, "Law, Love, and Civil Disobedience," p. 6.
111. Ibid.; also King, "Suffering and Faith," pp. 41-42.
112. King, *Stride*, p. 85.
113. Ibid., p. 88.
114. King, "Nonviolence: The Only Road to Freedom," Washington, *A Testament of Hope*, pp. 54-61; also in *Ebony* 21 (October 1966): 27-30.
115. King, "Christmas Sermon on Peace," Washington, *A Testament of Hope*, p. 255.
116. King, *Where Do We Go from Here?*, pp. 56-59.
117. Ibid., p. 59.
118. Ibid., pp. 52, 61.
119. King, "Nonviolence: The Only Road to Freedom," pp. 57-58.
120. See later discussion in this chapter regarding King's radicalism. See also Harold Cruse, *Rebellion or Revolution?* (New York: William Morrow and Co., 1968), pp. 60-63.
121. King, "The Negro and the American Dream," p. 3; Hanes Walton, Jr., *The Political Philosophy of Martin Luther King, Jr.* (Westport, Connecticut: Greenwood Publishing Co., 1971), p. 31.
122. King, "Nonviolence: The Only Road to Freedom," pp. 58-59.
123. King, *Where do We Go from Here?*, pp. 57, 132-34.
124. *Ibid.*, p. 61.
125. *Ibid.*, pp. 61-62, 188-91.
126. Henry D. Thoreau, "Civil Disobedience," in *Thoreau: Walden and Other Writings*, edited and with an Introduction by Joseph Wood Krutch (New York: Bantam Books, 1962), p. 94. Ansbro, *Making of a Mind*, pp. 113-14.
127. King, *Why We Can't Wait*, p. 82.
128. King, "Love, Law, and Civil Disobedience," p. 8.
129. Ibid.
130. King, "Nonviolence: The Only Road to Freedom," p. 60.
131. Ansbro, *Making of a Mind*, pp. 110-62.
132. See earlier Thurman discussion on nonviolence.
133. King, *Why We Can't Wait*, pp. 80-82.
134. King, "Nonviolence: The Only Road to Freedom," pp. 60-61.

135. King, "Some Things We Must Do," President's Address, Montgomery Improvement Association, Montgomery, Alabama, December 5, 1957.

136. King, "Nonviolence: The Only Road to Freedom," p. 60.

137. Hanes Walton, *Political Philosophy of Martin Luther King, Jr.*, pp. 77–102; see also earlier discussion of criticism of Black Power advocates and Malcolm X. In "The Death of Evil on the Seashore," King clearly outlines the unwillingness of oppressors to relinquish power without struggle; see esp. pp. 76-77, 82-83.

138. King, *Stride*, p. 82.

139. Martin Luther King, Jr., *The Trumpet of Conscience* (New York: Harper and Row, 1967), p. 15.

140. Early in his ministry, King foresaw the need to go beyond the false dichotomy between education and legislation as means to achieving equality within American society. King, *Stride*, pp. 17-19. Ansbro, *Making of a Mind*, pp. 136-37; see also earlier discussion on "Montgomery: Proving Ground." He insisted instead on the need for economic and political organization in order to bring about genuine community. King, "Nonviolence: The Only Road to Freedom" pp. 60-61. See also Frank Morris, "A Dream Unfulfilled," in Cartwright, *Essays in Honor of Martin Luther King, Jr.*

141. Smith and Zepp, *Search for Beloved*, pp. 137-38.

142. King, *Where Do We Go from Here?*, pp. 172-91.

143. King, "Nonviolence: The Only Road to Freedom" p. 61.

144. King sermon, "Unfulfilled Dreams," p. 5.

145. King, "What Is Man?" p. 12.

146. See earlier discussion on sin as a barrier to community.

147. King, "What Is Man," pp. 10-16.

148. King, "The Answer to a Perplexing Question," in *Strength to Love*, pp. 128-30; see also "What Is Man?" pp. 9-15.

149. King, *Stride*, p. 82.

150. King, "What Is Man,", p. 15.

151. King, "Unfulfilled Dreams," p. 6.

152. King, "Transformed Nonconformist," p. 23.

153. King writes, "To be a Christian, one must take up his cross, with all its difficulties and agonizing and tragedy-packed content, and carry it until that very cross leaves its marks upon us and redeems us to that more excellent way which only comes through suffering." Ibid., p. 25.

154. King, "Loving Your Enemies," pp. 53-54.

155. King, "Paul's Letter to American Christians," p. 141.

156. King, "A Knock at Midnight," *Strength to Love*, pp. 58-60.

157. King, *Where Do We Go from Here?*, p. 253; see also King, Stride, p. 88.
158. King, "Transformed Nonconformist," p. 18.
159. King, *Where Do We Go from Here?*, p. 190; see also King, "A Christmas Sermon on Peace," p. 253.
160. King, Stride, p. 10; see also King, "A Knock at Midnight," *Strength to Love*, p. 63.
161. King, "Letter from a Birmingham Jail," in *Why We Can't Wait*, p. 91; see also King, "A Knock at Midnight," *Strength to Love*, p. 62.
162. Ibid., p. 63.
163. Ibid., p. 62.
164. King, "Transformed Nonconformist," p. 18.
165. King, "Playboy Interview: Martin Luther King, Jr.," in Washington, *A Testament of Hope*, p. 345; King, "Love in Action," pp. 42-43.
166. King, "Transformed Nonconformist," p. 21; King, "Letter from a Birmingham Jail," pp. 90-91; "A Knock at Midnight," *Strength to Love*, p. 61.
167. King, "Transformed Nonconformist," p. 19.
168. King, "A Knock at Midnight," *Strength to Love*, pp. 62-63; King sermon, "Some Things We Must Do," pp. 6-21.
169. King, "Playboy Interview: Martin Luther King, Jr.," p. 347.
170. See King, *Stride*, p. 73; Ansbro, *Making of a Mind*, pp. 163-82; and earlier discussion on the influence of the black church.

Chapter 7

1. This claim follows the logic of Blackwell, *The Black Community*, pp. xi, 5. See Introduction.
2. In fact, Katie G. Cannon has shown how the formal features of the theological ethics of Thurman and King can serve as resources for a constructive womanist ethic. She identifies their common ethical themes as *imago dei*, love grounded in justice, and the nature of community. Cannon, *Black Womanist Ethics*, pp. 159-175.
3. Mary E. Goodwin, "Racial Roots and Religion." p. 533.
4. Frederick Douglass, *The Life and Times of Frederick Douglass*, with a new introduction by Rayford W. Logan (New York: Collier Books, 1962), p. 79. Reprint from revised edition of 1892.
5. These lectures were originally given at UCLA during the fall quarter of 1969 for her class, "Recurring Philosophical Themes in Black Literature," pp. 10-11.
6. See earlier discussion in chap. 5 under section entitled "The Conception of Community."

7. Thurman, *The Luminous Darkness*, p. 3.
8. King, "Autobiography," p. 12.
9. The discussion will return to this important dimension of their thoughts in the next chapter on conclusions.
10. Mozella Mitchell, *Spiritual Dynamics of Howard Thurman's Theology*, pp. 53-55.
11. Stephen Larsen, *The Shaman's Doorway: Opening the Mythic Imagination to Contemporary Consciousness* (New York: Harper and Row, 1976), pp. 9-10.
12. Mitchell, *Spiritual Dynamics of Howard Thurman's Theology*, p. 88.
13. Smith and Zepp, *Search for Beloved*, p. 113.
14. Thurman devotes an entire chapter to "The Outwardness of Religion" in *The Creative Encounter*, chap. 2, pp. 56-91. The "outwardness of religion" is the externalization of the individual's response to the divine initiative within. See Thurman, *The Creative Encounter*, p. 91, and the earlier discussion in chap. 2, The Nature of Community in Howard Thurman.
15. Thurman, "The Inwardness of Religion" in *The Creative Encounter*, pp. 19- 55. See earlier discussions of the influence of Rufus M. Jones on Thurman's understanding of community.
16. Thurman, "Mysticism and Social Change," *Eden Seminary Bulletin*, pp. 3-34.
17. Howard Thurman, "In Memoriam: Dr. Martin Luther King, Jr." Audio-Tape Cassette, The Fellowship Church For All Peoples. 7 April 1968. Special Collections, Mugar Memorial Library, Boston University.
18. Howard Thurman, "He Looked For A City." Audio-Tape Cassette. Marsh Chapel, Boston University, 2 January 1955. Special Collections, Mugar Memorial Library, Boston University.
19. Walter G. Muelder, *Foundations of the Responsible Society* (Nashville: Abingdon, 1954), p. 19.
20. Gibson Winter is helpful: "Personality is shaped by the communal relationships which it helps to create. This interdependence of person and community, personal good and societal order, is the subject matter of social ethical reflection." Gibson Winter, "Religion, Ethics, and Society," in *Social Ethics: Issues in Ethics and Society*, Gibson Winter, ed. (New York: Harper and Row, Publishers, 1968), p. 7.
21. Thurman says that freedom is "the will and ability to act at any moment in time as to determine the future." Moreover, it is "the sense of options or alternatives." The "sense of options" refers to the experience of the inner self located in the will. See earlier discussion

and example used by Thurman under "Freedom and Responsibility" in chap. 2.

22. King, *Where Do We Go From Here?* pp. 97-98.
23. For examples, see Thurman, "The Declaration of Independence," a series of four taped sermons, the Fellowship Church For All Peoples. 29 July-26 August 1951, Special Collections, Mugar Memorial Library, Boston University; "The American Dream," taped sermon. Marsh Chapel, Boston University, 6 July 1958, Special Collections, Mugar Memorial Library, Boston University.
24. Enoch H. Oglesby, *Ethics and Theology From the Other Side: Sounds of the Moral Struggle*, pp. 20- 22. Cornel West writes, "Afro-American Christianity is Christocentric to the core: yet Jesus Christ is not simply understood as an agent of deliverance, but also a human examplar of pain and agony. The crucified Christ looms as large as the risen Christ." *Prophetic Fragments*, p. 162. See also James H. Cone, *God of the Oppressed* (New York: Seabury Press, 1975), pp. 108-138.
25. Cauthen, *Impact of American Religious Liberalism*, p. 29.
26. Cone, *God of the Oppressed*, p. 109.
27. Thurman, *With Head and Heart*, p. 39; Thurman, *Jesus and the Disinherited*, p. 13; King, *Stride Toward Freedom*, pp. 72-73.
28. King, "The Death of Evil Upon the Seashore," p. 82.
29. Smith and Zepp, *Search for Beloved*, p. 129.
30. King, "Shattered Dreams," p. 91.
31. King, "Loving Your Enemies," p. 49.
32. See King, "Unfulfilled Dreams," pp. 3-5. This is a product of King's dialectical treatment of anthropology. See earlier discussion.
33. See King, "The Answer to a Perplexing Question," *Strength to Love*, p. 134.
34. Smith, *Mystic as Prophet*, p. 58.
35. Thurman, *The Creative Encounter*, p. 147.
36. Muelder writes, "In Christology it is essential to emphasize both the cosmic Christ, i.e., the love and power of God revealed in Christ, and the historically powerful Jesus Christ who is thoroughly rooted in the whole community and especially in the Old Testament community." Muelder, *Moral Law*, p. 155.
37. King, *Stride*, p. 88; King, *Where Do We Go from Here?* pp. 190-91.
38. See Thurman's "Conception of Community" in chap. 2.
39. Mitchell aptly states Thurman's position: "He acknowledges the divinity of Jesus but maintains that we all possess the same quality of divinity within ourselves. He does not deal with Jesus's divinity, nor with his role as savior (the atonement), nor with him as a religious object. He does not deal with the resurrection, nor with

eschatology. Jesus, in Thurman's thinking, is a religious symbol of the achievement of close harmony with God. Jesus is himself a religious subject, and as religious subject he has begun a process which we ourselves are in a position to complete." Mitchell, "The Dynamics of Howard Thurman's Relationship to Literature and Theology," p. 222.

40. See earlier discussion of nonviolence under King.
41. Erwin Smith, *The Ethics of Martin Luther King, Jr.*, pp. 53-54; see also earlier discussions in chap. 5, "The Totality" and chap. 6, "Overcoming The Barriers To Community."
42. Thurman, *The Creative Encounter*, p. 135.
43. Fairclough, *To Redeem the Soul of America*, p. 1.

Chapter 8

1. Mozella Gordon Mitchell, *Spiritual Dynamics of Howard Thurman's Theology*, p. 52. See also Luther Smith, "Black Theology and Religious Experience," *The Journal of the Interdenominational Theological Center* VII, no. 1 (Fall 1980): 59-72.
2. See Thurman, "The Centering Moment," *For the Inward Journey*, pp. 275, 279-280.
3. Thurman, *Lawrence Lectures*, p. 26; Smith, *Mystic as Prophet*, p. 133. This criticism is not justifiable. An informed view of Thurman's perspective on social transformation would see him primarily as an interpreter and enabler for those involved in social transformation.
4. Gibson Winter's definition of "social ethics" is helpful in underlying this crucial distinction between Thurman and King. In the language of Winter, "social ethics" could more properly be called "societal ethics." "The term ('social') should really be societal, since it is the evaluation of societal organization and public policy in the shaping of society with which social ethics is concerned ... In general, then, social ethics deals with issues of the social order—good, right, and ought in the organization of human communities and the shaping of social policies." From "Religion, Ethics, and Society," *Social Ethics: Issues in Ethics and Society*, Gibson Winter, ed. (New York: Harper and Row, 1968), pp. 5-6. Parentheses added.
5. King, *Stride*, p. 77.
6. King, "What a Christian Should Think about the Kingdom of God," Special Collections, Boston University, p. 2. Quoted in Smith and Zepp, *Search for Beloved*, p. 129; King, *Stride*, p. 87.
7. See earlier discussion of "transformed nonconformist" in chap. 6.

3. Vincent Harding, *There is a River: The Black Struggle for Freedom in America* (New York and London: Harcourt, Brace, Jovanovich, 1981), p. xxiii.

9. In the language of Muelder, "social solidarity rightly conceived is markedly pluralistic. Interdependence, mutual aid, group discipline, and freedom belong in the concrete whole. Social ethics must therefore consider community as an organic pluralism." Muelder, *Moral Law*, pp. 46-47. This view bears some affinity with the "personal, mutual model" of community proposed by Frank G. Kirkpatrick in *Community: A Trinity of Models* (Washington, D.C., Georgetown University Press, 1987).

10. See earlier discussions of the influences of Cross and Schreiner on Thurman, chap. 2.

11. For examples see King's sermons, "Transformed Nonconformist," pp. 18, 24; and "A Knock at Midnight," *Strength to Love*, p. 59.

12. Thurman, "Mysticism and Social Change," *Eden Seminary Bulletin*, p. 27. Italics added.

13. Muelder, *Moral Law*, pp. 46-47.

14. Muelder, "Philosophical and Theological Influences in the Thought and Action of Martin Luther King, Jr.," ed. Ronald Lee Carter, *Debate and Understanding* (Fall 1977): 184.

15. At places in his writings and preaching, Thurman articulates the necessity of organizing for political and economic power, but it is not the major emphasis of his thought. See "Black Pentecost III," *Footprints of the Disinherited*, Taped Message, Eliot Congregational Church, Roxbury, MA, 31 May 1972, "The Negro in the City," n.d., n.p., Thurman Papers, Boston Collection; "Desegregation, Integration, and the Beloved Community," Morehouse College Speech, n.d., Thurman Papers, Boston Collection, p. 7; *Deep Is the Hunger*, pp. 51–52; *Habbakuk*, p. 981; and *Disciplines of the Spirit*, pp. 111-21. See earlier treatment of the relationship between love, justice and power in Thurman in chap. 3.

16. James P. Hanigan, "Martin Luther King, Jr.: The Shaping of a Mind," *Debate and Understanding* (Fall 1977), p. 200.

17. Mary E. Goodwin, "Racial Roots and Religion." *pp.* 533-35. Parentheses mine. Howard Thurman, *The Growing Edge* (New York: Harper and Row, 1956; Richmond, IN: Friends United Press, 1974), p. 68; Howard Thurman, *The Creative Encounter* (New York: Harper and Row, 1954; Richmond, IN: Friends United Press, 1972), p. 115.

18. Thurman, *With Head and Heart*, p. 160.

19. Ibid., pp. 254-55; see also, "Howard Thurman to Martin Luther King, Jr.," October 1958 and "Martin Luther King, Jr. to Howard Thurman," 8 November 1958.

20. See Harold Dean Trulear's excellent article, "The Lord Will Make a Way Somehow: Black Worship and the Afro-American Story," *The Journal of the Interdenominational Theological Center* 13:1 (Fall 1985): 87–104; and Hortense J. Spillers, "Martin Luther King, Jr. and the Style of the Black Sermon," in *The Black Experience In Religion: A Book of Readings*, C. Eric Lincoln, ed. (New York: Anchor Books, Anchor Press/Doubleday, 1974), pp. 76-98; Carl H. Marbury, "An Excursus on the Biblical and Theological Rhetoric of Martin Luther King" in *Essays In Honor of Martin Luther King, Jr.*, John Cartwright, ed., pp. 14–28.

21. Archie Smith, Jr., *The Relational Self: Ethics and Therapy from a Black Church Perspective* (Nashville: Abingdon Press, 1982); Edward P. Wimberly and Anne Streaty Wimberly, *Liberation and Wholeness: The Conversion Experiences of Black People in Slavery and Freedom* (Nashville: Abingdon, 1986); and Cheryl Townsend Gilkes, "The Black Church As A Therapeutic Community," *The Journal of the Interdenominational Theological Center* (Fall 1980), 32-42.

22. For Thurman, see "Good News for the Underprivileged," *Religion in Life*, Summer Issue 4:3 (Summer 1935): 403-09; "The Fascist Masquerade," in *The Church and Organized Movements*, chap. 4, ed. Randolph Crump Miller, "The Interseminary Series" (New York: Harper and Brother, 1946), pp. 82-100; *The Creative Encounter*, pp. 141-53; *The Luminous Darkness*, pp. 101-13; *Footprints of a Dream*, pp. 19-24, 137–57, "A Faith to Live By," nos. 6 and 7 ("Democracy" and "Democracy and the Individual," respectively), 19 and 26 October 1952, The Fellowship Church, San Francisco, Thurman Collection, Mugar Library, Boston University. For King, see "Letter from a Birmingham Jail"; "Love in Action," pp. 43-44; "Paul's Letter to American Christians," pp. 141-43; "A Knock at Midnight," pp. 61-62 in *Strength to Love*; and "Discerning the Signs of History," p. 9.

23. Both Thurman and King fall easily into the category which Cornel West describes as "weak exceptionalism," this being a sub-category of one of four theoretical constructs West outlines as Afro-Americans' traditional responses to American racism. Cornel West, *Prophesy Deliverance!: An Afro-American Revolutionary Christianity* (Philadelphia: The Westminster Press, 1982, pp. 72-78. For West, the self-image of Afro-Americans in the exceptionalist tradition is "one of pride, self-congratulation, and often heroism. Afro-Americans are considered to be more humane, meek, kind, creative, spontaneous, and nonviolent than members of other racial groups; less malicious, mendacious, belligerent, bellicose, and avaricious. This tradition posits Afro-American superiority, not over all others, but specifi-

cally over white Americans" (p. 72). West rejects this tradition in favor of what he calls "the humanist response," which is "a promotion of an individuality strengthened by an honest encounter with the Afro-American past and the expansion of democratic control over the major institutions that regulate lives in America and abroad." (p. 90).

24. See Peter Paris's interesting discussion in *The Social Teaching of the Black Churches*, especially chaps. 1 and 2.
25. Robert W. Bellah, "Civil Religion in America," in *American Civil Religion*, eds. Russell Richey and Donald Jones (New York: Harper and Row, 1974), p. 21, parentheses added. Gehrig, *American Civil Religion*; see also, Gail Gehrig, "The American Civil Religion Debate: A Source for Theory Construction," *Journal for the Scientific Study of Religion*, 1981, 20(1): 51-63; and Ellis M. West, "A Proposed Neutral Definition of Civil Religion," *Journal of Church and State* (Winter 1980): 23-40.
26. Bellah, *The Broken Covenant* (New York: Seabury Press, 1975), pp. 13–15.
27. Bellah, "Religion and Polity in America," *Andover Newton Quarterly* 15 (November 1974): 108ff.
28. See Bellah, *The Broken Covenant*, chaps. 1 and 2.
29. Bellah, "Civil Religion in America," p. 28.
30. Ibid.," p. 40.
31. See especially King, *Where Do We Go from Here?*. pp. 67-83, where he analyzes the tragic "schizophrenic personality" of America on the question of race. King writes, "She (America) has been torn between selves—a self in which she proudly professed the great principles of democracy and a self in which she sadly practiced the antithesis of democracy." Ibid., p. 68. Parentheses added.
32. King, "Facing the Challenge of a New Age," Phylon (April 1957): 25–34; also in Washington, *A Testament of Hope*, pp. 135-44.
33. Lewis, *King: A Critical Biography*, pp. 294-96.
34. Cornel West, "Martin Luther King, Jr.: Prophetic Christian as Organic Intellectual," in *Prophetic Fragments*, p. 11. In this essay, West also identifies American civil religion as a major resource for King's thought. See earlier treatment of King's views under the experiential sources of his ideal of community in chap. 3. See esp. sections entitled "The American Dream" and "The World House." See also King, "Where Do We Go From Here?" and "Remaining Awake Through a Great Revolution" in Washington, *A Testament of Hope*, pp. 245-52 and 268–78; "Address of the Reverend Dr. Martin Luther King, Jr." New York State Civil War Centennial Commission, Park Sheraton

Hotel, New York City, 12 September 1962, King Library and Archives, Atlanta, GA; "The Negro and the American Dream," NAACP Public Meeting, Charlotte, NC, 25 September 1960, King Library and Archives, Atlanta, GA, pp. 1-3; and "The American Dream," in Washington, *A Testament of Hope*, pp. 208-16. John Cartwright sees King in the tradition of the "democratic faith" of American civil religion. See Cartwright, "An Affirmative Exposition of American Civil Religion," Research Report N. 001 (Evanston: Bureau of Social and Religious Research, Garrett-Evangelical Theological Seminary, 1976), p. 18; see also John Dixon Elder, "Martin Luther King and American Civil Religion," *Harvard Divinity School Bulletin* (Spring 1968): 17-18.

35. See Thurman, "America in Search of a Soul," "The American Dream," Taped Sermon, Marsh Chapel, Boston University, 13 June 1958, Thurman Collection, Mugar Library, Boston University. Compare with Bellah, "Evil in the American Ethos," Conference on the Legitimation of Evil, Grace Cathedral, San Francisco, 22 February 1970; "Reflections on Reality in America," *Radical Religion* I (1974); and "American Civil Religion in the 1970's," in *American Civil Religion*, Richey and Jones, eds., p. 269.

36. See Thurman's treatment of the dilemma of "outsiders" living in the midst of "insiders" and the inherent conflict this presents for the nation. Thurman, *The Search for Common Ground*, pp. 86-88.

37. See Thurman, "Human Freedom and the Emancipation Proclamation," *Pulpit Digest* (December 1962): 13-14; Thurman, "Freedom Under God," Washington University, Second Century Convocation, February 1955, Thurman Papers, Boston University; Thurman, "The Fascist Masquerade"; Thurman, *The Creative Encounter*, pp. 125-34.

38. Thurman, "Freedom Under God," p. 4. Parentheses added.

39. This speech was presented during the Robbins Lecture Series at the University of Redlands, Redland, California, January 1976; Taped Recording is also available at the Howard Thurman Educational Trust Fund, San Francisco, CA.

40. King, *Where Do We Go from Here?*, pp. 186-91.

41. Bellah, "Reflections on Reality in America," p. 48.

42. See chap. 4, section entitled, "The World House"; and King, "The Trumpet of Conscience," in Washington, *A Testament of Hope*, p. 647.

43. King, "I See the Promised Land," in Washington, *A Testament of Hope*, p. 280.

44. Thurman, *Search for Common Ground*, p. 103.

45. Ibid., p. 104.

46. Bellah, "Civil Religion in America," p. 40.

47. John T. Watts, "Robert N. Bellah's Theory of America's Eschatological Hope," *Journal of Church and State* (Winter 1980): 5-22.

48. Cartwright, "An Affirmative Exposition of American Civil Religion," p. 13.

49. Charles H. Long, "Civil Rights—Civil Religion: Visible People and Invisible Religion," in *American Civil Religion*, eds. Jones and Richey, pp. 211-21.

50. Ibid., p. 219.

51. See especially, Bellah, "Reflections on Reality in America," pp. 44-45; and "Evil in the American Ethos," pp. 7-11.

52. In addition to earlier references, see Thurman, *The Luminous Darkness* and King, *Where Do We Go from Here?*, chap. 3, "Racism and the White Backlash," pp. 67-101.

53. Robert W. Bellah et al, *Habits of the Heart: Individualism and Commitment in American Life* (New York: Perennial Library, Harper and Row, 1985).

54. Ibid., p. 270.

55. Ibid., 256.

56. "*Playboy* Interview: Martin Luther King, Jr.," in Washington, *A Testament of Hope*, pp. 346-47; "The Negro and the American Dream," NAACP Public Meeting, Charlotte, NC, 25 September 1960, King Library and Archives, Atlanta, GA, pp. 1-3; King, "The American Dream," in Washington, *A Testament of Hope*, pp. 208-16.

57. Thurman, *The Search for Common Ground*, pp. 87-88; see also his conversation with Gandhi in *With Head and Heart*, p. 132; and Thurman, "Black Pentecost III," *Footprints of the Disinherited*, Taped Message, 31 May 1972, Howard Thurman Listening Room, Boston University; and "The Negro in the City," n.d., n.p., Thurman Papers, Boston Collection.

58. Thurman, "Good News for the Underprivileged," *Religion in Life* 4:3 (Summer Issue, 1935): 409; *The Growing Edge*, pp. 174-80; *The Search for Common Ground*, pp. 88-104; *Deep River and the Negro Spiritual Speaks of Life and Death*, pp. 39-40, 63-65; *Creative Encounter*, p. 130; "The Negro and the City"; and *Deep Is the Hunger*, p. 2.

59. Thurman, *With Head and Heart*, p. 255.

BIBLIOGRAPHY

Acton, H.B. "Idealism." *The Encyclopedia of Philosophy*. Vol. 3. Edited by Paul Edwards. New York: Macmillan Publishing Co. and The Free Press, 1967.

Ahlstrom, Sydney E. *A Religious History of the American People*. New Haven and London: Yale University Press, 1973.

Ancelet-Hastache, Jeanne. *Master Eckhart and the Rhineland Mystics*. Translated by Hilda Graef. New York: Harper Torchbooks, 1957.

Ansbro, John. *Martin Luther King, Jr.: The Making of a Mind*. Maryknoll: Orbis Books, 1982.

Baillie, Donald M. *God Was in Christ*. New York: Charles Scribner's Sons, 1948.

Baldwin, James. *The Fire Next Time*. New York: Dell Publishing Co., 1962.

Baldwin, Lewis V. "Martin Luther King, Jr., the Black Church, and the Black Messianic Vision." *The Journal of the Interdenominational Theological Center* 12:1-2 (Fall 1984/Spring 1985): 93-108.

_____. "The Minister as Preacher, Pastor, and Prophet: The Thinkings of Martin Luther King, Jr." *American Baptist Quarterly* 7:2 (June, 1988): 79–97

_____. "Understanding Martin Luther King, Jr. Within the Context of Southern Black Religious History." *Journal of Religious Studies* 13:2 (Fall 1987):1-26.

Baldwin, Lewis V. ed. *Martin Luther King and South Africa*. Unpublished Manuscript, 1988.

Bellah, Robert N. *The Broken Covenant*. New York: Seabury Press, 1975.

_____. "Evil in the American Ethos." Conference on the Legitimation of Evil. Grace Cathedral, San Francisco, 22 February 1970.

_____. "Reflections on Reality in America." *Radical Religion* I (1974): 38- 49.

_____. "Religion and Polity in America." *Andover Newton Quarterly* 15 (November 1974): 107-23.

Bellah, Robert N. et al. *Habits of the Heart: Individualism and Commitment in American Life*. New York: Perennial Library, Harper and Row, 1985.

Bennett, John. *The Christian and the State*. New York: Charles Scribner's Sons, 1958.

Bennett, Lerone, Jr. "Howard Thurman: Twentieth Century Holy Man." *Ebony* (February 1978): 68-70, 72, 76, 84-85.

_____. *What Manner of Man*. 2nd rev. ed. Chicago: Johnson Publishing Co., 1976.

_____. "When the Man and the Hour Are Met." In *Martin Luther King, Jr.: A Profile*. Edited by C. Eric Lincoln. New York: Hill and Wang, 1970.

Billingsley, Andrew. *Black Families in White America*. Englewood Cliffs, New Jersey: Prentice-Hall, 1968.

Blackwell, James E. *The Black Community: Diversity and Unity*. New York: Dodd, Mead, and Co., 1975.

Bonino, Jose Miguez. *Doing Theology in a Revolutionary Situation*. Philadelphia: Fortress Press, 1975.

Brewer, James Mason. *American Negro Folklore*. New York: New York Times Book Co., 1968.

Bridges, Hal. *American Mysticism: From William James to Zen*. New York: Harper and Row, 1970.

Brightman, Edgar S. *A Philosophy of Religion*. New York: Prentice-Hall, Inc., 1940.

_____. *Moral Law*. New York: Abingdon Press, 1933.

_____. *Nature and Values*. Nashville: Abingdon Press, 1945.

Broderick, Francis L. and Meier, August. *Negro Protest Thought in the Twentieth Century*. New York: The Bobbs-Merrill Coc., 1965.

Brown, Stuart G., ed. *The Religious Philosophy of Josiah Royce*. Syracuse: Syracuse University Press, 1952.

Brown, William Adams. *The Essence of Christianity: A Study in the History of Definition*. New York: Charles Scribner's Sons, 1913.

Bullard, Muriel. *The Church for the Fellowship for All People*. San Francisco, California. Interview. 11 August 1982.

Burden, Jean. "Howard Thurman." *The Atlantic Monthly* (October 1953): 39-44.

Cannon, Katie. *Black Womanist Ethics*. American Academy of Religion Series No. 6. Atlanta: Scholars Press, 1988.

Carmichael, Stokley, and Hamilton, Charles. *Black Power*. New York: Vintage Books, 1967.

Carney, Frederick S. "Deciding What Is Required." *Norm and Context in Christian Ethics*, pp. 3-16. Edited by Gene Outka and Paul Ramsey. New York: Charles Scribner's Sons, 1968.

Carter, George E. "Martin Luther King: Incipient Transcendentalist." *Phylon* (December 1979): 318-24.

Carter, Ronald L., ed. *Debate and Understanding*. "The Philosophical and Theological Influences in the Thought and Action of Martin Luther King, Jr." 1:3 (Semester 2, 1977). Martin Luther King, Jr. Afro-American Center, Boston University.

Cartwright, John H. "An Affirmative Exposition of American Civil Religion." Research Report No. 001. Evanston: Bureau of Social and Religious Research, Garrett-Evangelical Theological Seminary, 1976.

_____. "Foundations of the Beloved Community." *Debate and Understanding*, pp. 171-78. Edited by Ronald L. Carter. Vol. 1, No. 3 (Semester 2, 1977). Boston University, Martin Luther King, Jr. Afro-American Center.

_____. "The Social Eschatology of Martin Luther King, Jr." In *Essays in Honor of Martin Luther King, Jr.*, pp. 9-13. Edited by John H. Cartwright. Evanston: Garrett-Evangelical Theological Seminary, Leiffer Bureau of Social and Religious Research, 1971.

_____. "The Religious Ethics of Howard Thurman." *The Journal of the Interdenominational Theological Center* (Fall 1984-Spring 1985): 22-34.

Cauthen, Kenneth. *The Impact of American Religious Liberalism.* New York: Harper and Row, 1962.

Cone, James H. *Black Theology and Black Power.* New York: Seabury Press, 1969.

_____. *A Black Theology of Liberation.* New York: J.B. Lippincott Co., 1970.

_____. *God of the Oppressed.* New York: Seabury Press, 1975.

_____. "Martin Luther King, Jr. and Malcolm X." Lectures delivered at Partners in Ecumenism Conference, National Council of Churches. Howard Inn, Washington, D.C. 26 September 1984.

_____. "Martin Luther King, Jr., Black Theology—Black Church." *Theology Today* (January 1984): 409-20.

_____. *Spirituals and the Blues.* New York: Seabury Press, 1972.

Cone, James H., and Wilmore, Gayraud. *Black Theology: A Documentary History*, 1966-1979. New York: Orbis, 1979.

Corbett, Jan. "Howard Thurman: A Theologian for Our Time." *The American Baptist* (December 1979): 10-12.

Cross, George. *Christian Salvation: A Modern Interpretation.* Chicago: University of Chicago, 1925.

_____. *Creative Christianity: A Study of the Genius of Christian Faith.* New York: Macmillan Co., 1922.

_____. *What Is Christianity? A Study of Rival Interpretations.* Chicago: University of Chicago Press, 1918.

Cruse, Harold. *Rebellion or Revolution?* New York: William Morrow and Co., 1968.

Davis, Angela. "Lectures on Liberation." New York Committee to Free Angela Davis. Originally Lectures from Class, "Recurring Philosophical Themes in Black Literature." UCLA (Fall 1969).

DeVeaux, William P. "Immanuel Kant, Social Justice, and Martin Luther King, Jr." *The Journal for Religious Thought* (1970): 5-15.

deVries, Egbert. *Man in Community.* New York: Association Press, 1966.

DeWolf, Harold L. *The Religious Revolt Against Reason.* New York: Greenwood Press, 1968.

_____. *A Theology for the Living Church.* New York: Harper and Row, 1968.

Dillenberger, John, and Welch, Claude. *Protestant Christianity Interpreted Through Its Development*. New York: Charles Scribner's Sons, 1954.

Dixon, Christa. *Negro Spirituals: From Bible to Folk Song*. Philadelphia: Fortress Press, 1976.

"Dr. King Mentor Remembered." *Boston Globe* (15 January 1982): 13-14.

Dodson, Jualynne. "Conceptualizations of Black Families." In *Black Families* pp. 23-35. Edited by Harriette Pipes McAdoo. Beverly Hills: Sage Publications, 1981.

Douglass, Frederick. *The Life and Times of Frederick Douglass*. With New Introduction by Rayford W. Logan. New York: Collier Books, 1962. Reprint from Rev. Ed., 1892.

DuBois, W.E.B. *The Souls of Black Folk*. Introduction by Saunders Redding. Greenwich, Connecticut: Fawcett, 1961.

Eckhart, Meister. *Meister Eckhart Speaks*. Otto Karrer, ed. New York: Philosophical Library, 1957.

_____. *The Works of Meister Eckhart, Doctor Ecstaticus*. Translation by C. de B. Evans. London: John M. Watkins, 1952.

Elder, John Dixon. "Martin Luther King and American Civil Religion." *Harvard Divinity School Bulletin* (Spring 1968): 17-18.

Fairclough, Adam. *To Redeem the Soul of American: The Southern Christian Leadership Conference and Martin Luther King, Jr.* Athens and London: The University of Georgia Press, 1987.

First, Ruth, and Scott, Ann. *Oliver Schreiner*. New York: Schocken Books, 1980.

Fosdick, Harry Emerson, ed. *Rufus Jones Speaks to Our Time: An Anthology*. New York: The Macmillan Co., 1952.

Frazier, E. Franklin. "Inferiority Complex and the Quest for Status." Reprint in Frazier, E. Franklin, *On Race Relations*. pp. 239- 55. Selected Papers. Edited and with Introduction by G. Franklin Edwards. Chicago: University of Chicago Press, 1968.

_____. *The Negro Family in the United States*. Chicago: University of Chicago Press, 1939.

Fox, George, *George Fox: An Autobiography*. Edited and with introduction and notes by Rufus M. Jones. London: Hadley Brothers, 1904.

Fullwinder, S.P. *The Mind and Mood of Black America*. Homewood, Illinois: The Dorsey Press, 1969.

Gandhi, Mohandas K. *All Men Are Brothers*. Compiled and Edited by Krishna Kripalani with Introduction by Sarvepalli Radhakrishnan. New York: Continuum, 1982.

_____. *An Autobiography: The Story of My Experiments with Truth*. Boston: Beacon Press, 1957.

_____. *Non-Violent Resistance*. New York: Schocken Books, 1961.

Gandy, Samuel Lucius, ed. *Common Ground: Essays in Honor of Howard Thurman*. San Francisco: Common Ground Press, 1976.

Garber, Paul R. "King Was a Black Theologian." *Journal of Religious Thought* 31 (Fall-Winter): 16-32.

Garrow, David. *Bearing the Cross: Martin Luther King, Jr., and the Southern Christian Leadership Conference*. New York: William Morrow and Co., 1986.

_____. *The FBI and Martin Luther King, Jr.: From "Solo" to Memphis*. New York: W.W. Norton and Co., 1981.

Gehrig, Gail. "The American Civil Religion Debate: A Source for Theory Construction." *Journal for the Scientific Study of Religion* 20:1 (1981): 51-63.

_____. *American Civil Religion: An Assessment*. Society for the Scientific Study of Religion Monograph Series, No. 3, 1981.

Gilkes, Cheryl Townsend. "The Black Church As A Therapeutic Community." *The Journal of the Interdenominational Theological Center* (Fall 1980): 32-42.

Goodwin, Mary E. "Racial Roots and Religion: An Interview with Howard Thurman." *The Christian Century* (9 May 1973): 535-35.

Gossett, Thomas F. *Race: The History of an Idea in America*. New York: Schocken Books, 1965.

Graham, Hugh Davis, and Gurr, Ted. R. *Violence in America*. New York: Signet, 1969.

"Great Preachers." *Ebony* (July 1954): 29.

"Great Preachers." Editors of *Life* (6 April 1953): 128.

Greer, Barnett J.W. "Howard Thurman: An Examination and Analysis of Thurman's Idea of Community and the Viability of the Fellowship Church." Doctor of Ministry Project, Claremont School of Theology, May 1983.

Greer, Scott and David W. Minar, compilers. *The Concept of Community: Readings With Interpretations* Chicago: Aldine, 1969.

Gustafson, James. *Ethics from a Theocentric Perspective*. 2 vols. Chicago: The University of Chicago Press, 1981, 1984.

_____. "Moral Discernment in the Christian Life," pp. 17-36. In *Norm and Context in Christian Ethics*. Edited by Gene Outka and Paul Ramsey. New York: Charles Scribner's Sons, 1968.

Halberstam, David. "When `Civil Rights' and `Peace' Join Forces," pp. 187-211. In *Martin Luther King, Jr.: A Profile*. Edited by C. Eric Lincoln. New York: Hill and Wang, 1970.

Handy, Robert T. *The Social Gospel in America*. New York: Oxford University Press, 1966.

Hanes, Walton, Jr. *The Political Philosophy of Martin Luther King, Jr.* Westport, Connecticut: Greenwood Publishing Co., 1971.

Hanigan, James P. "Martin Luther King, Jr.: The Shaping of a Mind." In *Debate and Understanding*. pp. 190- 206. Edited by Ronald L. Carter. 1:3 (Semester 2 1977). Martin Luther King, Jr. Afro-American Center, Boston University.

Harding, Vincent. "The Religion of Black Power," pp. 3-38. In *The Religious Situation: 1968*. Edited by Donald R. Cutler. Boston: Beacon Press, 1968.

_____. *There Is a River: The Black Struggle for Freedom in America*. New York and London: Harcourt, Brace, Jovanovich, 1981.

Harvey, Van. *A Handbook of Theological Terms*. New York: Macmillan, 1964.

Hauerwas, Stanley. *A Community of Character: Toward A Constructive Christian Social Ethic*. South Bend, Indiana: University of Notre Dame Press, 1981.

Hegel, G.W.F. *The Phenomenology of Mind*. New York: Harper and Row, 1962.

Hick, John. *Evil and the God of Love*. New York: Harper and Row, 1966.

Hill, Robert B., and Shackleford, Lawrence. "The Black Extended Family Revisited." *In The Black Family: Essays and Studies*. pp. 201-06. 2d. Ed. Edited by Robert Staples. Belmont, California: Wadsworth Publishing Co., 1971.

Hinshaw, David. *Rufus Jones: Master Quaker*. New York: G.P. Putnam's Sons, 1951.

Hiskes, Richard. *Community Without Coercion: Getting Along With the Minimal State*. Newark, New Jersey: University of Delaware Press, 1982.

Hocking, William Ernest. "The Meaning of Liberalism: An Essay in Definition." *Liberal Theology: An Appraisal*. Edited by David E. Roberts and Henry Pitney Van Dusen. New York: Charles Scribner's Sons, 1942.

Hoffman, Manfred. "Martin Luther: Resistance to Secular Authority." *The Journal of the Interdenominational Theological Center* 12:1-2 (Fall 84-Spring 85): 35-49.

Holt, Rackham. *Mary McLeod Bethune: A Biography*. Garden City, New York: Doubleday and Co., 1964.

Howard Thurman to Martin Luther King, Jr. 20 October 1958. Special Collections, Mugar Memorial Library, Boston University.

Jackson, Jacquelyne. "Black Grandparents in the South." *The Black Family: Essays and Studies*. Robert Staples, ed. Belmont, California: Wadsworth Publishing Co., Inc., 1971; 1978.

James, William. *The Varieties of Religious Experience*. Introduction by Reinhold Niebuhr. New York: Collier Books, 1961.

Jennes, Mary. "A Leader of Students." In *Twelve Negro Americans*, pp. 145-60. Free Port, New York: Books for Libraries Press, 1936; 1969.

Johnson, James W. *God's Trombones*. New York: Penguin, 1978.

Jones, Edward O. *A Candle in the Dark: A History of Morehouse College*. Valley Forge: Judson Press, 1967.

Jones, Lawrence N. "Black Christians in Antebellum America: In Quest of the Beloved Community." *The Journal of Religious Thought* 12:2 (1985): 12-19.

_____. "Hope for Mankind: Insights from Black Religious History in the United States." *The Journal of Religious Thought* 34:2 (Fall-Winter 77-78): 59- 65.

_____. "Urban Black Churches: Conservators of Value and Sustainers of Community." *The Journal of Religious Thought* 39:2 (Fall-Winter 82-83): 41-50.

Jones, Rufus M. *The Double Search: Studies in Atonement and Prayer*. Philadelphia: J.C. Winston, 1906.

_____. *Finding the Trail of Life*. New York: The Macmillan Co., 1927.

_____. *The Inner Life*. New York: The Macmillan Co., 1916.

_____. "Liberalism in the Mystical Tradition." In *Liberal Theology: An Appraisal*, pp. 121-36. Edited by David E. Roberts and Henry Pitney Van Dusen. New York: Charles Scribner's Sons, 1942.

_____. *The Luminous Trail*. New York: Macmillan Co., 1947.

_____. *Social Law in the Spiritual World: Studies in Human and Divine Inter-Relationship*. Philadelphia: J.C. Winston Co., 1904.

_____. *Studies in Mystical Religion*. London: Macmillan and Co., 1923.

Jones, William R. *Is God a White Racist?* New York: Doubleday, 1973.

Jordan, Winthrop D. *White Over Black: American Attitudes Toward the Negro, 1550-1812*. Baltimore: Penguin Books, 1968; 1969.

Kant, Immanuel. *Critique of Pure Reason*. Unabridged Edition, translated by Norman Kemp Smith. New York: St. Martin's Press, 1929; 1965.

_____. *Fundamental Principles of the Metaphysic of Morals*. New York: Bobs Merrill, 1949.

Kelsey, George D. *Racism and the Christian Understanding of Man*. New York: Charles Scribner's Sons, 1965.

King, Coretta Scott. *My Life with Martin Luther King, Jr*. New York: Holt, Rinehart and Winston, 1969.

King, Martin Luther, Jr. "A Comparison of the Conceptions of God in the Thinking of Paul Tillich and Henry Nelson Wieman." Ph.D. dissertation, Boston University, 1955.

_____. "Address to the Initial Mass Meeting of the Montgomery Improvement Association." Holt Street Baptist Church, Montgomery, Alabama, 5 December 1955.

_____. "An Address Before the National Press Club." *Congressional Record* 108 (20 July 1962): 14247-49.

_____. "Answer to a Perplexing Question." Ebenezer Baptist Church, Atlanta, Georgia, 3 March 1963. King Archives, Atlanta, Georgia.

_____. "An Autobiography of Religious Development." n.p., n.d. King Papers, Special Collections, Mugar Memorial Library, Boston University.

_____. "Discerning the Signs of History." Ebenezer Baptist Church. Atlanta, Georgia. 15 November 1964. King Archives, Atlanta, Georgia.

_____. "Equality Now." *The Nation* (4 February 1961): 91-95.

_____. "Excerpts from Address by Dr. Martin Luther King, Jr. at Public Meeting of Charlotte, North Carolina Branch NAACP." 25 September 1960. King Archives, Atlanta, Georgia.

_____. "Facing the Challenge of a New Age." *Phylon* 28 (April 1957): 24-34.

_____. "I Have a Dream," p. 218. Lincoln Memorial, Washington, D.C., 28 August 1963. *Martin Luther King, Jr.: A Documentary... Montgomery to Memphis.* Edited by Flip Schulke with Introduction by Coretta Scott King. New York: W.W. Norton and Co., Inc., 1976.

_____. "Is the Universe Friendly?" Ebenezer Baptist Church, 12 December 1965. King Archives, Atlanta, Georgia.

_____. "Love, Law, and Civil Disobedience." *New South* (December 1961): 3- 11.

_____. "The Meaning of Hope." Dexter Avenue Baptist Church, Montgomery, Alabama. 10 October 1967. King Archives, Atlanta, Georgia.

_____. *The Measure of a Man.* Philadelphia: The Christian Education Press, 1959.

_____. "The Negro and the American Dream." NAACP Public Meeting. Charlotte, North Carolina, 25 September 1960. King Archives, Atlanta, Georgia.

_____. "New York State Civil War Centennial Commission." Park Sheraton Hoten, New York, 12 September 1962. King Archives, Atlanta, Georgia.

_____. "Nobel Prize Acceptance Speech," p. 219. Oslo, 10 December 1964. In *Martin Luther King, Jr.: A Documentary...Montgomery to Memphis.* Edited by Flip Schulke with Introduction by Corretta Scott King. New York: W.W. Norton and Co., Inc., 1976.

_____. "The Only Road to Freedom." *Ebony* 21 (October 1966): 27–30.

_____. "Press Conference." Biltmore Hotel, Los Angeles, California. 12 April 1967. King Archives, Atlanta, Georgia.

_____. Reinhold Niebuhr's Ethical Dualism." 9 May 1952. King Papers, Special Collections, Mugar Memorial Library, Boston University.

_____. "Religion's Answer to the Problem of Evil," King Papers, Special Collections, Mugar Memorial Library, Boston University.

_____. "Sermon on Gandhi." Dexter Avenue Baptist Church, Montgomery, AL. 22 March 1959. King Archives, Atlanta, Georgia.

_____. "Some Things We Must Do." President's Address, Montgomery Improvement Association. Montgomery, Alabama, 5 December 1957. King Archives, Atlanta, Georgia.

_____. "Statement to American Baptist Convention." 7 August 1959. King Papers, Special Collections, Mugar Memorial Library, Boston University.

_____. "Statement to Freedom Rides Rally." First Baptist Church, Montgomery, Alabama. 21 May 1961. King Archives, Atlanta, Georgia.

_____. *Strength to Love*. Philadelphia: Fortress Press, 1981.

_____. *Stride Toward Freedom: The Montgomery Story*. New York: Harper and Row, 1958; 1964.

_____. "Thou Fool." Mt. Pisgah Baptist Church, Chicago. 27 August 1967. King Archives, Atlanta, Georgia.

_____. "Unfulfilled Dreams." Ebenezer Baptist Church, Atlanta, Georga. 3 March 1968. King Archives, Atlanta, Georgia.

_____. "What a Christian Should Think About the Kingdom of God." King Papers, Special Collections. Mugar Memorial Library, Boston University.

_____. *Where Do We Go From Here? Chaos or Community*. Boston: Beacon Press, 1967.

_____. "Who Speaks for the South?" *Liberation* (March 1958): 13-14.

_____. *Why We Can't Wait*. New York: Signet Books, The New American Library, 1964.

King, Martin Luther, Jr., Roosevelt, Eleanor, and Pike, James A. "Declaration of Conscience: The Apartheid Issue." 10 December 1957. Special Collections, Mugar Memorial Library, Boston University.

King, Martin Luther, Sr. *Daddy King: An Autobiography*. Written with the assistance of Clayton Riley. New York: William Morrow and Co., 1980.

Kirkpatrick, Frank G. *Community: A Trinity of Models*. Washington, D.C.: Georgetown University Press, 1986.

Kytle, Calvin. *Gandhi: Soldier of Non-Violence: An Introduction*. Cabin John, Maryland and Washington, D.C.: Seven Locks Press, 1969; 1982.

Larsen, Stephen. *The Shaman's Doorway: Opening the Mythic Imagination to Contemporary Consciousness*. New York: Harper and Row, 1976.

Levine, Lawrence W. *Black Culture and Black Consciousness*. Oxford: University Press, 1977.

Lewis, David L. *King: A Critical Biography*. 2d edition. Urbana: University of Illinois Press, 1970; 1978.

The Life and Thought of Howard Thurman. A Documentary Film in Two Parts. The British Broadcasting Company, 1976.

Lincoln, C. Eric. *The Black Muslims in America*. Boston: Beacon Press, 1961.

_____, ed. *The Black Experience in Religion*. New York: Doubleday, 1974.

_____, ed. *Martin Luther King, Jr.: A Profile*. New York: Hill and Wang, 1970.

Logan, Rayford W. *Howard University: The First One Hundred Years, 1867–1967*. New York: New York University Press, 1969.

Lomax, Louis. "When `Nonviolence' Meets `Black Power,'" pp. 157-80. In *Martin Luther King, Jr.: A Profile*. Edited by C. Eric Lincoln. New York: Hill and Wang, 1970.

Long, Charles H. "Civil Rights—Civil Religion: Visible People and Invisible Religion." In *American Civil Religion*. pp. 211-21. Edited by Russel Richey and Donald G. Jones. New York: Harper and Row, 1974.

Long, Edward Leroy. *A Survey of Christian Ethics*. New York: Oxford Press, 1967.

Lovell, John, Jr. *Black Song: The Forge and the Flame: The Story of How the Afro-American Spiritual Was Hammered Out*. New York: The Macmillan Co., 1971.

Lukes, Steven. *Individualism*. New York: Harper Torchbooks, Harper and Row, 1973.

Lyght, Ernest S. *The Relgious and Philosophical Foundations in the Thought of Martin Luther King, Jr*. New York: Vantage Press, 1972.

MacIntyre, Alasdair. *After Virtue*. South Bend, Indiana: University of Notre Dame Press, 1984.

MacIver, R.M. *Community: A Sociological Study*. 2d Edition. London: Macillan and Co., 1920.

McAdoo, Harriette Pipes, ed. *Black Families*. Beverley Hills: Sage Publications, 1981.

Martin Luther King, Jr. to Albert Luthuli. 8 December 1959. Special Collections, Mugar Memorial Library, Boston University.

Martin Luther King, Jr. to Howard Thurman. 8 November 1958. Special Collections, Mugar Memorial Library, Boston University.

Marty, Martin. "Mysticism and the Religious Quest for Freedom." *Christian Century* 100:8 (16 March 1983): 242-46.

_____. "Mysticism and the Religious Quest for Freedom." *God and Human Freedom*. Edited by Henry J. Young. Richmond, Indiana: Friends United Press, 1983.

Massey, James E. "Bibliographical Essay: Howard Thurman and Rufus M. Jones, Two Mystics." *The Journal of Negro History* (April 1972): 190-95.

Matthews, Basil S. "Whole-Making: Tagore and Thurman." *The Journal of Religious Thought* 34:2 (Fall-Winter, 77-78): 34-41.

Mays, Benjamin E. *Born to Rebel: An Autobiography*. New York: Charles Scribner's sons, 1971.

_____. *The Negro's God: As Reflected in His Literature*. Boston: Chapman and Grimes, 1938. Reprint, Westport, Connecticut: Greenwood Press, 1969.

Melvin H. Watson to Martin Luther King, Jr. 14 August 1952. King Papers, Special Collections. Mugar Memorial Library, Boston University.

Miller, William Robert. "The Broadening Horizons: Montgomery, America, the World." In *Martin Luther King, Jr.: A Profile*, pp. 40-71. Edited by C. Eric Lincoln. New York: Hill and Wang, 1970.

Millett, Ricardo A., ed. *Debate and Understanding*. "Simmering on Calm Presence and Profound Wisdom of Howard Thurman." Special Edition. (Spring, 1982). Martin Luther King, Jr. Afro-American Center, Boston University.

Mitchell, Henry. *Black Preaching*. San Francisco: Harper and Row, 1979.

Mitchell, Mozella Gordon. "The Dynamics of Howard Thurman's Relationship to Literature and Theology." Ph.D. dissertation. Emory University, 1983.

_____. "Howard Thurman and Olive Schreiner: Post Modern Marriage Post- Mortem." *Journal of Religious Thought* 38:1 (Spring 1981): 63-72.

_____. *Spiritual Dynamics of Howard Thurman's Theology*. Bristol, Indiana: Wyndham Hall Press, 1985.

Morris, Frank L. "A Dream Unfulfilled: The Economic and Political Policies of Martin Luther King, Jr." Garrett-Evangelical Theological Seminary, Evanston, Illinois (January 1977). (Mimeograph)

_____. "A Dream Unfulfilled: The Economic and Political Policies of Martin Luther King, Jr." *Essays in Honor of Martin Luther King, Jr.*, pp. 41-63. Edited by John H. Cartwright. Evanston: (Leiffer Bureau of Social and Religious Research) Garrett-Evangelical Theological Seminary.

Moxley, Irving S. "An Examination of the Mysticism of Howard Thurman and Its Relevance to Black Liberation." Ph.D. dissertation. Louisville Presbyterian Theological Seminary, 1974.

Muelder, Walter G. "Apostles of Growth." Thurman Papers, Special Collections. Mugar Memorial Library, Boston University.

_____. "Apostles of Growth." *Nexus* 25 (November 1965) 9:1.

_____. Boston University School of Theology. Interviews. May 1983 and November 1983.

_____. *Foundations of a Responsible Society*. Nashville: Abingdon, 1954.

_____. "Martin Luther King, Jr. and the Moral Laws." Morehouse College, 24 March 1983. (Mimeographed.)

_____. *Moral Law in Christian Social Ethics*. Richmond, Virginia: John Knox Press, 1966.

_____. "Reinhold Niebuhr's Conception of Man." *The Personalist* 36 (1945): 282-93.

_____. "The Structure of Howard Thurman's Religious Social Ethics." In *Debate and Understanding*. Edited by Ricardo A. Millett. Special Edition (Spring 1982): 7-13.

Nelson, William S., ed. *The Christian Way in Race Relations*. New York: Harper and Brothers, 1948.

New York Times (22 March 1953): 79.

Niebuhr, H. Richard. *Christ and Culture*. New York: Harper and Brothers, 1951.

_____. *The Meaning of Revelation*. New York: Macmillan, 1941.

_____. *Radical Monotheism and Western Culture*. New York: Harper and Row, 1943.

_____. *The Responsible Self*. New York: Harper and Row, 1963.

_____. *The Social Sources of Denominationalism*. New York: The New American Library, 1929; 1957; 1975.

Niebuhr, Reinhold. *An Interpretation of Christian Ethics*. New York: Seabury Press, 1979.

_____. *Love and Justice: Selections from the Shorter Writings of Reinhold Niebuhr*. D.B. Robertson, ed. Glouster, Massachussettes: Peter Smith, 1976.

_____. *Moral Man and Immoral Society*. New York: Charles Scribner's, 1932.

_____. "Must We Do Nothing?" *The Christian Century* (30 March 1932).

____. *The Nature and Destiny of Man*. 2 Vols. New York: Charles Scribner's Sons, 1941, 1943; Reprints, 1963, 1964.

Nietzsche, Friedrich. *Beyond Good and Evil*. New York: Vintage, 1967.

_____. *On the Genealogy of Morals*. New York: Vintage, 1967.

_____. *The Will to Power*. New York: Vintage, 1968.

Nisbet, Robert A. *The Quest for Community*. New York: Oxford University Press, 1953.

Nozick, Robert. *Anarchy, State, and Utopia*. New York: Basic Books, 1974.

Oates, Stephen B. *Let the Trumpet Sound: The Life of Martin Luther King, Jr.* New York: New American Library, 1982.

"Offering of the Heart." *Yankee* (December 1953): 19-22.

Oglesby, Enoch H. *Ethics and Theology from the Other Side: Sounds of Moral Struggle.* Washington, D.C.: University Press of America, 1979.

Oliver Tambo to Martin Luther King, Jr. 18 November 1957. Special Collections, Mugar Memorial Library, Boston University.

Otto, Rudolph. *The Idea of the Holy.* London: Oxford University Press, 1950.

Outka, Gene H., and Ramsey, Paul, eds. *Norm and Context in Christian Ethics.* New York: Charles Scribner's Sons, 1968.

Paris, Peter. *The Social Teaching of the Black Churches.* Philadelphia: Fortress Press, 1985.

Pfeiffer, Franz. *Meister Eckhart.* Translation with some omissions and additions by C. de B. Evans. London: John M. Watkins, 1947.

Quarles, Benjamin. *The Negro in Making of America.* New York: The Macmillan Co., 1964.

Rader, Melvin. *Ethics and Human Community.* Holt, Rinehart and Winston, 1964.

Rauschenbusch, Walter. *The Righteousness of the Kingdom.* New York: Abingdon Press, 1968.

_____. *A Theology for the Social Gospel.* New York: Macmillan Company, 1918.

Rawls, John. *A Theory of Justice.* Cambridge: The Belknap Press of Harvard University Press, 1971.

Reddick, Lawrence D. *Crusader Without Violence: Martin Luther King, Jr.* New York: Harper and Row, 1959.

Richardson, Herbert. "Martin Luther King, Jr.: Unsung Theologian." *New Theology*, No. 6. Edited by Martin Marty and Dean Peerman. New York: Macmillan Co., 1969.

Richey, Russel, and Jones, Donald G., eds. *American Civil Religion.* New York: Harper and Row, 1974.

Roberts, David E., and Van Dusen, Henry P. *Liberal Theology: An Appraisal—Essays in Honor of Eugene William Lyman.* New York: Charles Scribner's Sons, 1942.

Roberts, J. Deotis. *Liberation and Reconciliation: A Black Theology.* Philadelphia: The Westminster Press, 1971.

Roth, John K., ed. *The Philosophy of Josiah Royce.* New York: Thomas J. Crowell Co., 1972.

Royce, Josiah. *The Problem of Christianity.* Introduction by John Smith. Chicago: University of Chicago Press, 1968.

Russell, E.S. "The Directiveness of Organic Activities." The Zoology Section of the British Association, 1934.

Schreiner, Olive. "The Dawn of Civilization." *The Nation and the Athenaeum* (26 March 1921).

_____. "From Three Dreams in the Desert." In *A Track to the Water's Edge: The Olive Schreiner Reader*, pp. 53-56. Edited by Howard Thurman. New York: Harper and Row, 1973.

_____. "The Hunter," pp. 84-95. In *A Track to the Water's Edge: The Olive Schreiner Reader*. Edited by Howard Thurman. New York: Harper and Row, 1973.

Shulke, Flip. *Martin Luther King, Jr.: A Documentary...Montgomery to Memphis*. Introduction by Coretta Scott King. New York: W.W. Norton and Co., 1976.

Sidgwick, Henry. *The Methods of Ethics*. Chicago: University of Chicago Press, 1962.

Smith, Archie, Jr., ed. *The Relational Self: Ethics and Therapy from a Black Church Perspective*. Nashville: Abingdon Press, 1982.

Smith, Ervin. *The Ethics of Martin Luther King, Jr.* New York and Toronto: The Edwin Mellen Press, 1981.

Smith, Kenneth L., and Zepp, Ira G., Jr. *Search for the Beloved Community: The Thinking of Martin Luther King, Jr.* Valley Forge: Judson Press, 1974.

Smith, Luther E. "An American Prophet: A Critical Study of the Thought of Howard Thurman." Ph.D. dissertation, St. Louis University, 1979.

_____. "Black Theology and Religious Experience." *The Journal of the Interdenominational Theological Center* 7:1 (Fall 1980): 59-72.

_____. "Community Partnership, Freedom and Responsibility." *God and Human Freedom*. Edited by Henry J. Young. Richmond, Indiana: Friends United Press, 1983.

_____. *Howard Thurman: The Mystic as Prophet*. Washington, D.C.: University Press of America, 1981.

Smith, Timothy L. "Slavery and Theology: The Emergence of Black Christian Consciousness in Nineteenth-Century America." Reprint from *Church History* 41:4 (December 1972).

Smith, Wallace Charles. *The Church in the Life of the Black Family*. Valley Forge: Judson, 1985.

Smylie, James H. "On Jesus, Pharoahs, and the Chosen People: Martin Luther King as Biblical Interpreter and Humanist." *Interpretation* 34 (January 1970): 77-91.

Soelle, Dorothee. *Revolutionary Patience*. Translated by Rita and Robert Kimber. Maryknoll: Orbis Books, 1969; 1974. English copyright, 1977.

Spillers, "Martin Luther King, Jr. and the Style of the Black Sermon." In *The Black Experience In Religion: A Book of Readings*. Edited by C. Eric Lincoln., New York: Anchor Books, Anchor Press/Doubleday, 1974.

Steger, Jane. *Leaves from a Secret Journal*. Dublin, Indiana: Printit Press, 1978.

Stewart, Carlyle Felding III. "A Comparative Analysis of Theological-Ontology and Ethical Method in the Theologies of James H. Cone and Howard Thurman." Ph.D. dissertation, Northwestern University, 1982.

Stuckey, Sterling. *Slave Culture: Nationalist Theory and the Foundations of Black America*. New York: Oxford University Press, 1987.

Sudarkasa, Niara. "Interpreting the African Heritage in Afro-American Family Organization," pp. 37-53. In *Black Families*. Edited by Harriette Pipes McAdoo. Beverly Hills: Sage Publications, 1981.

"This is SCLC." Leaflet, Southern Christian Leadership Conference, rev. ed., 1964. In *Negro Protest Thought in the Twentieth Century*. pp. 269-70. Edited by Francis L. Broderick and August Meier. New York: The Bobbs-Merrill Company, 1965.

Thoreau, Henry David. "Civil Disobedience." In *Thoreau: Walden and Other Writings*. Edited by Joseph Wood Krutch. New York: Bantam Books, 1962. 13th printing.

Thurman, Anne Spencer, ed. *The Listening Ear: A Newsletter of the Howard Thurman Educational Trust* 16:2 (Summer 1985).

Thurman, Howard. "The American Dream." Taped Sermon. Marsh Chapel, Boston University. 6 July 1958. Special Collections, Mugar Memorial Library, Boston University.

_____. "America in Search of a Soul." *The Robbins Lecture Series*. University of Redlands, Redlands, California. 20 January 1976. Thurman Papers, Special Collections. Mugar Memorial Library, Boston University.

_____. *Apostles of Sensitiveness*. Boston: American Unitarian Association, 1956.

_____. *The Centering Moment*. Richmond, Indiana: Friends United Press, 1980.

_____. "The Christian Minister and the Desegregation Decision." *The Pulpit Digest* (May 1957): 13-19.

_____. "The Circle of Life." Audio-Tape Cassette. 65-8. Howard Thurman Educational Trust Fund, San Francisco.

_____. "Community and Will of God, 3-8." Audio-Tape Cassette, n.d. Howard Thurman Educational Trust Fund, San Francisco, California.

_____. "Convocation Address." Pittsburgh Theological Seminary. November 1971. Thurman Papers, Special Collections, Mugar Memorial Library, Boston University.

_____. "Community and the Will of God." Mendenhall Lectures. DePauw University, February 1961. Thurman Papers, Special Collections, Mugar Memorial Library, Boston University.

_____. *The Creative Encounter*. New York: Harper and Row, 1954; Richmond Publishers, 1972.

_____. "The Declaration of Independence." Taped Sermon Series. The Fellowship Church For All Peoples, San Francisco, California. 29 July-26 August 1951. Special Collections, Mugar Memorial Library, Boston University.

_____. *Deep Is the Hunger*. New York: Harper and Brothers, 1951; pb. ed., Richmond, Indiana: Friends United Press, 1975

_____. *Deep River and the Negro Spiritual Speaks of Life and Death*. Richmond, Indiana: Friends United Press, 1975.

_____. "Desegregation, Integration, and the Beloved Community." Morehouse College, n.d. Thurman Papers, Special Collections, Mugar Memorial Library, Boston University.

_____. *Disciplines of the Spirit*. New York: Harper and Row, 1963; pb. ed., Richmond, Indiana: Friends United Press, 1973.

_____. "The Divine Encounter, 1-3." Audio-Tape Cassette, n.d. Howard Thurman Educational Trust. San Francisco, California.

_____. "Eulogy for Mary McLeod Bethune." Taped Recording, Thurman Papers, Special Collections. Mugar Memorial Library, Boston University.

_____. Evanston, Illinois. Interview. May 1979.

_____. "Exposition to the Book of Habbukuk." In *The Interpreter's Bible*. pp. 979-1002. Edited by George A. Buttrick. Nashville: Abingdon Press, 1956.

_____. "Exposition to the Book of Zephaniah," In *The Interpreter's Bible*, Vol. 6. pp. 1013-34. Edited by George A. Buttrick. Nashville: Abingdon Press, 1956.

_____. "A Faith to Live By—Democracy and the Individual." The Fellowship Church, San Francisco. 19 and 26 October 1952. Taped Recording, Nos. 6 and 7, Thurman Papers, Boston University.

_____. "The Fascist Masquerade," pp. 82-100. In *The Church and Organized Movements*. Chapter 4. Edited by Randolph Crump Miller. ("The Interseminary Series"). New York: Harper and Brothers, 1946.

_____. *Footprints of a Dream: The Story of the Church for the Fellowship of All Peoples*. New York: Harper and Row, 1959.

_____. "Footprints of the Disinherited: Black Pentecost." Audio-Tape Cassette. Eliot Congregational Church, Roxbury, Massachusetts, 30-31 May 1942. Special Collections, Mugar Memorial Library, Boston University.

_____. *For the Inward Journey: The Writings of Howard Thurman*. Selected by Anne Spencer Thurman. New York: Harcourt, Brace Jovanovich, 1984.

_____. "The Freedom of the Human Spirit." Carmel Valley Manor, January 24, 1971. Thurman Papers, Special Collections. Mugar Memorial Library, Boston University.

_____. "Freedom Under God." Second Century Convocation, Washington University. February 1955. Thurman Papers, Special Collections, Mugar Memorial Library, Boston University.

_____. "Good News for the Underprivileged." Religion in Life 4:3 (Summer Issue, 1935): 403-09.

_____. *The Greatest of These*. Mills College, California: Eucalyptus Press, 1944.

_____. *The Growing Edge*. New York: Harper and Row, 1956; Richmond, Indiana: Friends United Press, 1974.

_____. "He Looked for a City." Taped Sermon. Marsh Chapel, Boston University, 2 January 1955. Special Collections, Mugar Library, Boston University.

_____. "Human Freedom and the Emancipation Proclamation." *Pulpit Digest* (December 1962): 13-16.

_____. "The Inner Life and World-Mindedness." n.p., n.d. Thurman Papers, Special Collections. Mugar Memorial Library.

_____. "The Inner Light." Audio-Tape Cassette, n.p., n.d. Howard Thurman Educational Trust Fund, San Francisco, California.

_____. Editor and with introduction. *Why I Believe There Is a God: Sixteen Essays by Negro Clergymen*. Chicago: Johnson Publishing Co., 1965.

_____. *The Inward Journey*. New York: Harper and Row, 1961; paperback, Richmond, Indiana: Friends United Press, 1971.

_____. *Jesus and the Disinherited*. Nashville: Abingdon Press, 1949; paperback, Richmond, Indiana: Friends United Press, 1981.

_____. "Judgment and Hope in the Christian Message," pp. 229-35. In *The Christian Way in Race Relations*. Edited by William Stuart Nelson. New York: Harper and Brothers, 1948.

_____. "Keep Alive the Dream." Audio-Tape Cassette, n.d. Howard Thurman Educational Trust. San Francisco, California.

_____. "Litany and Words in Memoriam for Martin Luther King, Jr." Fellowship Church, San Francisco, California, 7 April 1968.

_____. "Love and a Sense of Awareness." Audio-Tape Cassette, n.d. Howard Thurman Educational Trust Fund. San Francisco, California.

_____. "Love and a Sense of Fact." Audio-Tape Cassette, n.d. Howard Thurman Educational Trust Fund. San Francisco, California.

_____. "The Love of God." Audio-Tape Cassette, n.d. Howard Thurman Educational Trust Fund. San Francisco, California.

_____. "Love's Climate." Audio-Tape Cassette, n.d. Howard Thurman Educational Trust Fund. San Francisco, California.

_____. *The Luminous Darkness: A Personal Interpretation of the Anatomy of Segregation and the Ground of Hope*. New York: Harper and Row, 1965.

_____. "Man and the Experience of Community." California State College, Long Beach, California, n.d. Thurman Papers, Special Collections. Mugar Memorial Library, Boston University.

_____. "Man and the Experience of Freedom." California State College, Long Beach, California. 19 March 1969. Thurman Papers, Special Collections. Mugar Memorial Library, Boston University.

_____. "Man and Social Change—Violence and Nonviolence." California State College, Long Beach, California. 28 March 1961. Thurman Papers, Special Collection. Mugar Memorial Library, Boston University.

_____. "Man's Equity in Life." Audio-Tape Cassette, n.d. Howard Thurman Educational Trust Fund. San Francisco, California.

_____. "The Meaning of Commitment, No. 5: The Strength of Corporate Worship." Taped Sermon. The Fellowship Church For All Peoples, San Francisco, California. 8 April 1951. Special Collections, Mugar Memorial Library, Boston University.

_____. *Meditations of the Heart*. New York: Harper and Row, 1953; paperback ed., Richmond, Indiana: Friends United Press, 1976.

_____. *The Mood of Christmas*. New York: Harper and Row, 1973.

_____. "Mysticism and Ethics." *The Journal of Religious Thought* 27:2 (Summer Supplement, 1970): 23-30.

_____. *Mysticism and the Experience of Love*. Pendle Hill Pamphlet No. 115. Wallington, Pennsylvania: Pendle Hill, 1961.

_____. "Mysticism and Social Action." *The Lawrence Lectures on Religion and Society*. First Unitarian Church, Berkeley, California (13 October 1978).

_____. "Mysticism and Social Change," pp. 3-34. In *Eden Theological Seminary Bulletin* (Spring 1939).

_____. "Mysticism and Social Change." n.p., n.d. Thurman Papers, Special Collections, Boston University.

_____. "The Negro in the City." n.d., n.p. Thurman Papers, Special Collection. Mugar Memorial Library, Boston University.

_____. "The Public and Private Results of Collegiate Education in the Life of Negro Americans—An Interpretation of the Significance of Education in a Segregated Society." The Centennial Banquet of Morehouse College. 15 February 1967. Thurman Papers, Special Collections. Mugar Memorial Library, Boston University.

_____. "Quality of Life." Audio-Tape Cassette, n.d. Howard Thurman Educational Trust Fund. San Francisco, California.

_____. "Religion in a Time of Crisis." *The Garrett Tower* 43:4 Garrett Biblical Institute, Evanston, IL, (August 1943): 1-3.

_____. *The Search for Common Ground: An Inquiry Into the Basis of Man's Experience of Community*. New York: Harper and Row, 1971.

_____. "The Search for God in Religion." *Laymen's Movement Review* (November- December 1962).

_____. "A Seed Upon the Wind." Audio-Tape Cassette, n.d. Howard Thurman Educational Trust Fund. San Francisco, California.

_____. "Storms of Life." Audio-Tape Cassette, n.d. Howard Thurman Educational Trust Fund. San Francisco, California.

_____. *Temptations of Jesus: Five Sermons.* San Francisco: Lawton, Kennedy, 1962.

_____. "We Believe" (Television Series). Thurman Papers, Special Collections. Mugar Memorial Library, Boston University.

_____. "What Can I Believe In?" *The Journal of Religion and Health* 12 (November 1972): 111-19.

_____. "What Can I Believe In?" Thurman Papers, Special Collections. Mugar Memorial Library, Boston University.

_____. "Who Are You?" Audio-Tape Cassette, n.d. Howard Thurman Educational Trust Fund. San Francisco, California.

_____. "Windbreak Against Existence." *Bostonia* 34:2 (Fall 1960): 8-9.

_____. *With Head and Heart: The Autobiography of Howard Thurman.* New York: Hartcourt, Brace, Jovanovich, 1979.

_____, ed. *The First Footprints: The Dawn of the Idea of the Church for the Fellowship of All Peoples: Letters Between Alfred Fisk and Howard Thurman, 1943-1944.* San Francisco, California: Lawton and Alfred Kennedy, 1975.

_____, ed. *A Track to the Water's Edge: The Olive Schreiner Reader.* New York: Harper and Row, 1973.

Thurman, Sue Bailey. Howard Thurman Educational Trust. San Francisco, California. Interview. 11 August 1982.

Tillich, Paul. *Love, Power, and Justice.* New York: Oxford University Press, Galaxy Books, 1960. First published in 1954.

Topkin, Edgar A. *A Biographical History of Blacks in America Since 1528.* New York: David McKay Co., 1969; 1971.

Trulear, Harold Dean. "The Lord Will Make a Way Somehow: Black Worship and the Afro-American Story." *The Journal of the Interdenominational Theological Center* 13:1 (Fall 1985): 87-104.

Tucker, Robert C., ed. *The Marx-Engels Reader.* 2d ed. New York: W.W. Norton and Co., 1978.

Underhill, Evelyn. *Mysticism: A Study in the Nature and Development of Man's Spiritual Consciousness.* New York: E.P. Dutton, 1961.

Vining, Elizabeth Gray. *Friend of Life: The Biography of Rufus M. Jones.* Philadelphia: J.B. Lippincott Co., 1958.

Washington, James Melvin, ed. *A Testament of Hope: The Essential Writings of Martin Luther King, Jr.* San Francisco: Harper and Row, 1986.

Washington, Joseph R., Jr. *Black Religion: The Negro and Christianity in the United States*. Boston: Beacon Press, 1964.

Watley, William D. *Roots of Resistance: The Nonviolent Ethics of Martin Luther Kind, Jr*. Valley Forge: Judson Press, 1985.

Watson, Melvin H. "Howard Thurman, Teacher-Preacher." In *God and Human Freedom*. Edited by Henry J. Young. Richmond, Indiana: Friends United Press, 1983.

_____. Liberty Baptist Church, Atlanta, Georgia. Interview. 28 December 1982.

Watts, John T. "Robert N. Bellah's Theory of America's Eschatological Hope." *Journal of Church and State* (Winter 1980): 5-22.

West, Cornel. *Prophesy Deliverance!: An Afro-American Revolutionary Christianity*. Philadelphia: The Wesminster Press, 1988.

_____. *Prophetic Fragments*. Grand Rapids, Michigan: Eerdmans Publishing Co. and Trenton, New Jersey: African World Press, 1988.

West, Ellis M. "A Proposed Neutral Definition of Civil Religion." *Journal of Church and State* (Winter 1980): 23-40.

White, Ronald C., Jr., and Hopkins, C. Howard. *The Social Gospel: Religion and Reform in Changing America*. Philadelphia Temple University Press, 1976.

Williams, John A. *The King God Didn't Save: Reflections on the Life and Death of Martin Luther King, Jr*. Coward, McCann and Ceoghegan, Inc., 1970.

Williams, Robert C. "Moral Suasion and Militant Aggression in the Theological Perspective of Black Religion." *Journal of Religious Thought* 30:2 (1973-74): 27- 50.

_____. "Self, God, and Existence," In *God and Human Freedom*, pp. 44-56. Edited by Henry J. Young. Richmond, Idiana: Friends United Press, 1983.

_____. "Worship and Anti-Structure in Thurman's Vision of the Sacred." *The Journal of the Interdenominational Theological Center* 14 (Fall 86-spring 87): 161-74.

Wilmore, Gayrand S. *Black Religion and Black Radicalism*. Rev. ed. C. Eric Lincoln Series on Black Religion. Garden City, New Jersey: Doubleday and Co., 1983.

Wimberly, Anne Streaty, and Wimberly, Edward P. *Liberation and Wholeness: The Conversion Experiences of Black People in Slavery and Freedom*. Nashville: Abingdon, 1986.

Winter, Gibson. "Religion, Ethics, and Society." In *Social Ethics: Issues in Ethics and Society*. Edited and with Introduction by Gibson Winter. New York: Harper and Row, 1968.

X, Malcolm. *The Autobiography of Malcolm X*. With the Assistance of Alex Haley and Introduction by M.S. Handler. New York: Grove Press, 1964; 1965.

_____. *Malcolm X Speaks: Selected Speeches and Statements*. George Breitman, ed. New York: Grove Prses, 1965.

Yates, Elizabeth. *Howard Thurman: Portrait of a Practical Dreamer*. New York: John Day Co., 1964.

Young, Henry Jr., ed. *God and Human Freedom: A Festschrift in Honor of Howard Thurman*. Richmond, Idiana: Friends United Press, 1983.

_____. *Major Black Religious Leaders, 1755-1940*. Nashville: Abingdon, 1970.

_____. *Major Black Religious Leaders since 1940*. Nashville: Abingdon, 1979.